Canada
since 1867

Canada
since 1867

a bibliographical guide edited by
J.L. Granatstein and Paul Stevens

Second Edition, Completely Revised

SAMUEL STEVENS
HAKKERT & COMPANY
TORONTO & SARASOTA
1977

Design by Peter Maher

Canadian Cataloguing in Publication Data

Canada since 1867

Includes index.
ISBN 0-88866-583-0 bd. ISBN 0-88866-584-9 pa.

1. Canada-History-1867-   -Bibliography.
I. Granatstein, J.L., 1939 –   II. Stevens, Paul,
1938-

Z1385.G7 1977   016.971   C77-001217-5

A.M. Hakkert, Ltd.
554 Spadina Crescent
Toronto, Ontario M5S 2J9

Samuel Stevens & Co.
3807 Bond Place, P.O. Box 3899
Sarasota, Florida 33578

Printed in Canada

Contents

Preface

The intent of this much revised and expanded second edition of *Canada Since 1867: A Bibliographical Guide* remains the same as that of the first edition: to pick out the best works and to focus on the most recent research and writing in the major areas of Canadian historical writing. We try to say what is good and why. We try to locate the sources of articles and the publishers of books still in print. And we try to facilitate everyone's task, thus leaving more time for reading, research and writing.

We recognize that there are omissions in this book. The section on the North, for example, is too brief to be of real value. Our intention was good, however, and we sought for someone to do a full-length chapter that would do justice to an important topic and satisfactorily resolve one of the major complaints directed at the first edition. Unfortunately our search for an author was not successful. And as readers of Michael Bliss' excellent chapter will note, he feels that he can give too little space to labour history, one of the "boom" areas of current research. We agree, and in the third edition we hope to resolve this problem too.

Nonetheless we continue to believe that *Canada Since 1867* is the best available guide to the field of Canadian history. To compare this edition with the first is to be struck by the new work that has emerged in just two and a half years. There is more in some areas than in others, to be sure, but research and publication is underway in every aspect of Canada's past.

As in the first edition, the organization of chapters and subheadings has been preserved. A new, fuller and more conventional index has been added in response to criticism, and it should now be relatively simple to find all books and articles dealing with, for example, Sir Wilfrid Laurier, simply by looking his name up in the alphabetical index.

In the text abbreviations have been used for certain places and publishers as follows:

Places

T.—Toronto
M.—Montreal
L.—London
N.Y.—New York

Publishers

KP—King's Printer
QP—Queen's Printer
Mac.—Macmillan
UTP—University of Toronto Press
OUP—Oxford University Press
M&S—McClelland and Stewart
CIIA—Canadian Institute of International Affairs

Journals

CHR—*Canadian Historical Review*
CHAR—*Canadian Historical Association Annual Report (Historical Papers)*
TRSC—*Transactions of the Royal Society of Canada*
CJEPS—*Canadian Journal of Economics and Political Science*
JCS—*Journal of Canadian Studies*
QQ—*Queen's Quarterly*
RHAF—*Revue d'Histoire de l'Amerique Française*
OH—*Ontario History*

Once again, we urge users of this book to remember that this is only a partial listing and that the bibliographies and footnotes of the works cited herein should be thoroughly plumbed for additional material. We urge our users to remember too that the judgments expressed by the writers of these chapters are their own, not gospel. What one writer thinks less than valuable, another may find immensely useful.

And finally, the editors are pleased to welcome their colleague, Ramsay Cook, whose new chapter on French Canada was prepared on short notice when René Durocher was unable because of other commitments to prepare revisions for this edition.

JLG
PDS

Canada
since 1867

National Politics

Paul Stevens and J. L. Granatstein

Political history has dominated the writing of Canadian historians since the turn of the century. Excessively national in scope, too heavily biographical in approach, overly episodic, based on an insufficient understanding of the country's social and economic development, and lacking in the application of the tools and methodologies historians elsewhere have begun to make use of, it can yet be easily justified. In a country artificially created to expedite the economic exploitation of an otherwise inaccessible transcontinental expanse, persistently differentiated in the racial and religious composition of its dominant components, politics has been the core of its historical development. Politics in Canada has provided the milieu in which the deepest passions of religion, race and economic ambition have been harmonized and adjusted without resort to the destructive agencies of civil war and revolution which at different times have disrupted the political development of the three nations from which Canada has derived her national heritage.

INTRODUCTION

The political history of Canada has not lacked distinguished interpreters and annalists. For the student of Canadian history there are a number of general texts where he can begin his study. Edgar McInnis, *Canada: A Political and Social History* (T., Holt, Rinehart and Winston, 1959), is an objective and well-balanced history from the founding of New France to the Conservatives' victory in March, 1958. *Canada: A Story of Challenge* (Cambridge, Cambridge Univ. Press, 1953), by J. M. S. Careless, is the second volume in the British Commonwealth Series, intended "to tell young students in each part of the Commonwealth about the history of the other parts." Written in a clear and simple style, it fulfills its purpose extremely well, without indulging in patriotic excesses. A. R. M. Lower, *Colony to Nation: A History of Canada* (T., Longmans, 1946), is an interesting study, the old story of the development of Dominion Status. More provocative, however, is Donald Creighton, *Dominion of the North: A History of Canada* (T., Mac., 1944). Elaborating on the thesis conceived by Harold Innis and developed in his earlier study, *The Commercial Empire of the St. Lawrence, 1760-1850* (T., Ryerson, 1937), Creighton looks at Canada as the gradual expansion of the commercial empire based on the economic system of the St. Lawrence region, and argues that the success of this system was the primary factor in the survival of Canada, both French and British. His "The Decline and Fall of the Empire of the St. Lawrence" (*CHAR*, 1969), and *Canada's First Century* (T., Mac., 1970), supplement the text, and the conclusions he comes to are somewhat foreboding. The most comprehensive single-volume history of Canada yet published, however, is W. L. Morton, *The Kingdom of Canada: A General History from Earliest Times* (T., M&S, 1963). Although he was critical of the Laurentian historians in his earliest writing, Morton accepts almost completely the main lines of their thesis in this book.

There are some other texts as well which might be consulted. The best is *Canada: a Modern Study*, by Ramsay Cook with John Saywell and John Ricker (T., Clarke, Irwin 1964). Kenneth McNaught concentrates on economic expansion, national unity and Canadian-American relations in *The Pelican History of Canada* (T., Longmans, 1969). Two other texts incorporate some of the themes and conclusions of more recent scholarship: Paul Cornell, Jean Hamelin, Fernand Ouellet, and Marcel Trudel, *Canada: Unity in Diversity* (T., Holt, Rinehart & Winston, 1967), and D. M. L. Farr and J. S. Moir, *The Canadian Experience* (T., Ryerson, 1968).

Also useful as an introduction to the field are the volumes published in the Canadian Centenary Series. In *The Critical Years: The Union of British North America, 1857-1873* (T., M&S, 1964), W. L. Morton describes the events of the decade of ferment leading up to confederation, and carries the narrative down to the defeat of the Macdonald government, the weakest chapters in the book. Peter Waite's *Canada 1874-1896: Arduous Destiny* (T., M&S, 1971) is a sound, rather conventional political history, providing numerous fresh anecdotes, but little in the way of new interpretations. The colourful story of Canadian expansion into the northern frontiers is told in Morris Zaslow, *The Opening of the Canadian North: 1870-1914*, (T., M&S, 1971). The most valuable book in this important series is R. C. Brown and Ramsay Cook, *Canada 1896-1921: A Nation Transformed* (T., M&S, 1974). Based on a wide range of primary and secondary sources, it is an impressive synthesis of the major themes in the years between the election of Wilfrid Laurier and the resignation of Robert Borden. In *Canada 1939-1957: The Forked Road* (T., M&S, 1976), Donald Creighton once again pounds home the argument that Canada "simply exchanged the free and equal association of the Commonwealth for an increasing economic and military dependence on the United States" during World War II and in the years that followed.

A number of interpretive essays and surveys should also be mentioned. Although they vary in quality, the chapters surveying each of the decades since 1860 in J. M. S. Careless and R. C. Brown, eds., *The Canadians 1867-1967* (T., Mac., 1967), are extremely valuable as an introduction to the post-confederation period, particularly the chapters on the 1890s and the 1900s. F. H. Underhill's *The Image of Confederation* (T., CBC, 1964), a series of six half-hour radio lectures broadcast as the third series of the Massey Lectures, contain some brilliant insights into some of the major controversies about Canada's national purposes and goals, as does his *In Search of Canadian Liberalism* (T., Mac., 1960). Another valuable study is W. L. Morton, *The Canadian Identity* (T., UTP, 1961), an historian's attempt to define the character of Canadian nationhood. Indispensable to the student of Canadian history, as well, are two collections of essays by Ramsay Cook, *Canada and the French-Canadian Question* (T., Mac., 1966), in which Cook writes of the relations between French and English Canadians, and *The Maple Leaf Forever: Essays on Nationalism and Politics in Canada* (T., Mac., 1971), an attempt to view

Canadian nationality in terms of the distinction between a nationalist state and the nation state. Murray Beck's *Pendulum of Power: Canada's Federal Elections* (T., Prentice-Hall, 1968) provides brief sketches of each of Canada's federal election campaigns since 1867 and a wealth of statistics to supplement the text. An important new book is Robert Presthus' *Elite Accommodation in Canadian Politics*, (T., Mac., 1973). Based on 1,123 interviews with federal and provincial legislators, senior civil servants and interest group leaders, the author concludes that public policy in Canada is largely shaped by accommodation among these three political elites, "motivated essentially by a managerial ethic, rather more than by ideological commitment," with little participation by back-benchers and citizens. The result, he contends, is the survival of Canada, despite its deep seated cleavages of regionalism, ethnicity and religion. Although there is little that is new in this interpretation of Canadian politics, it is the first major systematic attempt to document it using survey data.

Two other studies of French Canadian history are also important. The first is Robert Rumilly's 41 volume *Histoire de la province de Québec* (M., Fides, 1940-1969). The earlier volumes are based heavily upon newspaper sources, while the later volumes use information gathered from the author's personal interviews with leading public figures in the province of Quebec. Rumilly also had access to a number of private archives and collections in the preparation of the *Histoire*. Mason Wade's *The French Canadians 1760-1945* (T., Mac., 1955) is the most complete study in English of French Canadian history for this period, but it contains little that is original.

THE POLITICS OF NATION BUILDING

It was a fragile union which the politicians of the sixties had pieced carefully together. And the predominant figure, whose task was to preside over its destiny, was Sir John A. Macdonald. The most important book in the post-confederation period is the second volume of Donald Creighton's biography of Macdonald, *John A. Macdonald: The Old Chieftain* (T., Mac., 1955). Beginning in 1867 and ending with Macdonald's death in 1891, there are few aspects of

Canadian life in the intervening years which Professor Creighton does not cover. It is based primarily on the Macdonald papers, but Creighton has also used the wide range of sources which were available to him in the Canadian and British archives. And it is written with the clarity and charm which has characterized all of his work. The most controversial aspect is his treatment of Louis Riel. The Métis leader stood in the way of Macdonald's plans for the opening of the West, and Creighton treated him with scorn and contempt. Still valuable, as well, is the official biography of Macdonald by his former secretary and literary executor, Joseph Pope, *The Memoirs of Sir John A. Macdonald* (2 vols., Ottawa, 1894), Sympathetic, sound, and solidly based on the Macdonald papers, it was written too close to the events it described, and consists primarily of extracts from Sir John's personal correspondence strung together in a loose narrative form. A more popular biography, P. B. Waite, *Macdonald: His Life and World.* (T., McGraw-Hill Ryerson, 1975) follows the general lines of interpretation laid down by Creighton. An important primary source is Pope's *Correspondence of Sir John Macdonald 1840-1891* (T., OUP, 1921), and Sir John Willison's review, "The Correspondence of Sir John A. Macdonald" (*Dalhousie Review*, 1922).

There are some other studies of Macdonald which should also be consulted: A. L. Burt, "Peter Mitchell on John A. Macdonald" (*CHR*, 1961); J. A. Roy, "John A. Macdonald, barrister and solicitor" (*Canadian Bar Review*, 1945); T. W. L. MacDermot, "The Political Ideas of John A. Macdonald" (*CHR*, 1933); and two articles by Peter Waite, "The Political Ideas of John A. Macdonald," in Marcel Hamelin, *The Political Ideas of the Prime Ministers of Canada* (Ottawa, Univ. of Ottawa Press, 1969), and "Sir John A. Macdonald, the man," in H. L. Dyck and H. P. Krosby, eds., *Empire and Nations: Essays in Honour of F. H. Soward* (T., UTP, 1969). Donald Creighton has written a number of essays on Macdonald, most of which he completed while preparing the biography of Sir John. Particularly useful are "Sir John Macdonald and Kingston" (*CHR* 1950), and "Sir John A. Macdonald and Canadian Historians" (*CHR*, 1948).

Macdonald's Conservative colleagues have been less

adequately dealt with: E. M. Saunders, *The Life and Letters of Sir Charles Tupper* (2 vols., N.Y., 1916); J. Castell Hopkins, *Life and Work of Sir John Thompson*, (T., 1895); O. D. Skelton, *The Life and Times of Sir A. T. Galt* (T., OUP, 1920); and John Boyd, *Sir Etienne Cartier, Bart. His Life and Times*, (T., Mac., 1914) are not without value. But each of these figures deserves more scholarly treatment based on the sources now available. More interest has been shown in recent years in the activities of Macdonald's associates in Quebec. Alastair Sweeney's *George-Etienne Cartier: A Biography* (T., M&S, 1976) suffers from a lack of Cartier papers, but it is the most thorough study of Macdonald's Quebec lieutenant. Barbara Fraser, "The political career of Sir Hector Langevin" (*CHR*, 1961) is a fine article on Sir John's principal lieutenant, while Andrée Désilets, *Hector-Louis Langevin. Un père de la confédération canadienne 1826-1906* (Québec, Laval Univ. Press, 1969), is a comprehensive survey of his political career. Langevin's rival in Quebec for political influence in the Conservative caucus, J. A. Chapleau, has been studied in an excellent article by H. B. Neatby and J. T. Saywell, "Chapleau and the Conservative party in Quebec" (*CHR*, 1956). Also useful are Jacques Gouin, "Histoire d'une amitié: correspondence intime entre Chapleau et De Celles, 1875-1898" (*RHAF*, 1964), and F. Ouellet, "Lettres de J. A. Chapleau, 1870-1896" (*Rapport de l'Archiviste de la province de Québec*, 1959-1960). The most important study of Israël Tarte is an unpublished Ph.D. dissertation, Laurier Lapierre's "Politics, race and religion in French Canada: Joseph Israël Tarte" (University of Toronto, 1962). Also useful are two articles by Lapierre, "Joseph Israël Tarte: Relations Between the French Canadian Episcopacy and a French Canadian Politician, 1874-1896" (*Canadian Catholic Historical Association Report*, 1958) and "Joseph Israël Tarte and the McGreevy-Langevin Scandal" (*CHAR*, 1961).

The most immediate problem confronting the new Prime Minister was the formation of a cabinet, and two articles by W. L. Morton fill in many of the details: "The Formation of the First Federal Cabinet" (*CHR*, 1955); and "The Cabinet of 1867," in F. W. Gibson, *Cabinet Formation and Bi-cultural Relations. Seven Case Studies. Vol. 6,*

Studies of the Royal Commission on Bilingualism and Bi-culturalism. (Ottawa, QP, 1970). The agitation for repeal of the confederation agreement in Nova Scotia has prompted a number of studies: L. J. Burpee, "Joseph Howe and the Anti-Confederation League" (*TRSC*, 1916); D. C. Harvey, "Incidents of the Repeal Agitation in Nova Scotia" (*CHR*, 1934); and two articles by J. M. Beck, "Joseph Howe: Opportunist or Empire Builder?" (*CHR*, 1960), and "Joseph Howe and Confederation: Myth and Fact" (*TRSC*, 1964). Morton's work on Manitoba and the Riel resistance is extremely important for an understanding of the problems involved in that province's joining confederation. His brilliant analysis of the Red River rebellion in the introduction to *Alexander Begg's Red River Journal*, (T., Champlain Society, 1956), in *Manitoba: A History* (T., UTP, 1957), and in *The Birth of a Province* (Altona, Man., *Records of the Manitoba Historical Society*, 1970) tell the story with considerable skill. Also of use are: George Stanley, *The Birth of Western Canada* (1936: T., UTP, 1960); D. F. Warner, "Drang nach Norden —The United States and the Riel Rebellion" (*Mississippi Valley Historical Review*, 1953); and A. C. Glueck, *Minnesota and the Manifest Destiny of the Canadian Northwest* (T., UTP, 1966). The best study on British Columbia and its entry into confederation is to be found in Margaret Ormsby's *British Columbia: a History* (T., Mac., 1958), while F. W. P. Bolger, *Prince Edward Island and Confederation* (Charlottetown, St. Dunstan's Univ. Press, 1968), provides a thorough account of the debate on the Island. Macdonald also had considerable dealings with the American government during his first term of office and particularly useful are: Goldwin Smith, *The Treaty of Washington: A Study in Imperial History* (Ithaca, Cornell Univ. Press, 1941); R. S. Longley, "Peter Mitchell, Guardian of the North Atlantic Fisheries, 1867-1871" (*CHR*, 1941); C. P. Stacey, "Britain's Withdrawal from North America" (*CHR*, 1955); and M. M. Robson, "The Alabama Claims and Anglo-American Reconciliation, 1865-1871" (*CHR*, 1961).

There are other studies as well which should also be considered to understand the nature of Macdonald conservatism in the first years of confederation. The most important, perhaps, is Donald Creighton's "Conservatism and National Unity," in R. Flenley, ed., *Essays in Canadian History Presented to George MacKinnon Wrong*, (T., Mac., 1939), in which he attempts to distinguish conservative doctrines from those of the other parties. Also useful are the articles by A. D. Lockhart, "The Contribution of Macdonald Conservatism to National Unity 1854-78" (*CHAR*, 1939) and J. I. Cooper, "The Political Ideas of George Etienne Cartier" (*CHR*, 1942). An important study on the development of the Canadian political party system is F. H. Underhill, "The Development of National Political Parties in Canada" (*CHR*, 1935). Underhill's conclusions about the nature of the party system in Canada have been largely accepted by historians in Canada and much of their work has been written within the conceptual framework laid down by Underhill. Another useful essay is Escott Reid's "The Rise of National Parties in Canada" (*Papers and Proceedings of the Canadian Political Science Association*, 1932), in which he describes the fragility of political parties at confederation and the lack of sophistication in their organizational techniques.

The Liberal Party had little success against the wily Macdonald and the biographies of its leaders tell part of the story. The basic book on George Brown after confederation is J. M. S. Careless, *Brown of the Globe, Vol. II: Statesman of Confederation, 1860-1880*, (T., Mac., 1963). Not only does it present a thorough and well-balanced study of mid-nineteenth century politics, it illustrates Careless's views about the contribution of British ideas to Canadian liberalism and about the growing influence of Toronto over its metropolitan hinterlands. Dale Thomson's *Alexander Mackenzie. Clear Grit*, (T., Mac., 1960) tells the story of Brown's successor in the leadership of the Liberal party. Although Thomson fails to probe the reasons for the party's political collapse in 1878 after five years in office, and particularly the responsibility Mackenzie may have borne for it, the book is a well-written account of the Liberal leader and of his prime ministership from 1873 to 1878. Joseph Schull's two volume biography, *Edward Blake: The Man of the Other Way*, (T., Mac., 1975) and *Edward Blake: Leader in Exile* (T., Mac., 1976) is an interesting portrait of the intellectually brilliant but politically unsophisticated Ontario lawyer who became the party's leader in 1880. More penetrating in analysis are two fine essays by F. H. Underhill: "Edward Blake," in C. T. Bissell, ed., *Our Living Tradition, First Series*, (T., UTP, 1957); and "Edward Blake and Canadian Liberal Nationalism," in Flenley, *Essays in Canadian History in Honour of G. M. Wrong*. J. D. Livermore, "The Personal Agonies of Edward Blake," (*CHR*, 1975) examines some of the physical and emotional problems which contributed to his erratic behavior as a political leader.

There are a number of books and articles which supplement these studies and throw further light on the development of Canadian liberalism during the later part of the nineteenth century. Of primary importance are: W. R. Graham, "Liberal Nationalism in the 1870's" (*CHAR*, 1946); W. S. Wallace, ed., "Edward Blake's Aurora Speech" (*CHR*, 1921); and two articles by Underhill, "Political Ideas of the Upper Canadian Reformers, 1867-1878" (*CHAR*, 1942) and "Edward Blake, The Supreme Court Act and the Appeal to the Privy Council 1875-1876" (*CHR*, 1938). Sister T. A. Burke describes Mackenzie's difficulties in forming his cabinet in "Mackenzie and his Cabinet, 1873-1878" (*CHR*, 1960), while Margaret Ormsby tells the story of his dealings with British Columbia in "Prime Minister Mackenzie, The Liberal party and the Bargain with British Columbia" (*CHR*, 1945). Another important source for the railway question is C. W. de Kiewiet and F. H. Underhill, eds., *The Dufferin-Carnarvon Correspondence, 1874-1878* (T., Champlain Society, 1955). M. Ayearst, "The Parti Rouge and the Clergy" (*CHR*, 1934) describes some of the problems faced by the Liberals in Quebec, but students should also read Jean-Paul Bernard, *Les Rouges: Libéralisme, Nationalisme et Anti-cléricalisme au Milieu du XIXe Siècle*, (M., Université de Québec, 1971), for the background to the problem. One explanation for the defeat of the party in the general election of 1878 is provided in D. Lee, "Dominion General Election of 1878 in Ontario" (*OH*, 1959).

There are numerous studies on the economic background to the origins and development of the national policy. Particularly important are Donald Creighton, *British North America at Confederation* (Ottawa, KP,1939), and W. A. Mackintosh, *The Economic Background of Dominion-Pro-*

vincial Relations, (Ottawa, KP, 1939), both appendices to *The Report of the Royal Commission on Dominion-Provincial Relations*. O. J. Firestone, *Canadian Economic Development* (L., Bowes & Bowes, 1953), and O. J. MacDiarmid, *Commercial Policy in the Canadian Economy* (Cambridge, Harvard Univ. Press, 1946), are also helpful. The leading critic of the national policy is John Dales. In "Canada's National Policies," in his *The Protective Tariff in Canada's Development*, (T., UTP, 1966), Dales challenges the assumption it was of general benefit to the country. Another critic of the policy of tariff protection is Michael Bliss, "Canadianizing American business: The Roots of the Branch Plant," in Ian Lumsden, ed., *Close the 49th Parallel etc: The Americanization of Canada*, (T., UTP, 1970). Also important are: two articles by Creighton, "Economic Nationalism and Confederation" (*CHAR*, 1942), and "George Brown, Sir John Macdonald and the Workingman" (*CHR*, 1943); Bernard Ostry's "Conservatives, Liberal, and Labour in the 1870's" (*CHR*, 1960), and "Conservatives, Liberals and Labour in the 1880s" (*CJEPS*, 1961); and R. C. Brown, "The Nationalism of the National Policy," in Peter Russell, *Nationalism in Canada*, (T., McGraw-Hill, 1966).

The building of the Canadian Pacific Railway has been written about several times. Although he concentrates heavily on the financial aspects of the line, the best account is still H. A. Innis, *A History of the Canadian Pacific Railway*, (L., P. S. King & Son, 1923). G. P. de T. Glazebrook, *A History of Transportation in Canada*, (T., Ryerson, 1938), traces the story of transportation through Canadian history, describing the methods and relating them to the rise of Canadian civilization. J. M. Gibbon, *The Romantic History of the Canadian Pacific: The Northwest Passage of To-day* (N.Y., Tudor, 1937), is also useful. A good biography of George Stephen, through whose financial genius the railway was achieved, is Heather Gilbert's *Awakening Continent: The Life of Mount Stephen. Vol. 1.* (Aberdeen, Aberdeen Univ. Press, 1965). L. B. Irwin, *Pacific Railways and Nationalism in the Canadian-American Northwest, 1845-1873* (Philadelphia, 1939), tells the early story of the Canadian Pacific and Northern Pacific Railways and describes their influence on the political history of the Northwest before the panic of 1873. The most recent and widely publicized book on the question is Pierre Berton, *The National Dream: The Great Railway, 1871-1881* (T., M&S, 1970) and *The Last Spike: The Great Railway, 1881-1885* (T., M&S, 1971). In a colorful narrative account, Berton mistakenly assumes that there was no feasible alternative to the expensive line and that the national interest was identical with the interests of central Canada.

Indeed, one of the most striking features of Canadian politics during the decade of the 1880s was the reappearance and growth of regional and particularist feeling. The background to the discontent is described in the *Report of the Royal Commission on Dominion-Provincial Relations: Book 1* (Ottawa, KP, 1940), while J. A. Maxwell, *Federal Subsidies to the Provincial Governments in Canada* (Cambridge, Harvard Univ. Press, 1937), provides a well-balanced account of federal-provincial financial relations. The best study of the rise of the provincial rights movement in Ontario is J. A. Morrison, "Oliver Mowat and the Development of Provincial Rights in Ontario," in *Three History Theses* (T., Ontario Department of Public Records and Archives, 1961). This should be supplemented with Christopher Armstrong, "The Mowat Heritage in Federal-Provincial Relations," in Donald Swainson, ed., *Oliver Mowat's Ontario* (T., Mac., 1972). Robert Rumilly's *Mercier* (M., Zodiaque, 1936) picks up the story in Quebec, but Ramsay Cook's *Provincial Autonomy: Minority Rights and the Compact Theory, 1867-1921* (Ottawa, QP, 1969), a study of the origins, development and uses of the idea that confederation represented a compact of provinces or cultures, provides a much fuller account. Unrest in the Maritime provinces is described in: S. A. Saunders, *The Economic History of the Maritime Provinces, A Study Prepared for the Royal Commission on Dominion-Provincial Relations* (Ottawa, KP, 1939); Murray Beck, *The Government of Nova Scotia* (T., UTP, 1957); and Beck, *History of Maritime Union: A Study of Frustrations* (Fredericton, QP, 1969). In addition to Morton's *Manitoba*, J. A. Maxwell, "Financial relations between Manitoba and the Dominion, 1870-1886" (*CHR*, 1934), is important for the movement in Manitoba. Students should also consult John Saywell's first-rate study, *The Office of Lieutenant-Governor*

(T., UTP, 1957), and Eugene Forsey, "Disallowance of Provincial Acts, Reservation of Provincial Bills, and Refusal of Assent by Lieutenant-Governors since 1867" (*CJEPS*, 1938).

Unrest in the West took another form and brought into question the cultural modus vivendi worked out by the fathers of confederation. George Stanley's *The Birth of Western Canada* and his *Louis Riel* (T., Ryerson, 1963) tell the story well. In contrast to Creighton, Stanley views Riel as a tragic hero of the frontier West rather than the fanatical half-breed rebel embodying the nationalism of the Métis. To Quebec, Riel was the defender of the French and Catholic tradition in the West, and R. E. Lamb, *Thunder in the North: Conflict over the Riel Risings, 1870-1885* (N.Y., 1957), and Rumilly's *Mercier* and his *Mgr Laflèche et son temps* (M., Zodiaque, 1938) describe the *nationaliste* response in "la belle province." Arthur Silver's "French Quebec and the Métis Question, 1869-1883," in C. Berger and R. Cook, *The West and the Nation: Essays in Honour of W. L. Morton*, (T., M&S, 1976) should also be consulted. In *The Jesuits' Estates Question, 1760-1888: a Study of the Background For the Agitation of 1889* (T., UTP, 1968), Roy Dalton explores the origins of another issue which aggravated the relations between the French and the English, while F. Landon, "D'Alton McCarthy and the Politics of the Later Eighties" (*CHAR*, 1932), looks at the reaction in Ontario. Also important are two articles by J. R. Miller, "The Jesuits' Estates Act Crisis," (*JCS*, 1974), and "Honoré Mercier, la minorité protestante du Québec et la loi relative au règlement de la question des biens des Jésuites," (*RHAF*, 1974). There are three articles which should also be consulted, all of which place the problem in a somewhat larger context: W. L. Morton, "The Conservative Principle in Confederation" (*QQ*, 1965); Donald Creighton, "John A. Macdonald, Confederation and the Canadian West" (*Historical and Scientific Society of Manitoba*, 1966-1967); and Ralph Heintzman, "The Spirit of Confederation: Professor Creighton, Biculturalism, and the Use of History" (*CHR*, 1971).

The reciprocity issue and the question of Canada's commercial relations with the United States represented another challenge to the basic foundations of confederation. The standard source is C. C. Tansill, *Canadian-American*

Relations, 1875-1911 (New Haven, Yale Univ. Press, 1943), but it must now be supplemented by Craig Brown's excellent study, *Canada's National Policy, 1883-1900: A Study in Canadian-American Relations*, (Princeton, Princeton Univ. Press, 1964). Based primarily on Canadian sources, Brown emphasizes the major impact of Canadian politics on Canadian-American diplomacy. D. F. Warner, *The Idea of Continental Union: Agitation for the Annexation of Canada to the United States 1849-1893* (Lexington, Univ. of Kentucky Press, 1960), surveys the movements for the annexation of Canada to the United States from the manifesto of 1849 to the election of 1891, but it is episodic in approach and uneven in its research. A more satisfactory treatment of the ideas of at least one continentalist is Ian Grant, "Erastus Wiman: a Continentalist Replies to Canadian Imperialism" (*CHR*, 1972). The origins of the movement for commercial union are discussed in R. C. Brown, "The Commercial Unionists in Canada and the United States" (*CHAR*, 1963), while W. R. Graham, "Sir Richard Cartwright, Wilfrid Laurier and the Liberal Party Trade Policy, 1887" (*CHR*, 1952), looks at the Liberal party's decision to adopt reciprocity as an issue. Three articles by F. H. Underhill are also important: "Edward Blake, The Liberal Party and Unrestricted Reciprocity" (*CHAR*, 1939); "Laurier and Blake, 1882-1891" (*CHR*, 1939); and "Laurier and Blake 1891-1892" (*CHR*, 1943). Students should also take a look at one contemporary source: Goldwin Smith, *Canada and the Canadian Question* (T., 1891).

Only recently have historians realized the critical nature of the 1890s and the subtle and complex interrelationship of forces that shaped the decade. Imperialism and nationalism, racism and nativism, continentalism and anti-Americanism battled for supremacy, though the alliances were often strange and the generalship uncertain. The Manitoba Schools question brought many of these forces into play, and one of the best treatments of the problem is John Saywell's introduction to the *Canadian Journal of Lady Aberdeen 1893-1898* (T., Champlain Society, 1960). Saywell and H. B. Neatby's earlier article, "Chapleau and the Conservative Party in Quebec," (*CHR*, 1956); Saywell's "The Crown and the Politicians: The Canadian Succession Question," (*CHR*, 1956); and Barbara Fraser's "The Political Career of Sir Hector Louis Langevin," (*CHR*, 1961), remain valuable. Lovell Clark, *The Manitoba School Question: Majority Rule or Minority Rights?* (T., Copp Clark, 1968), is a useful compendium of documents, while his "The Conservative Party in the 1890's" (*CHAR*, 1961), and "Macdonald's Conservative Successors, 1891-1896," in John Moir, ed., *Character and Circumstance: Essays in Honour of Donald Grant Creighton*, (T., Mac., 1970), examine the decline of the Conservative Party after the death of Macdonald. An important new book is Paul Crunican, *Priests and Politicians: Manitoba Schools and the Election of 1896*, (T., UTP, 1974), a study solidly based upon the rich resources of the ecclesiastical archives and the private papers of the politicians involved. It also adds another dimension to the historiographical controversy surrounding the election of 1896. While confirming Saywell and Neatby's earlier hypothesis that the Conservatives lost Quebec because of divisions in the party and a lack of leadership in the province, Crunican argues that the clergy played a pivotal role in the outcome of the campaign. Division within the hierarchy of the Quebec bishops and the resulting weakness of their *mandement* allowed Laurier to convince enough voters that the gap between what the bishops were demanding and what the Liberals were promising was not as wide as Bishop Laflèche and the Conservatives were painting it. Also of use for the politics of the early 1890s are: J. T. Watt, "Anti-Catholic nativism in Canada: The Protestant Protective Association" (*CHR*, 1967); J. W. Lederle, "The Liberal Convention of 1893" (*CJEPS*, 1950); and R. Stamp, "J. D. Edgar and the Liberal Party: 1867-1896" (*CHR*, 1964).

THE POLITICS OF NATIONAL UNITY

The Laurier years were of critical importance in the development of Canada. During this period, in which the destinies of the country were, for the first time, presided over by a member of the minority race, the national economic expansion, optimistically promised by the Fathers of Confederation to have followed immediately upon the creation of the Union, finally took place. In both its domestic and external affairs, Canada arrived at a cross-roads as well.

Confronting the Canadian people and their political repre-
sentatives were two closely-related problems: what was the
exact nature of the connection between Canada and Great
Britain? And was the maintenance of this connection com-
patible with the existence of a bicultural state?

The starting point for any examination of Laurier's
career must be the official biography by Professor O. D.
Skelton, the *Life and Letters of Sir Wilfrid Laurier* (2 vols.,
T., OUP, 1921). This was "official biography" in every sense
of the word; it was undertaken at Laurier's request and was
solidly based on the vast mass of the Laurier papers and
long talks with Sir Wilfrid on the important aspects of his
career. For the 1920s it was a fine book. But Skelton was
much too close to the subject of his study and too restricted
in the sources he was able to use to produce anything other
than a partisan work. In his determination that Laurier
should emerge as a symbol of national unity and racial har-
mony, he overlooked important aspects of both the man and
his career. There is more than one instance when his objec-
tivity must be questioned. On some occasions he has rear-
ranged quotations to make Laurier's views appear more coherent; on other occasions he has simply left out controversial sentences. Skelton's sympathy for Laurier also led him
to minimize Sir Wilfrid's responsibility for some of the important decisions taken by his government. And he has virtually ignored Laurier's relationship with the Roman Catholic church, despite an abundance of material in the Laurier
correspondence.

Other biographies have also been published. But they
are incomplete in their research, and with the exception of
John Dafoe's analytical essay, *Laurier: A Study*, (T., 1922),
have followed the lines of interpretation laid down by Professor Skelton. J. S. Willison's *Sir Wilfrid Laurier and the
Liberal Party* (2 vols., T., 1903) was written in the aftermath of the federal election of 1900, in which the Liberal
party suffered humiliating losses in the province of Ontario,
and was an attempt to demonstrate that English-speaking
voters had been unfair to Laurier, and that he should be
viewed in the light of his efforts to unify and consolidate
confederation. Joseph Schull's more recent study, *Laurier:
The First Canadian* (T., Mac., 1965), develops a similar

theme. In an effort to show that Sir Wilfrid embodied the spirit of Canada more completely and satisfactorily than any of his predecessors, he drew a sympathetic picture of the Liberal leader, more boldly sketched and more dramatically presented than that of Skelton's, but basically the same Laurier. And nowhere does Schull question the achievements of his subject, nor the tactics he used.

Only recently have other historians begun to fill in the picture. Although he has accepted many of Skelton's conclusions, H. B. Neatby looked at Laurier's management of the Liberal Party in the province of Quebec in *Laurier and a Liberal Quebec: A Study in Political Management* (T., M&S, 1973). Developing the theme in an essay entitled "Wilfrid Laurier: Politician," in *The Political Ideas of the Prime Ministers of Canada*, Paul Stevens argued that Laurier's statesmanship was dependent upon his success as a politician, and he began to analyze the approaches and techniques the Liberal leader developed. In each of these studies, the authors quote with approval Dafoe's conclusion that the final appraisal would show Laurier "an abler man, but one not quite so preternaturally good; a man who had affinities with Machiavelli as well as with Sir Galahad." An article by Marc La Terreur, "Correspondence Laurier–Mme Joseph Lavergne, 1891-1893" (*CHAR*, 1964), provides one insight at least into Laurier's personal life.

There are surprisingly few biographies of Laurier's political associates to supplement these studies. John Dafoe's *Clifford Sifton in relation to His Times* (T., Mac., 1931) is still the most useful, while A. H. U. Colquhoun, *Press Politics and People, The Life and Letters of Sir John Willison* (T., Mac., 1935), and Willison's *Reminiscences, Political and Personal* (T., M&S, 1919) provide some interesting insights into the politics of the era. But C. B. Fergusson's biography of Laurier's Minister of Finance, W. S. Fielding, *Mr. Minister of Finance* (Windsor, Nova Scotia, Lancelot Press, 1971), is disappointing, particularly in view of the important role he played throughout the period. Laurier's one-time protégé, Henri Bourassa, has been the subject of a number of studies: Robert Rumilly, *Henri Bourassa*, (M., Chantecler, 1953); Casey Murrow, *Henri Bourassa and French Canadian Nationalism* (M., Harvest House, 1968);

Joseph Levitt, *Henri Bourassa and the Golden Calf: The Social Program of the Nationalists of Quebec, 1900-1914* (Ottawa, Univ. of Ottawa Press, 1969); and Martin O'Connell, "The Ideas of Henri Bourassa" (*CJEPS*, 1953). But the most revealing work is a sensitive and subtle essay by André Laurendeau in R. L. McDougall, ed., *Our Living Tradition, Fourth Series* (T., UTP, 1962).

The dominant issue confronting Laurier and his colleagues was the question of imperialism. At the turn of the century, Canada looked out upon a world feverishly pursuing imperial grandeur. And Canadian historians have focussed considerable attention upon the different aspects of the problem. Two excellent essays by John T. Saywell and H. B. Neatby in Careless and Brown, *The Canadians, 1867-1967*, put the debate in its context, while useful background information can be found in: J. E. Tyler, *The Struggle for Imperial Unity, 1868-1895* (L., Mac., 1959); J. L. Garvin and J. Amery, *The Life of Joseph Chamberlain* (4 vols, L., Mac., 1934-1951); and D. G. Creighton, "The Victorians and the Empire" (*CHR*, 1938). André Siegfried, *The Race Question in Canada* (L., 1907), throws a penetrating light upon Canadian politics in the Laurier era, and upon imperialism in particular. Two other contemporary sources, George Parkin, *Imperial Federation: The Problem of National Unity* (L., 1892), and George T. Denison, *The Struggle for Imperial Unity: Recollections and Experiences*, (T., 1909), offer some revealing glimpses about the motives and ideas of the Canadian Imperialists.

Much of the writing about Canada's relations with the British Empire has emphasized political and diplomatic developments. R. M. Dawson, *The Development of Dominion Status 1900-1936* (L., OUP, 1937), details the paper-strewn path to national status, concentrating on Colonial Office dispatches, the records of Imperial conferences, and the centralizing tendencies of the British government. In *Canada and Imperialism, 1896-1899* (T., UTP, 1965), Norman Penlington took another tack. Rejecting the argument that Canada's participation in the Boer War was the result of Downing Street influence, Penlington argued that there were powerful forces within Canadian society which demanded involvement. Anti-Americanism, he concluded, was largely responsible for the enthusiasm for imperial unity and was the outlet for a form of jingoism that closely resembled that in the United States and Great Britain. Carl Berger, *The Sense of Power: Studies in the Ideas of Canadian Imperialism 1867-1914* (T., UTP, 1970), maintained that the problem was even more complex. In a brilliant analysis of the nature of Canadian imperialism, Berger contended that some Canadian imperialists saw nothing inconsistent between Canadian nationalism and closer relations with Great Britain, and believed that Canada could best achieve national status within a transformed empire. Ramsay Cook's "Stephen Leacock and the Age of Plutocracy, 1903-1921," in Moir, *Character and Circumstance: Essays in Honour of Donald Grant Creighton*; Richard Clippingdale, "J. S. Willison and Canadian Nationalism, 1886-1902," (*CHAR*, 1969); Douglas Cole, "John S. Ewart and Canadian Nationalism," (*CHAR*, 1969); Robert Page, "Canada and the Imperial Idea in the Boer War," (*JCS*, 1970); and Terry Cook, "George Parkin and Britannic Idealism," (*JCS*, 1975), provide further insights into the meaning of nationalism and imperialism at the turn of the century.

There are a number of studies of other aspects of Canada's imperial relations which students should consult. In "Sir Wilfrid Laurier and the British Preferential Tariff System" (*CHAR*, 1955), James Colvin examines the background to the preferential tariff of 1897. Exhaustive treatments of the question of imperial defence are D. C. Gordon, *The Dominion Partnership in Imperial Defense, 1870-1914* (Baltimore, Johns Hopkins Univ. Press, 1965) and R. A. Preston, *Canada and "Imperial Defense": A Study of the origins of the British Commonwealth's Defense Organization, 1867-1919* (T., UTP, 1967). Desmond Morton, *Ministers and Generals: Politics and the Canadian Militia, 1868-1904* (T., UTP, 1970) analyses the conflicts between the British General Officers Commanding the Canadian militia and their political superiors, and describes the process by which Canadians assumed the responsibility for framing their own policies. Anglo-American diplomacy leading to the settlement of the Alaska boundary dispute is dealt with in: Charles S. Campbell, *Anglo-American Understanding 1898-1903* (Baltimore, John Hopkins Univ. Press, 1957); A. E.

Campbell, *Great Britain and the United States, 1895-1903* (L., Longmans, 1960); Norman Penlington, *The Alaska Boundary Dispute: A Critical Reappraisal* (T., McGraw-Hill Ryerson, 1972); and F. W. Gibson, "The Alaska Boundary Dispute" (*CHAR*, 1945). On the debate over naval defence, G. N. Tucker, *The Naval Service of Canada* (Ottawa, KP, 1952), is particularly useful. Also of interest are: H. B. Neatby, "Laurier and Imperialism" (*CHAR*, 1955); R. C. Brown, "Goldwin Smith and Anti-Imperialism" (*CHR*, 1962); H. P. Gundy, "Sir Wilfrid Laurier and Lord Minto" (*CHAR*, 1952); and James Eayrs, "The Round Table Movement in Canada, 1909-1920" (*CHR*, 1957).

The problem of education in Canada and the relationship between the English-speaking majority and the French-speaking minority was a complex one as well. W. L. Morton, "Manitoba Schools and Canadian Nationality, 1890-1923" (*CHAR*, 1951), and Ramsay Cook, "Church, Schools, and Politics in Manitoba, 1903-1912" (*CHR*, 1958), describe the resolution of the Manitoba Schools question. The most detailed study of the school question in Alberta and Saskatchewan is Manoly R. Lupul, *The Roman Catholic Church and the North-West School Question: A Study in Church-State Relations in Western Canada, 1875-1905*, (T., UTP., 1974). The author's careful research in the ecclesiastical and clerical archives is impressive. But on the critical question of the educational clauses in the Autonomy bills, his conclusion that Laurier was guilty of nothing worse than carelessness in its drafting is open to question, as Evelyn Eager, "Separate Schools and the Cabinet Crisis of 1905," (*The Lakehead University Review*, 1969) and D. J. Hall, "A Divergence of Principle: Clifford Sifton, Sir Wilfrid Laurier and the North-West Autonomy Bills, 1905," (*Laurentian University Review*, 1974) have begun to suggest. Still useful as well is C. C. Lingard, *Territorial Government in Canada: The Autonomy Question in the Old North-West Territories* (T., UTP, 1946). Based largely on newspaper sources and personal interviews with the Territorial premier, Sir Frederick Haultain, it is a sympathetic presentation of the case for provincial rights and a vindication of their champion. Also interesting is Lupul, "The Campaign for a French Catholic School Inspector in the North-West Territories, 1898-1903"

(*CHR*, 1967), a study of the Roman Catholic hierarchy's attempts to secure a French-language school inspector for the denominational schools in the Territories. Franklin Walker, *Catholic Education and Politics in Ontario: A Documentary Study* (T., Nelson, 1964); Margaret Prang, "Clerics, Politicians, and the Bilingual Schools Issue in Ontario, 1910-1917" (*CHR*, 1960); Marilyn Barber, "The Ontario Bilingual Schools Issue: Sources of Conflict" (*CHR*, 1966); and Peter Oliver, "The Ontario Bilingual Schools Crisis, 1919-1926" (*JCS*, 1972) describe the controversy in Ontario over bilingual schools.

The defeat of the Laurier government in 1911 has aroused considerable interest on the part of the historians as well. Still the most comprehensive survey of the reciprocity question is L. E. Ellis, *Reciprocity, 1911: A Study in Canadian-American Relations* (New Haven, Yale Univ. Press, 1939). Although he emphasized the role of the business and financial interests which implanted fears of annexation in the minds of many Canadians, Ellis accepted the view of most of his colleagues in the profession that reciprocity was the issue that broke the government's back. More recent research, however, has added another dimension to the question. In "The Conservative Party Machine and the Election of 1911 in Ontario" (*OH*, 1965), Robert Cuff maintained that the Conservative Party's organization in Ontario was sufficiently strong that the results would not have been much different whatever issue had emerged in the campaign. Looking at the Liberals, Paul Stevens, "Laurier, Aylesworth, and the Decline of the Liberal Party in Ontario" (*CHAR*, 1968), argued that the party was in considerable difficulty even before reciprocity became the centre of political controversy. Lack of leadership and party division, he contended, seriously undermined the Liberal campaign to sell reciprocity and forced valuable ground to be yielded to the opposition as the debate unfolded. Stevens has also assembled the important primary and secondary sources on the election campaign in his *The 1911 General Election: A Study in Canadian Politics* (T., Copp Clark, 1970).

There is still no complete official biography of Robert Borden. Students must rely on Henry Borden, ed., *Robert*

Laird Borden: His Memoirs (T., Mac., 1938) for the only account covering all of Borden's long career, but the *Memoirs* are largely unanalytical and unreflective. Much more valuable for the period to 1914 is the first volume of R. Craig Brown's significant study, *Robert Laird Borden, A Biography 1854-1914* (T., Mac., 1975). This is a well-written and well-researched political account that treats Borden as a less-than-perfect but well-meaning politician. The book can be supplemented by Brown's articles: "The Political Ideas of Robert Borden," in Hamelin, *The Political Ideas of the Prime Ministers of Canada*; and "'Whither are we being shoved'? Political Leadership in Canada during World War I," in J. L. Granatstein and R. D. Cuff, eds., *War and Society in North America* (T., Nelson, 1971). W. S. Wallace, *The Memoirs of the Rt. Hon. Sir George Foster*, (T., 1933), provides some material on one of Borden's principal colleagues, as does J. W. Dafoe, "The Political Career of Sir George Foster" (*CHR*, 1934), a review article of Wallace's book. But of much greater importance is W. R. Graham's *Arthur Meighen*, Vol. 1, *The Door of Opportunity* (T., Clarke Irwin, 1960). A sympathetic treatment, Graham makes no attempt to conceal his conclusion that Meighen was an intellectual giant amongst political pygmies. Although he sees issues and personalities through the eyes of Meighen and adopts most of the conclusions reached by his subject, it is a well-written account of Meighen's early career. Equally important is Margaret Prang's *N. W. Rowell: Ontario Nationalist* (T., UTP, 1975), a massive study of the Ontario Liberal leader who entered Borden's coalition in 1917. The book is a steady, reliable guide to the politics of the period, but it fails to provide much insight into the motivation of Rowell and his powerful and wealthy Methodist friends.

W. R. Graham, "The Cabinet of 1911," in Gibson, *Cabinet Formation and Bicultural Relations*, is an interesting account of the problems Borden confronted in forming his cabinet. But most of the studies available revolve around the conscription issue. The best work on the subject is still Elizabeth Armstrong, *The Crisis of Quebec, 1914-1918*, (N.Y., Columbia Univ. Press, 1937), an analysis of French-Canadian opinion during the period. There are a number of good articles on the subject as well. The most suggestive, perhaps, is one by A. M. Willms, "Conscription 1917: A Brief for the Defence" (*CHR*, 1956), in which the author argues that conscription was militarily necessary and politically unpopular. Others include: Ramsay Cook, "Dafoe, Laurier, and the Formation of Union Government," (*CHR*, 1961); J. M. Bliss, "The Methodist Church and World War I" (*CHR*, 1968); Martin Robin, "Registration, Conscription, and Independent Labour Politics, 1916-1917" (*CHR*, 1966); and W. R. Young, "Conscription, Rural Depopulation, and the Farmers of Ontario, 1917-1919" (*CHR*, 1972). Labour unrest following the end of the war has drawn the attention of historians as well. D. C. Masters, *The Winnipeg General Strike*, (T., UTP, 1950) has been supplanted as the standard source for the notorious strike by David Bercuson's well-done *Confrontation at Winnipeg* (M., McGill-Queen's, 1974) and by Bercuson and Kenneth McNaught, *The Winnipeg Strike: 1919* (T., Longmans, 1974). Also useful is Norman Penner, ed., *Winnipeg 1919* (T., James Lewis and Samuel, 1973), an account of the strike, prepared by the strikers' defence committee.

AFTER THE GREAT WAR

The political and social ferment in Canada after the Great War was unprecedented in intensity. The war had left Laurier Liberalism in tatters and the reactionary policies of Union government had tarnished both Union Tories and Liberals. The situation was ideal for the emergence of a new political movement, and the farmers, long feeling left out of the progress and profits of the boom years of the century, were quick to take advantage.

The basic book on *The Progressive Party in Canada* (T., UTP, 1950) is still that by W. L. Morton. For almost a quarter-century this well-researched and well-written volume has effectively dominated the field, and his analysis of the political and economic basis of Progressivism is still sound. Students should also refer to Morton's numerous articles on the Progressives, including his "The Western Progressive Movement and Cabinet Domination" (*CJEPS*, 1946), "The Western Progressive Movement 1919-21" (*CHAR*, 1946), and "Direct Legislation and the Origins of the Progressive Movement" (*CHR*, 1944), as well as to his *Manitoba: A History* (T., UTP, 1957).

Four recent collections of essays on the West contain articles that are useful in understanding the discontent that produced the farmers' revolt. S. M. Trofimenkoff, ed., *The Twenties in Western Canada* (Ottawa, National Museum, 1972), contains a number of articles, and most particularly an essay on T. A. Crerar, a classic Liberal-Progressive, by Foster Griezic, and an essay on Prairie cooperatives by Ian Macpherson. David Gagan, ed., *Prairie Perspectives* (T., Holt Rinehart and Winston, 1970), has a useful brief article by Denis Smith on "Liberals and Conservatives on the Prairies, 1917-68." *Prairie Perspectives 2* (T., 1973), ed. by A. W. Rasporich and H. C. Klassen, brings together a large number of essays, including a sweeping interpretation of "The West and the Nation, 1870-1970" by Professor Morton. Finally, there are two good bibliographical essays on the Prairies in Richard Allen, ed., *A Region of the Mind: Interpreting the Western Canadian Plains* (Regina, Univ. of Sask. Press, 1973).

Among still useful contemporary books are two by William Irvine, *Cooperative Government* (Ottawa, 1929) and *The Farmers in Politics* (T., 1920). Another is L. A. Wood, *A History of Farmers' Movements in Canada* (T., 1924; reprinted, T., UTP, 1975). Paul F. Sharp, *The Agrarian Revolt in Western Canada* (Minneapolis, Univ. of Minn. Press, 1948), deliberately sets out to draw American parallels, and largely succeeds. There is first-class material in Ramsay Cook, ed., *The Dafoe-Sifton Correspondence* (Altona, Man., *Manitoba Record Society Publications*, 1966), and in W. K. Rolph, *Henry Wise Wood of Alberta* (T., UTP, 1950), the only study of the Alberta leader. For the Ontario Progressives, students should use E. C. Drury, *Farmer Premier* (T., M&S, 1966), and W. C. Good, *Farmer Citizen* (T., Ryerson, 1958), neither of which is very satisfactory or analytical about events in which both men participated.

Politics in Ottawa in this period were dominated by the battle between Arthur Meighen and Mackenzie King. The brilliant and lucid Meighen fought against King's puffy platitudes and lost repeatedly. Meighen's biography by Roger Graham, especially *Arthur Meighen*, Vol. II: *And Fortune Fled* (T. Clarke Irwin, 1963), is also brilliant and lucid, but partisan in the extreme. Meighen's letters and speeches are used to build an effective portrait of the Conservative leader, but what Graham finds admirable, readers may dislike. Also useful are Graham's articles, "Meighen and the Montreal Tycoons: Railway Policy in the Election of 1921" (*CHAR*, 1957), "Arthur Meighen and the Conservative Party in Quebec" (*CHR*, 1955), "Comments on a Credible Canadian" (*CHR* 1958), and "Some Political Ideas of Arthur Meighen," in *The Political Ideas of the Prime Ministers of Canada*. Meighen's speeches are collected in the characteristically titled *Unrevised and Unrepented* (T., Clarke Irwin, 1949), and while they convey something of the spirit of the man, Meighen at his biting best should be read in House of Commons *Debates*.

Only the brave should try to read Mackenzie King in *Hansard*. It is much more rewarding to turn to the official biography where King's exercises in circumlocution have been sorted out. The first volume, covering the period from 1874 to 1923, is by R. MacGregor Dawson; the second, for 1924-32, and the third, for 1932-39, are by H. Blair Neatby (T., UTP, 1958, 1963, 1976). The biographers are generally sympathetic to King, Dawson perhaps a shade more so than Neatby, but there is no real attempt to hide Mr. King's many warts. Neatby's description of the constitutional crisis of 1926 or King's waffling policies in the 1930s are admirably fair, although both areas have been the subject of polemics in the past. The three volumes show appreciation for King's political skills and his sensitivity to the national— or regional —mood, and the official biography forms the best foundation for the revisionist approaches to King that are now underway. King collected his speeches in several volumes. For the 1920s, see *The Message of the Carillon* (T., Mac., 1927). To understand King's conception of *Industry and Humanity*, reference should be had to the re-issued version (T., UTP, 1973) with its sympathetic introduction by D. J. Bercuson. The one popular biography of King's whole career that has lasted is Bruce Hutchison's *The Incredible Canadian* (T., Longmans, 1952). Based on shrewd observation and access to memoranda of conversations with King and other ministers prepared by Hutchison's newspaper colleague, Grant Dexter, this biography has some first class material in it. For King's early years before he became Premier, there are three very different interpretations. H.

S. Ferns and B. Ostry, writing without access to King's papers, did a hatchet job on King in *The Age of Mackenzie King: The Rise of the Leader* (1955; T., Lorimer, 1976), and only some of the damage was repaired by F. A. McGregor, King's longtime secretary, in *The Fall and Rise of Mackenzie King: 1911-1919* (T., Mac., 1962). Completely different from these books, although nearer in tone to Ferns and Ostry than to McGregor, is C. P. Stacey's *A Very Double Life: The Private World of Mackenzie King* (T., Mac., 1976). Some readers may feel uncomfortable at this less-than-sympathetic prying into King's sexual life and into his dabblings in spiritualism.

To understand the things that moved King, as Stacey well realized, recourse must be had to his massive and informative diaries. All the diary up 1931 is available in a microfiche edition from the University of Toronto Press. But unfortunately only those for the period 1939 to 1948 have been published as J. W. Pickersgill, ed., *The Mackenzie King Record*, Vols. I-IV (T., UTP, 1960-70). *The Record* provides personal material in abundance, and is extremely useful too for reliable comment on events, meetings and persons. Some useful articles on King include: Blair Neatby's fine study of "Mackenzie King and National Unity," in Dyck and Krosby, *Empire and Nations*; and his "The Political Ideas of . . . King," in *The Political Ideas of the Prime Ministers of Canada*; J. A. Gibson's "Mr. Mackenzie King and Canadian Autonomy, 1921-1946" (*CHAR*, 1951); J. W. Pickersgill's " Mackenzie King's Speeches" (*QQ*, 1950); and the articles by John Courtney and J. E. Esberey on "Prime Ministerial Character" (*CJPS*, 1975). As a corrective to these accounts, students should see Eugene Forsey's roundhouse assaults in "Mr. King and Parliamentary Government" (*CJEPS*, 1951), and in his *The Royal Power of Dissolution of Parliament in the British Commonwealth* (T., OUP, 1968). Senator Forsey's analysis of the King-Byng affair of 1926 is classic academic vituperation. For additional material, Roger Graham's documents book, *The King-Byng Affair 1926* (T., Copp Clark, 1967), collects the relevant sources.

Much additional useful material on King, Meighen and the politics of the 1920s exists, of course. *Les Mémoires du Senateur Raoul Dandurand (1861-1942)* (Quebec, Laval

Univ. Press, 1967) unfortunately tells us little, but no student should miss the brilliant essays by F. H. Underhill, many of which have been collected in his *In Search of Canadian Liberalism*. Many of the Underhill pieces first appeared in *The Canadian Forum* and its backfiles are very good for left-centre comment throughout the 1920s and 1930s. Ramsay Cook's *The Politics of J. W. Dafoe and the Free Press* (T., UTP, 1963) is an excellent look at the influential Winnipeg editor as is his article "John W. Dafoe: Conservative Progressive" (*CHAR*, 1961). Also excellent is James Eayrs' *In Defence of Canada*: Vol. I: *From the Great War to the Great Depression* (T., UTP, 1964), a brilliant study of defence policy in the 1920s. And, although it is easy to become lost in a maze of abbreviations, William Rodney's *Soldiers of the International: A History of the Communist Party of Canada 1919-29* (T., UTP, 1968) is based on excellent research and may be contrasted with Ivan Avakumovic, *The Communist Party in Canada: A History* (T., M&S, 1975).

THE DEPRESSION

The easy and casual prosperity of the 1920s disappeared with stunning suddenness in late 1929, and until war restored prosperity Canada went through an agonizing period. There are several general books and articles with which students should begin their study of this period. One of the newest is Blair Neatby's *The Politics of Chaos: Canada in the Thirties* (T., Mac., 1972), a collection of TV lectures that provides a useful overview of the decade. Also valuable and enjoyable to browse through is Michiel Horn's fine documents collection, *The Dirty Thirties* (T., Copp Clark, 1972), and Victor Hoar, ed., *The Great Depression* (T., Copp Clark, n.d.). Particularly useful in the Hoar collection is Neatby's article on early Keynesian tendencies in budget making, "The Liberal Way: Fiscal and Monetary Policy in the 1930's." A soul-destroying book—and one that few will be able to push through to the end—is Linda Grayson and J. M. Bliss, eds., *The Wretched of Canada: Letters to R. B. Bennett 1930-35* (T., UTP, 1971). The poor wrote to the Prime Minister asking for aid, and surprisingly often Bennett responded with cash.

His policies, however, left something to be desired when it came to dealing with the Depression. Perhaps in reaction to this there has been relatively little in the way of scholarship on either Bennett or his five years in power. The two biographies are unsatisfactory. Lord Beaverbrook's *Friends* (L., Heinemann, 1959) adds nothing beyond silly judgments, while Ernest Watkins, *R. B. Bennett* (T., Kingswood House, 1963), does not appear to be based on substantial research. More useful is J. R. H. Wilbur's collection of documents and articles on *The Bennett New Deal* (T., Copp Clark, 1968) his book *H. H. Stevens* (T., UTP, 1977) and his articles "H. H. Stevens and R. B. Bennett, 1930-34" (*CHR*, 1962) and "H. H. Stevens and the Reconstruction Party" (*CHR*, 1964). Stevens broke with Bennett in late 1934 in response to his failure to win any action from the Prime Minister in meeting the needs of small businessmen. Once Stevens organized his own Reconstruction Party, stealing away hundreds of thousands of potentially Conservative voters, Bennett was doomed. Wilbur's articles tell the story quite well. Bennett's successor as Conservative leader, Dr. R. J. Manion, wrote an autobiography, *Life Is an Adventure* (T., Ryerson, 1936) which has a brief, frank portrait of Bennett. Another book of value is Marc LaTerreur, *Les Tribulations des conservateurs au Québec* (Quebec, Laval Univ. Press, 1973), an analysis of Quebec's weak Tories from Bennett's period to Diefenbaker's. One revelation in Lita-Rose Betcherman, *The Swastika and the Maple Leaf: Fascist Movements in Canada in the Thirties* (T., Fitzhenry and Whiteside, 1975) is that the Conservatives supported financially the Arcand fascists in Quebec, a somewhat frightening state of affairs.

THE CCF

Out of the despair of the depression came a socialist party, the Cooperative Commonwealth Federation. And, like most of the third parties in our recent history, the CCF has received substantial attention from scholars. There are several overall surveys of the party, of which much the best is Walter Young's excellent *The Anatomy of a Party: The National CCF 1932-61* (T., UTP, 1969). Based on solid research, Young grapples with the problems faced by a social movement that tries to act like a political party, and he is very effective in analyzing the role of party bureaucracy. He has also written a brief survey volume, *Democracy and Discontent* (T., Ryerson, 1969) that puts the CCF into a western perspective. Still useful is Dean McHenry, *The Third Force in Canada* (T., OUP, 1950), an early scholarly look at the party, and S. M. Lipset's study of the CCF in Saskatchewan, *Agrarian Socialism*. Originally published in 1950, Lipset has been up-dated and supplemented with a series of essays in a new edition (N.Y., Doubleday, 1968). His article, "Political Participation and the Origin of the CCF in Saskatchewan" (*CJEPS*, 1948), should also be examined for its discussion of the very broad support the CCF gathered among elite groups.

There are still more books on the party. Gerald Caplan's *The Dilemma of Canadian Socialism* (T., M&S, 1973) is really a study of the CCF's failure in Ontario, and unfortunately omits much recent research. Leo Zakuta's *A Protest Movement Becalmed* (T., UTP, 1964) is a study of change in the CCF and one that annoyed party members when it appeared, in part because of its hostile attitude and also because it reproduces *in extenso* conversations on which no notes or recordings were apparently taken. Gad Horowitz' *Canadian Labour in Politics* (T., UTP, 1968) examines the role played by labour unions in the development of the CCF and NDP, though he says little about that segment of labour which did not support that party and hardly mentions Quebec where the labour movement has stayed aloof. He also expounds brilliantly the red-tory thesis, but Irving Abella's *Nationalism, Communism and Canadian Labour* (T., UTP, 1973) is better in its treatment of labour.

In terms of frankly political material, the student should look at David Lewis and Frank Scott, *Make This Your Canada* (T., 1943), a book written in the full flush of CCF optimism during the war, as was M. J. Coldwell's *Left Turn, Canada* (N.Y., Duell, Sloan and Pearce, 1945). There are also several politically committed historical essays in L. LaPierre, *et al.,* *Essays on the Left* (T., M&S, 1971). For a sampling of antisocialist literature, B. A. Trestrail, *Stand Up and Be Counted* (T., M&S, 1944) is a classic in scurrility, while R. T. Ferguson, *We Stand on Guard* (M., 1945) is a bit more restrained.

There are also several CCF biographies. Much the best is K. W. McNaught's fine study of J. S. Woodsworth, *A Prophet in Politics* (T., UTP, 1959). Woodsworth's daughter, Grace McInnis, wrote *J. S. Woodsworth, A Man to Remember* (T., Mac., 1953). There is also the warmly sympathetic but severely flawed *Tommy Douglas* (T., M&S, 1975) by Doris Shackleton. Douglas is the *nonpareil* fighting evil inside the party and without but the research is sometimes sloppy and the errors abound. Biographies of other figures include Dorothy Steeves' study of Ernest Winch, *The Compassionate Rebel* (Vancouver, 1960) and two biographies of politicians who remained partly aloof from the CCF: Leo Heaps' biography of his father, A. A. Heaps, *The Rebel in the House* (L. Niccolo, 1970); and M. Stewart and D. French, *Ask No Quarter: The Story of Agnes Macphail* (T., Longman, 1959).

SOCIAL CREDIT

There is similarly a large body of literature on Social Credit, that other radical product of the Depression. The major works are to be found in the Social Science Research Council series, "Social Credit in Alberta," a ten-volume large-scale enterprise that looked widely into the origins and developments of the society of the West. The most valuable books in the series, from a political point of view are: J. R. Mallory, *Social Credit and the Federal Power in Canada* (T., UTP, 1954); J. A. Irving, *The Social Credit Movement in Alberta* (T., UTP, 1959); and C. B. Macpherson, *Democracy in Alberta: Social Credit and the Party System* (T., UTP, 1953). Irving succeeds in getting to the roots of William Aberhart's appeal to the Albertans of the 1930s. Macpherson erects the theory of the quasi-party to explain the phenomenon of one-party dominance in democratic states.

These last three authors also have numerous articles on Social Credit. Macpherson's "The Political Theory of Social Credit" (*CJEPS*, 1949) makes the complicated fiscal policies of Social Credit as simple as A + B. Irving's articles try to explain "The Appeal of Social Credit" (*QQ*, 1953), "The Evolution of the Social Credit Movement" (*CJEPS*, 1948), and to examine "Psychological Aspects of the Social Credit Movement in Alberta" (*Canadian Journal of Psychol-*

ogy, 1948). Mallory's article, "The Lieutenant Governor as a Dominion Officer ... " (*CJEPS*, 1948), looks at the reservation of three Social Credit measures in 1937, a theme that John Saywell studies in "Reservation Revisited: Alberta 1937" (*CJEPS*, 1962) and in *The Office of Lieutenant-Governor*.

Other studies of note are in the articles of Harold Schultz. His "The Social Credit Backbenchers' Revolt, 1937" *(CHR*, 1960) and "A Second Term, 1940" (*Alberta Historical Review*, 1962) look at the legislative happenings in Premier Aberhart's government, while his "Aberhart, The Organization Man" (*Alberta Historical Review*, 1959) tries to focus on the talents of the Premier. The one biography of *Aberhart of Alberta* (Edmonton, 1970) is by L. P. V. Johnson and Ola MacNutt, Aberhart's daughter. There is also N. B. James' humorous and revealing *The Autobiography of a Nobody* (T., Dent, 1947). James was a Social Credit M.L.A. John Finlay's *Social Credit: The English Origins* (M., McGill-Queens Univ. Press, 1972) focusses on Major Douglas and his ideas, while Hugh Whalen's article studies the nature of "Social Credit Measures in Alberta" (*CJEPS*, 1952). Mary Hallett, "The Social Credit Party and the New Democracy Movement, 1939-1940" (*CHR*, 1966), looks at Social Credit's abortive pro-conscription effort in national politics in the 1940 election.

THE SECOND WORLD WAR

The politics of the war years have not yet been thoroughly studied in detail. There is no history of the Liberal Party and no detailed biographies of Mackenzie King or his most important ministers. *The Mackenzie King Record* is, of course, an extremely valuable source, as is Norman Ward, ed., *A Party Politician: The Memoirs of Chubby Power* (T., Mac., 1966), a funny and frank look at King's Air Minister. John Hawkins, *The Life and Times of Angus L* (Windsor, N.S., Lancelot Press, 1969), a study of King's Navy Minister, Angus L. Macdonald, is an embarrassment, and the only biography of C. D. Howe, Leslie Roberts' *C.D.* (T., Clarke Irwin, 1957) is not much use. Dale Thomson's *Louis St. Laurent, Canadian* (T., Mac., 1967) is the first biography of King's successor, written by a former aide and McGill political scientist. Although Thomson apparently had access to private materials, the book does not succeed in lifting the pall of grey competence that blankets the period 1948-57, nor does it add anything to existing books about wartime politics. There is, however, interesting material in John Swettenham's *McNaughton*, Vol. II: *1939-43* and Vol. III: *1944-69* (T., Ryerson, 1969) particularly on political-military relations, the conscription crisis of 1944, and on McNaughton's brief period as Minister of National Defence. King's Ontario antagonist, *Mitch Hepburn*, is amusingly examined by Neil McKenty (T., M&S, 1967), and there is also some useful political information in: Vincent Massey, *What's Past is Prologue* (T., Mac. 1963); L. B. Pearson, *Mike*, Vol. I: *The Memoirs of the Rt. Hon. Lester Pearson 1897-1948* (T., UTP, 1972); and Arnold Heeney, *The Things that are Caesar's* (T., UTP, 1972). The one study of the wartime King government is J. L. Granatstein's *Canada's War: The Politics of the Mackenzie King Government 1939-1949* (T., OUP, 1975). This brings together material from British, American and Canadian sources and provides detailed overviews of conscription, politics and social welfare along with elections and the party struggles.

"Liberal Party Finances, 1935-45" have been studied by Granatstein in M. S. Cross and R. Bothwell, *Policy By Other Means* (T., Clarke Irwin, 1972), and there is additional material on this subject both in *The Report of the Committee on Election Expenses* (Ottawa, QP, 1966) and in *Studies in Canadian Party Finance* (Ottawa, QP, 1967). K. Z. Paltiel, the research director for the Committee, has published *Political Party Financing in Canada* (T., McGraw-Hill, 1970), a simple digest of the Committee's findings.

There is good material in J. L. Granatstein's *The Politics of Survival* (T., UTP, 1967), a study of the Conservative Party in the war years, and in his "Conservative Party Finances 1939-45," in *Studies in Canadian Party Finance*. John R. Williams, *The Conservative Party of Canada 1920-49* (Durham, Duke Univ. Press, 1956) was written before the important sources were available. Also useful are Granatstein's studies of conscription, *Conscription in the Second World War* (T., Ryerson, 1969), "The Conservative Party and Conscription in the Second World War" (*CHAR*, 1967), and "Le Québec et le plébiscite de 1942 sur la conscription" (*RHAF*, 1973). His "Mackenzie King and the Turn to Social Welfare, 1943-1945" (*Quarterly of Canadian Studies*, 1972) examines the move for family allowances, and his "The York South By-Election of 1942" (*CHR*, 1967) looks at the key by-election that started the CCF on their rise and that defeated Meighen for the last time. This period of Meighen's career is examined in Roger Graham, *Arthur Meighen*, Vol. III: *No Surrender* (T., Clarke Irwin, 1965), the least satisfactory of the three volumes in this biography. There is detailed information on the Conservative wartime conventions (and those of other parties, too) in John Courtney's *The Selection of National Party Leaders in Canada* (T., Mac., 1973). André Laurendeau's *La Crise de la conscription de 1942* is available in English in P. Stratford, ed., *André Laurendeau, Witness for Quebec* (T., Mac., 1973), and Robert Rumilly's massive *Duplessis et son temps* (M., Fides, 1973) is useful, as is his *Histoire de la province de Québec*, tomes XXXVIII-XLI (M., Fides, 1968-9).

POSTWAR POLITICS

The scholarly literature is thin while the journalistic studies abound for this period. *The Mackenzie King Record*, Vols. III and IV, is indispensable for the years 1945 to 1948, and the Thomson biography of St. Laurent sketches out the events of the period to 1957. J. W. Pickersgill's adulatory memoir of *My Years With Louis St. Laurent* (T., UTP, 1975) goes some distance to redress the prevailing view of 1948-57 as years of good, gray competence. The Pearson autobiography, *Mike* I, II and III (T., UTP, 1972-5) is also essential for the period although the last two volumes, posthumously ghosted for the most part, are lifeless by comparison with the first. John Diefenbaker's *One Canada* (2 vols., T., Mac., 1975-6) is a spirited defence of a sometimes bad, often good record. The Chief's bitterness shows through very frequently, most notably at Dalton Camp whose very fine memoir *Gentlemen, Players and Politicians* (T., M&S, 1970) unfortunately stops before Dief was dumped. Peter Stursberg's *Diefenbaker: Leadership Gained* (T., UTP, 1975) and *Diefenbaker: Leadership Lost* (T., UTP, 1976) are collages produced from oral history tapes. Both books have much useful information and capture the flavour of the time, but scissors and paste books that present edited versions of interviews have to be treated with some caution by students of the period. The Diefenbaker era has produced a large number of journalistic accounts of which the best is Peter Newman's *Renegade in Power* (T., M&S, 1963). Surprisingly good is Pierre Sevigny, *This Game of Politics* (T., M&S, 1965), a book that was written before public knowledge of Mr. Sevigny's role in the Munsinger affair.

Denis Smith's splendid biography of Walter Gordon, *Gentle Patriot*, (Edmonton, Hurtig, 1973) is a model of how to write biographies of contemporaries. It is fair but firm in its judgments, particularly those on Mr. Pearson, and it seems clear that the revisionists have already begun work. A bad biography, very British in form, is Robert Speaight, *Vanier: Soldier, Diplomat and Governor-General* (T., Collins, 1970). Joey Smallwood's idiosyncratic *I Chose Canada* (T., Mac., 1973) has some tart comments on federal politicians, but its length will wear out all but the hardiest.

For presently practising politicians, there are only journalistic studies. Geoffrey Stevens' *Stanfield* (T., M&S, 1973) is much the best of these, much better than Anthony Westell's *Paradox: Trudeau as Prime Minister* (T., Prentice-Hall, 1972) or the harshly critical *Shrug: Trudeau in Power* (T., New Press, 1971), by Walter Stewart.

The best guide to national and provincial politics from 1960 on is undoubtedly to be found in John Saywell, ed., *The Canadian Annual Review* (T., UTP, 1961-). Each year, the *CAR* brings out at least 100 pages of first-class analysis on national politics. A good history of the NDP, from its founding to 1973, is Desmond Morton's *NDP: The Dream of Power* (T., Hakkert, 1974). Some good newspapermen's accounts are: Peter Newman's *The Distemper of Our Times: Canadian Politics in Transition 1963-68* (T., M&S, 1968); Patrick Nicholson's *Vision and Indecision: Diefenbaker and Pearson* (T. Longman, 1968); Richard Gwyn's *The Shape of Scandal* (T., Clarke Irwin, 1965), a fine study of the scandals that wracked the Pearson government in its first two years; and Martin Sullivan's analysis of the Trudeau boom in 1968, *Mandate '68* (T. Doubleday, 1968). All these books are based on private sources, particularly the Nicholson book, which has the best inside account of the collapse of the Diefenbaker government in 1962-3 based on both Conservative and Social Credit leaks.

Among useful academic studies, John Meisel's work stands out. His *The Canadian General Election of 1957* (T., UTP, 1962) is a model election study, and his edited collection, *Papers on the 1962 Election* (T., UTP, 1964) is also very useful. More technical, but illustrative of the new political science methodology, is his *Working Papers on Canadian Politics* (M., McGill-Queens, 1972; rev. ed., 1973) which goes into some depth in analyzing the bases of party support in the 1968 election and which offers preliminary data on party images in Canada and on the 1972 election. One of the earliest academic pollster books was Peter Regenstreif's *The Diefenbaker Interlude* (T., Longmans, 1965). Other valuable books are Howard Penniman, ed., *Canada at the Polls: The General Election of 1974* (Washington, American Enterprise Institute, 1975), a collection of studies by Canadians on party finance, public opinion, the media and the parties; John C. Courtney, *The Selection of National Party Leaders in Canada* (T., Mac., 1973); Paul Pross, ed., *Pressure Group Behaviour in Canadian Politics* (T., McGraw-Hill, 1975); and C. Winn and J. McMenemy, *Political Parties in Canada* (T., McGraw-Hill, 1976), a collection of current political science approaches to the subject.

There are two good studies of Social Credit in Quebec in the 1950s and 1960s. Michael Stein's *The Dynamics of Right Wing Protest: A Political Analysis of Social Credit in Quebec* (T., UTP, 1973) is good on the party, but on less safe ground when the author tries to formulate a theory of right wing movements. Maurice Pinard's *The Rise of a Third Party* (Englewood, N.J., Prentice-Hall, 1971) is primarily an analysis of the dramatic Créditiste surge in Quebec in the 1962 election.

In a class by itself is Donald Creighton's *Canada 1939-1957: The Forked Road* (T., M&S, 1976), a volume in the Centenary Series. The country's greatest historian here presents a very personal, lightly researched and almost idiosyncratic look at the events since the beginning of the Second World War. Much of the analysis had been presented earlier in *Canada's First Century* (T., Mac., 1970) and as that volume stirred controversy so will this one, too.

Foreign and Defence Policy

J. L. Granatstein

The scholarly literature on foreign and defence policy in Canada is still not large. In part this is a reflection of the recent colonial past; more important, it is the result of the very small number of Canadian scholars who specialized in such fields. Until the 1960s the number of academic experts in these areas could be counted on two hands—with fingers to spare. Even today, there are probably not more than thirty-five specialists in the study of Canadian external policy.

To some extent, the non-availability of source materials limited the field. The records of the Department of External Affairs have only now been opened to scholars for the period up to 1946, and the papers of Prime Ministers and Cabinet ministers have only recently become available *in toto* for the same period. The result is that the history of Canadian external affairs and defence policy is in its infancy. Whether the new sources will force major revisions in our understanding of our past is not yet certain, but the likelihood is great that it will. And amen to that.

BIBLIOGRAPHIES

There is no detailed and critical bibliography of Canadian foreign and defence policy. The best source is undoubtedly Claude Thibault's massive *Bibliographia Canadiana* (T., Longman, 1973), a guide to the whole of Canadian history but one that suffers from a cumbersome organization and a serious lack of consistent cross-referencing. Nonetheless, every student should begin his research with this book.

For the period after 1945, the "golden age" of the foreign policy, there are two large bibliographies, both published by the Canadian Institute of International Affairs. The first, *A Reading guide to Canada in World Affairs* (T., 1972), is edited by Laurence Motiuk and Madeline Grant. The second, Donald M. Page's *A Bibliography of Works on Canadian Foreign Relations, 1945-1970* (T., 1973), is better arranged and organized than the Motiuk-Grant bibliography. The sole guide to work on defence policy is Laurence Motiuk's *Canadian Forces College Reading Guide for the Study of War, National Defence and Strategy* (T., Canadian Forces College, 1967). This volume is more of a "how not to do it" bibliography than a successful guide to the material, in part because articles are catalogued by journal, not by subject.

OFFICIAL SOURCES

Given the dearth of secondary sources, the researcher is forced to use the various materials published by the government. The basic source, of course, is the *Debates* of the House of Commons. Massive in size and occasionally tedious, the *Debates* have the solitary virtue of being well indexed. The same thing can be said of Senate *Debates*, especially the tedium. Both sources cover the whole post-confederation period. More useful than the *Debates* are the *Minutes* of the Standing Committee on External Affairs and National Defence of the House of Commons, an institution that was not set up until the mid-1960s. Here, for example, are the best published materials on the unification controversy.

Other sources that should be sought out are the *Reports* of the Departments of External Affairs and National Defence. No earth-shaking material here, but useful data on personnel, policy, budgetary matters. The Department of External Affairs has also from time to time published small collections of documents, often of British materials, on various crises. There are, to cite a few, collections on the Italo-Ethiopian Crisis (1936), on the Outbreak of War (1939), on Korea (1950, 1951) and on the Suez Crisis (1956, 1957). The Department also published for some twenty years after the Second World War a series of annual volumes on *Canada and the United Nations*. The early volumes are exceedingly useful compendiums of speeches and documents, but the more recent volumes are turgid government-speak. The Department's *Report on the United Nations Conference on International Organization... 1945* (Ottawa, 1945) is a valuable collection of documents on the San Francisco meeting that established the United Nations.

Easily the most valuable books published by External Affairs are the massive *Documents on Canadian External Relations*. The series, begun in 1967, has thus far produced eight fat volumes covering the period from the Department's founding in 1909 to the second year of war in 1941. The series is to be continued through the war and cold war years. The first six volumes suffer from serious flaws. Too often the space is devoted to tedious telegrams, treaties, and press releases. The source of the document is never cited, so that a researcher seeking the remainder of a file is doomed to long hours of searching. Occasionally the choice of document seems designed to obscure rather than to elucidate, and the introductions (as that in Vol. V) are sometimes silly. But these criticisms notwithstanding, the series is straightforward, well-indexed, and a very good source. An additional volume published by the Department of External Affairs must also be cited, P. A. Bridle, ed., *Documents on Relations Between Canada and Newfoundland 1936-49* (1974). This is the first of two volumes on the subject and a very good collection of documents indeed. The student should also be aware that Canadian material is often found in the similar American series, *Foreign Relations of the United States*, and less often in the *Documents on British Foreign Policy* and the *Documents on German Foreign Policy*.

Students should also know of the Department of External Affairs' magazines. *External Affairs* was started after 1945 as a repository for dusty speeches and press releases, although occasionally good material slipped through the censors and found its way into print. After the Trudeau government took power, the new image of the Department was reflected in *International Perspectives*, a glossier and much better journal with good articles. And if speeches are your idea of a source, *Statements and Speeches* are issued by the dozens each year by the Department. A good library should have a near-complete run.

National Defence has not published as freely as its counterpart. *The Canadian Defence Quarterly* was its journal in the interwar years, succeeded after the war by the *Canadian Army Journal*, the *Crowsnest* and the *Roundel*. After unification, the three were consolidated into the glossy *Sentinel*, a picture monthly, but one that occasionally has a detailed article, as for example its examination of the FLQ crisis in Quebec. The Department's White Papers, most notably that published in 1964 and that of 1971 (*Defence in the 70s*), are important policy documents, and current information is readily found in the yearly departmental reports, *Defence 71*, *Defence 72*, etc. Historical publications will be cited below.

GENERAL HISTORIES

The single general history of external relations is that by G. P. de T. Glazebrook, late of the Department of External Affairs and the University of Toronto. The first part of his *A History of Canadian External Relations* was published in 1942 and covered the period to the Great War. In 1950 an expanded version was published (T., OUP), that carried the story to the post-1945 world, and in 1962 the volume was reissued in paperback in two volumes. (T., M&S, 1962). Glazebrook's work is largely based on secondary sources and is notable primarily because it established the parameters within which virtually every other scholar has operated. The story follows the familiar path from colony to nation with elaborate by-ways into the murky materials of diplomacy. Glazebrook is certain to be superseded, particularly in his work on the period since 1900, but this is still the place to start.

The only other book that has made an attempt at covering the sweep of Canadian policy is R. A. MacKay and E. B. Rogers, *Canada Looks Abroad* (T., OUP, 1938). In many respects this book is better than Glazebrook—better written, more interesting and more pithy. Equally interesting is the little survey by Charles Stacey, *The Military Problems of Canada* (T., Ryerson, 1940), the sole survey of defence policy. This should be read in conjunction with G. F. G. Stanley's *Canada's Soldiers* (T., Mac., 1954), a popular history of Canada's wars and warriors.

A few additional general studies may be mentioned

here. J. Bartlet Brebner's *North Atlantic Triangle: The Interplay of Canada, the United States and Great Berlin* (T., Ryerson, 1945) is still a useful and suggestive interpretation whose title tells its purpose. Brebner's was but one of the many volumes in the great series, *The Relations of Canada and the United States*, edited by J. T. Shotwell for the Carnegie Endowment for International Peace. Also useful, though badly dated, of course, is H. A. Keenleyside, *Canada and the United States* (N.Y., Knopf, 1929). The author, later a member of External Affairs, is quite prescient in some of his comments on American influence in Canada. Of interest is Gerald Craig's *The United States and Canada* (Cambridge, Harvard Univ. Press, 1968) which is, however, less of a history of international relations than a history of Canada for Americans.

THE FIRST YEARS, 1867-1914

In this period when Canada could be said not to have had a foreign policy of her own, there is still much room for research. The result is that most books are either exceedingly narrow in focus or else so all inclusive as to be less than important for the student of external affairs.

The first place to begin is with the standard biographies of Prime Ministers, referred to in the National Politics section. Creighton's *Macdonald*, Thomson's *Alexander Mackenzie*, Skelton's *Laurier* and Brown's *Borden*, are all good books that have substantial material about Canada's relations with Britain and the United States in them. Skelton's *Laurier* is particularly fascinating for what it tells us about its author, O. D. Skelton, the Undersecretary of State for External Affairs from 1925 to 1941 and the creator of the modern Department of External Affairs. Joseph Schull's *Laurier: The First Canadian* (T., Mac., 1966) has not superseded Skelton's biography. Also worth note are Sir Charles Tupper, *Recollections of Sixty Years in Canada* (T., Cassell, 1914), the two volume *Life and Letters of Sir Charles Tupper* (T., Cassell, 1916), and the subsequent *Supplement to the Life and Letters* (T., Ryerson, 1926). In addition to a long political career that culminated briefly in the premiership, Tupper was High Commissioner in London for a long period.

Other biographies of importance are J. M. S. Careless'

fine *Brown of the Globe* (T., Mac., 1959, 1963) particularly for its discussion of the abortive negotiations with the Americans on reciprocity questions during the Mackenzie administration, and O. D. Skelton's *Life and Times of Sir Alexander Galt* (T., OUP, 1920), which carefully explores the financial links between British and Canadian capitalists and entrepreneurs. Sir John Wilson's study of *Sir George Parkin* (L., Mac., 1929) and W. L. Grant and Frederick Hamilton, *George Monro Grant* (T., Morang, 1905), are studies of Canadian imperialists of the turn of the century. Goldwin Smith's *Canada and the Canadian Question* (reprint; T., UTP, 1972) looks at the continentalist option of the same period.

Any consideration of imperialism and nationalism at this time must take into account the excellent study by Carl Berger, *The Sense of Power* (T., UTP, 1970). Intellectual history, social history and foreign policy—if one can describe the battle for the Canadian soul in this way—are brought into juxtaposition here. Berger has also collected documents together in his *Imperialism and Nationalism 1884-1914: A Conflict in Canadian Thought* (T., Copp Clark, 1969). The student should also read Norman Penlington's *Canada and Imperialism 1896-1899* (T., UTP, 1965), a book that anticipated some of Berger's arguments.

In this era, Governors General still had some importance, influence and power, and many hesitated not at all before using it. John Buchan, later a Governor General himself as Lord Tweedsmuir, wrote the life of *Lord Minto* (L., Nelson, 1925), and there are two interesting volumes in the publications of the Champlain Society. One is the *Dufferin-Carnarvon Correspondence 1874-1878*, edited by C. W. de Kiewiet and F. H. Underhill; the second is John Saywell's *The Canadian Journal of Lady Aberdeen, 1893-1898*, a marvelous, gossipy account by the wife of the Governor General.

For general histories of the period, all of which devote space to Canada's relations with Britain and the United States, the first place to turn is to the generally excellent volumes of the Centenary series, published by McClelland and Stewart. W. L. Morton's *The Critical Years . . . 1857-73* (1964), Peter Waite's *Canada 1874-96: Arduous Destiny* (1971), and R. C. Brown and Ramsay Cook's *Canada 1896-*

1921: A Nation Transformed (1974), cover the first half-century of Confederation in considerable detail. The first two volumes have extensive bibliographies; all have detailed footnotes.

For the period around Confederation, the reader should refer to Robin Winks' *Canada and the United States: The Civil War Years* (Baltimore, Johns Hopkins Univ. Press, 1960) and to David Farr, *The Colonial Office and Canada* (T., UTP, 1955). An extraordinary scholar, J. Mackay Hitsman completed *Safeguarding Canada 1763-1871* (T., UTP, 1968) although he was desperately ill. The last two chapters cover this period and very well indeed, as does Charles Stacey's excellent *Canada and the British Army 1846-71* (revised; T., UTP, 1963). Several of Stacey's voluminous articles cover the period, too, including "Fenianism and the Rise of National Feeling in Canada at the Time of Confederation" (*CHR*, 1931); "The Fenian Troubles and Canadian Military Development, 1865-71" (*CHR*, 1935); and "Britain's Withdrawal from North America, 1864-71" (*CHR*, 1955). As with all Stacey's works, these are marked by splendid prose style and thorough research. For strong views, no one should miss Donald Creighton. His polemic, *Canada's First Century* (T., Mac., 1970) covers this period and all others. His altering views on the United States and its influence on Confederation can be compared and contrasted with some of his earlier articles notably "Canada in the English-Speaking World" (*CHR*, 1945) and "The United States and Canadian Confederation" (*CHR*, 1958).

American intentions to Canada were not always benevolent in practice. Basic studies include L. B. Shippee, *Canadian-American Relations 1849-74* (New Haven, Yale Univ. Press, 1939), C. C. Tansill, *Canadian-American Relations 1875-1911* (New Haven, Yale Univ. Press, 1943) and L. E. Ellis, *Reciprocity 1911* (New Haven, Yale Univ. Press, 1939), all three being Carnegie series volumes and all three by American scholars. More useful, if more recent, are A. C. Glueck, *Minnesota and the Manifest Destiny of the American Northwest* (T., UTP, 1965) and the suggestive book by D. F. Warner, *The Idea of Continental Union* (Lexington, Univ. of Kentucky Press, 1960). R. C. Brown's *Canada's National Policy 1883-1900: A Study in Canadian-American Relations*

(Princeton, Princeton Univ. Press, 1964) is very detailed and valuable because, unlike most of the books hitherto cited, it attempts to relate external questions and domestic politics. Two studies that put Canada into place within an Anglo-American context are C. S. Campbell, *Anglo-American Understanding 1898-1903* (Baltimore, Johns Hopkins, 1957) and A. E. Campbell, *Great Britain and the United States 1895-1903* (L., Longman, 1960). For the complex Alaska Boundary dispute, reference can be made to John Munro, *The Alaska Boundary Dispute* (T., Copp Clark, 1970) and to Norman Penlington, *The Alaska Boundary Dispute: A Critical Appraisal* (T., McGraw-Hill Ryerson, 1972). The Munro volume is a documents collection, but there are substantial differences in interpretation on the merits of the Canadian and American cases and on the British role between him and Penlington. Another useful documents collection is Paul Stevens, *The 1911 General Election: A Study in Canadian Politics* (T., Copp Clark, 1970). Stevens assembles ample material to show the way commercial interests resisted any shift in the established trade patterns. In this same vein, students should read Robert Cuff's article, "The Toronto Eighteen and the Election of 1911" (*OH*, 1965).

There are other interesting articles scattered throughout the periodicals. Donald Creighton's "The Victorians and the Empire" (*CHR*, 1938) is still of value as is A. C. Cooke, "Empire Unity and Colonial Nationalism 1884-1911" (*CHAR*, 1955). James Eayrs' examination of "The Round Table Movement in Canada 1909-20" (*CHR*, 1957) should be supplemented by Carroll Quigley, "The Round Table Groups in Canada 1908-38" (*CHR*, 1962). The Articles by Neatby and Eayrs, among others, are collected in Carl Berger, ed., *Imperial Relations in the Age of Laurier* (Canadian Historical Readings No. 6; T., UTP, 1969), along with a useful introduction and additional bibliographical listings.

For military subjects, the Stacey and Hitsman books referred to above should be noted, as well as Richard Preston, *Canada and 'Imperial Defense'* (Durham, Duke Univ. Press, 1967), and his *Canada's RMC* (T., UTP, 1969), a well-done history of the Royal Military College, Kingston. An interesting curiosa is W. H. Russell's *Canada: Its Defences Condition and Resources* (L., 1865). On the Rebellion of

1885, the best source unquestionably is Desmond Morton's well-illustrated popular history, *The Last War Drum* (T., Hakkert, 1972), which can be supplemented with his and R. H. Roy's *Telegrams of the North-West Campaign 1885* (T., Champlain Society, 1972). Canada also despatched a party of voyageurs to the Nile expedition of 1884-5. On this, see Charles Stacey, *Records of the Nile Voyageurs 1884-5* (T., Champlain Society, 1959), and his article on the same subject (*CHR*, 1952).

There is no modern military history of the Boer War and the Canadian role in it, but Desmond Morton has published a biography of his ancestor, Gen. W. D. Otter, *The Canadian General* (T., Hakkert, 1974), which is the best account of this subject available. Morton's "Colonel Otter and the First Canadian Contingent in South Africa 1899-1900," in M. S. Cross and R. Bothwell, eds., *Policy By Other Means* (T., Clarke Irwin, 1972), is derived from his book. The able and prolific Morton's earlier book, *Ministers and Generals* (T., UTP, 1970), is the best study of military-political relations for this period. Three contemporary Boer War accounts are still readily available: T. G. Marquis, *Canada's Sons on Kopje and Veldt*; S. M. Brown, *With the Royal Canadians*; and Sandford Evans, *The Canadian Contingents*, all full of tales of derring-do and romantic Victorianism. Very useful and very suggestive is Carman Miller's, "A Preliminary Analysis of the Socio-Economic Composition of Canada's South African War Contingents," (*Social History*, 1975) a detailed breakdown of the kinds and classes of men who joined up in the last little war.

One classic is George Taylor Denison's *Soldiering in Canada* (T., 1900), an account of Canadian military history from 1812 along with a memoir by the wild-eyed nationalist/imperialist militia officer. Other contemporary items that are interesting and now almost humorous are J. H. Burnham, *Canadians in the Imperial Naval and Military Service Abroad* (T., 1891), brief biographies of Canadian officers from lieutenant to general serving the Queen-Empress; Maj.-Gen. C. W. Robinson, *Canada and Canadian Defence* (L., 1910), an account of the ways Canada could defend against (or attack) the United States; and Christopher West, *Canada and Sea Power* (T., 1913), essentially a religio-militaristic tract calling on Canadians to think carefully before automatically offering to support the imperial fleet.

For French-Canadian attitudes to militarism, imperialism and nationalism, Robert Rumilly's long biography of *Henri Bourassa* (M., Chantécler, 1953) and Bourassa's own writings should be referred to. A useful Bourassa collection, translated into English, is Joseph Levitt, *Henri Bourassa on Imperialism and Bi-Culturalism* (T., Copp Clark, 1970). Desmond Morton's two articles, "French Canada and the Canadian Militia 1868-1914" (*Social History*, 1969) and "French Canada and War, 1898-1917: The Military Background to the Conscription Crisis of 1917," in J. L. Granatstein and R. D. Cuff, eds., *War and Society in North America* (T., Nelson, 1971), are the best available analyses of the reasons Quebec was uneasy about military life, and there is additional material on this subject in his books cited above. Quebec scholarship on the subject has not been well done, as can be seen from an examination of C. M. Boissonault, *Histoire politico-militaire des Canadiens-francais* (Trois Rivières, Editions du Bien Public, 1967). An exception to this harsh comment is Jean-Yves Gravel, *L'Armée au Québec (1868-1900)* (M., Boréal Express, 1974), a worthy attempt at writing the social history of French Canada's relations with military life after Confederation.

THE GREAT WAR

Much of the literature about the Great War is ephemeral—patriotic books designed to rouse the home front, memoirs by soldiers, bad regimental histories and the like. These can be important to recapture the mood of a period, but for our purposes here, this type of literature cannot be surveyed.

The basic biographies for the war include Skelton on Laurier, referred to above, and Henry Borden, ed., *Robert Laird Borden: His Memoirs* (T., Mac., 1938). Based on Borden's diaries, the memoirs are not completely satisfactory as a source, being largely stripped down and unanalytical. Much better for the war years is Roger Graham, *Arthur Meighen*, Vol. I: *The Door of Opportunity* (T., Clarke Irwin, 1960). A partisan account, as commited as Meighen himself, the Graham biography is probably the best account of the war period in a biographical frame.

A few other biographies deserve mention. The commander of the Canadian Corps was General Sir Arthur Currie, a civilian in arms and a better general for it. Currie was badly treated by the politicians, but he has received sympathetic treatment from H. M. Urquhart, *Arthur Currie, A Biography* (T., Dent, 1950), and from A. M. J. Hyatt, "The Military Career of Sir Arthur Currie" (Ph.D. thesis, Duke University, 1965). General A. G. L. McNaughton was just beginning his long career in the Great War and in John Swettenham's massive biography *McNaughton*, Vol. I: *1887-1939* (T., Ryerson, 1968) his story is superbly told. One man for whom a good biography is desperately needed is Sam Hughes. The only book length studies of the Minister of Militia and Defence from 1911 to 1916 are C. F. Winter, *Lt. Gen. Sir Sam Hughes, Canada's War Minister* (T., Mac., 1931) and Alan R. Capon, *His Faults Lie Gently: The Incredible Sam Hughes* (Lindsay, Floyd Hall, 1969). Both are uncritical pieces of devotion, as is the Hon. Leslie Frost's little pamphlet, "The Record on Sir Sam Hughes Set Straight" (n.p., n.d.). Much, much better is Frost's *Fighting Men* (T., Clarke Irwin, 1967), a very good study of the effects of the war on Orillia, Ontario and on the men this little town sent to the front.

The official history of the army in the war is Col. G. W. L. Nicholson, *The Canadian Expeditionary Force 1914-19* (Ottawa, QP, 1962), a throughly balanced and careful account, well illustrated and with good maps. There had been an earlier attempt at producing an official history, but the outbreak of war in 1939 interfered and only one volume each of text and documents was ever produced. The text of Col. A. F. Duguid, *Official History of the Canadian Force in the Great War 1914-1919* (Ottawa, KP, 1938), covers the first year of the war and is no longer particularly helpful, but the documents volume is a splendid piece of social history in its own right. There is no air force history, although one is in process. *The Naval Service of Canada* (Ottawa, KP, 1952) by G. N. Tucker is a good conventional history. Volume I covers the period from the earliest beginnings of Canadian history to 1939, and the four war chapters sketch out the story. Tucker's account of the great Naval Bill controversy in the closing years of Laurier's administration and the beginning years of Borden's is well done. One other official source should be noted, the *Report of the Ministry, Overseas Military Forces of Canada* (L., 1919). This is a good contemporary account of operations and organization in the last year of the war.

For basic chronologies of the war and for extensive citations from newspapers and speeches, every researcher should be aware of J. Castell Hopkins' *The Canadian Annual Review*. Every year for most of the first four decades of this century, Hopkins almost singlehandedly turned out his massive guide to the year's events. The war volumes are particularly valuable, as is Hopkin's *Canada at War 1914-18* (T., 1919), and his *The Province of Ontario in the War* (T., 1919).

A few more books deserve mention. The very best popular account of the war fronts from a Canadian perspective (and the best defence of Currie) is John Swettenham's *To Seize the Victory* (T., Ryerson, 1965). Interesting, too, because its author had his own important career, is George Drew, *Canada's Fighting Airmen* (T., Maclean, 1930). The account is largely non-critical and somewhat hero-worshipping. Another later politician, Col. Herbert A. Bruce, also wrote about the war. *Politics and the C.A.M.C.* (T., 1919) is a resounding attack on patronage, politics, and Bruce's enemies who interfered with his efforts in the Canadian Army Medical Corps.

A few articles on military matters can be cited. A fine piece of scholarship, S. F. Wise's "The Borden Government and the Formation of a Canadian Flying Corps, 1911-16," in Cross and Bothwell, *Policy By Other Means*, skillfully mixes military and political sources together and produces a sophisticated study of policy and technology. Desmond Morton has examined "The Supreme Penalty: Canadian Deaths by Firing Squad in the First World War," (*QQ*, 1972) a grisly look at the twenty-five unfortunates executed by firing squad. And D. M. A. R. Vince has studied, somewhat legalistically, "The Acting Overseas Sub-Militia Council and the Resignation of Sir Sam Hughes" (*CHR*, 1950).

Conscription is the one subject that still stirs argument in discussions about the war. Was it necessary militarily or merely politically? The best study of the subject is Elizabeth Armstrong, *The Crisis of Quebec, 1914-18* (N.Y., Columbia Univ. Press, 1937), a judicious, balanced account that has survived for forty years. A number of the good articles on the subject have been collected in Carl Berger, *Conscription 1917* (Canadian Historical Readings No. 8; T., UTP, n.d.). Much the most suggestive of these articles is A. M. Willms, "Conscription 1917: A Brief for the Defence" (originally in *CHR*, 1956). This tough-minded article argues not always convincingly that conscription was at once militarily necessary and politically unpopular, and Willms defends the Borden government. Other articles in the collection focus on the church's attitude to war and on labour's reaction to the events of 1917. And for a good account of conscientious objectors in this war—and the next one—M. James Penton, *Jehovah's Witnesses in Canada* (T., Mac., 1976) should be consulted.

During the war, the country made substantial gains in autonomy. Under Borden's lead and in response to the pressures of the war, great changes took place. Borden's account of these is in his *Canadian Constitutional Studies* (T., 1922). An excellent collection of documents on the period, R. MacGregor Dawson's *The Development of Dominion Status, 1900-31* (first ed. 1937; reprint ed., Hamden, Conn., Archon, 1967), has maintained its usefulness, a very unusual state for usually ephemeral documents books. Other valuable studies include John Kendle's well-researched and well-written *The Round Table Movement and Imperial Union* (T., UTP, 1975), the best study of the imperialist movement that frightened or exhilarated so many Canadians. Kendle is also the author of the standard study on *The Colonial and Imperial Conferences 1887-1911* (L., 1967), essential background to the Imperial War Conference of 1917. Additionally, new material has been gathered in Margaret Prang's *N.W. Rowell: Ontario Nationalist* (T., UTP, 1975), the very long but definitive study of one of Borden's key ministers in the Union government. Among the academic articles on this subject, two of the best are R. C. Brown, "Sir Robert Borden, the Great War and Anglo-Canadian Relations," in J. S. Moir, ed., *Character and Circumstance* (T., Mac., 1970), and Brown and R. Bothwell, "The 'Canadian Resolution,'" in Cross and Bothwell, *Policy By Other Means*. Brown is preparing the official biography of Borden, and he has the best grasp of the massive war documentation. In the Brown and Bothwell article, for example, by careful textual analysis, Borden's primary responsibility for the crucial Resolution IX at the Imperial War Conference of 1917 is established. Bothwell has himself published "Canadian Representation at Washington: A Study in Colonial Responsibility" (*CHR*, 1972), a useful examination of the way Canada got its own representation in the United States. Other articles of some value include L. F. Fitzhardinge, "Hughes, Borden and Dominion Representation at the Paris Peace Conference" (*CHR*, 1968), R. M. Dawson, "Canada and Imperial War Cabinets," in Chester Martin, ed., *Canada in Peace and War* (T., OUP, 1941), Margaret Prang, "N. W. Rowell and Canada's External Policy, 1917-21" (*CHR*, 1960), and J. W. Dafoe, "Canada at the Peace Conference of 1919" (*CHR*, 1943). The one monograph on Canada at Paris is the brief *Canada at the Paris Peace Conference* (T., OUP, 1942), by G. P. de T. Glazebrook.

BETWEEN THE WARS

There are a number of good biographies dealing with the main figures of Canadian foreign and defence policy between the wars. The policy for the most part was that of Mackenzie King, the strange little giant who dominated Canada, Canadian politics, and to a large extent Commonwealth Policy from 1921 to 1948 and beyond. The official King biography has three volumes. *William Lyon Mackenzie King* Vol. I, by R. M. Dawson, covers the period 1874-1923 (T., UTP, 1958); Vol. II and III, by H. Blair Neatby, cover the period to 1939 (T., UTP, 1963, 1976). The Dawson volume is perhaps more favourable, more committed, but both books are calm and judicious and they establish a Mackenzie King who is somewhat different from the legend. Certainly this is not the anti-British King, wrecking the Empire. These two volumes are indispensable sources for putting together the story of King's attitudes and ideas on foreign policy. Equally useful are Kenneth McNaught's fine study of the pacifist CCF leader, J. S. Woodsworth, *A Prophet in Politics* (T., UTP, 1959), and Roger Graham's *Arthur Meighen*, Vol. II: *And Fortune Fled* (T., Clarke Irwin, 1963). Meighen was King's great antagonist through the 1920s on foreign and domestic policies, and the Meighen and

King biographies should be read together for an object lesson in the way different historians can draw on much the same sources to reach variant conclusions. Unfortunately, none of the biographies of Richard B. Bennett, Prime Minister from 1930 to 1935, are of any value whatsoever.

Although there are no memoirs by the Prime Ministers of the interwar years, one later Prime Minister has written about his role in the 1920s and 1930s. This is, of course, Lester Pearson, whose *Mike: The Memoirs of the Rt. Hon. Lester B. Pearson*, Vol. I: *1897-1948* (T., UTP, 1972) is at once charming and quite informative about Canadian foreign policy. Equally so in its look at the lingering Quebec attitude to conscription is Norman Ward, ed., *A Party Politician: The Memoirs of Chubby Power* (T., Mac., 1966). One of Mackenzie King's ministers from 1935 to 1944, Power was that rare political figure, an honest man. Very different are Vincent Massey's memoirs, *What's Past is Prologue* (T., Mac., 1963), which are designed to conceal as much as to reveal. There should be useful material in Marcel Hamelin, *Les Mémoirs du Senateur Raoul Dandurand* (Québec, Laval, 1967), for the Senator was an important figure at the League of Nations during the 1920s. Regrettably, nothing of value made its way into print. The same thing can be said of E. M. Macdonald, a Minister of National Defence under King in the same period. His *Recollections Political and Personal* (T., Ryerson, n.d.) are neither political nor personal. Fortunately, John Swettenham's *McNaughton*, Vol. I, has much useful material on defence policy. Also of merit is Ramsay Cook's fine study of *John W. Dafoe and the Free Press* (T., UTP, 1963), which tells us a good deal about Dafoe's views on nationalism and foreign policy in the interwar decades.

The very best source on defence policy in the interwar years is undoubtedly James Eayrs, *In Defence of Canada*, Vol. I: *From the Great War to the Great Depression* and Vol. II: *Appeasement and Rearmament* (T., UTP, 1964, 1965). Eayrs has seen almost all the private papers and government records, and he has produced a brilliant, opinionated look at policy, policy-making and policy-makers that is indispensable for researchers into the period. The confusion and mismangement stand out in sharp detail, and

Mackenzie King is generally the villain against whom occasionally far-sighted generals struggle. Some of the military, however, such as Col. J. Sutherland Brown, are revealed in a dream world of their own, planning strikes against the United States by mobile columns.

By comparison other studies of the period are lacklustre. Aloysius Balawyder's *Canadian-Soviet Relations between the World Wars* (T., UTP, 1972) is marred by impenetrable prose and a penchant for minutiae. Equally, Michael Fry's *Illusions of Security: North Atlantic Diplomacy 1918-22* (T., UTP, 1972) and Richard Kottman, *Reciprocity and the North Atlantic Triangle 1932-38* (Ithaca, Cornell Univ. Press. 1968), are difficult books to push through, although like Balawyder they are based on extensive use of primary sources. One interesting book covering a little-known subject is Victor Hoar's *The Mackenzie-Papineau Battalion* (T., Copp Clark, 1969), an account of the Canadians who went to Spain in the late 1930s to fight Franco's fascism.

Several others studies are quite valuable. Ian Drummond, *Imperial Economic Policy 1917-1939* (T., UTP, 1974) is a superbly researched examination of a very complex subject. Richard Veatch, *Canada and the League of Nations* (T., UTP, 1975) is a somewhat flawed look at an important subject, the first scholarly book on the League. As such it replaces S. Mack Eastman's *Canada at Geneva* (T., Ryerson, 1946). These two volumes should be supplemented by the 30-year old study by Gwendolyn Carter, *The British Commonwealth and International Security* (T., Ryerson, 1947), a thorough-going look at Commonwealth League attitudes and policy with good sections on Canada. An indispensable source for the entire period—and one that is generally flattering to Mackenzie King—is Nicholas Mansergh's *Survey of British Commonwealth Affairs: Problems of External Policy* (L., OUP, 1952). In the same *Survey* series, the volumes by Sir Keith Hancock, *Problems of Nationality 1918-36* (L., OUP, 1937) and *Problems of Economic Policy 1918-39, Part I* (L., OUP, 1942), are somewhat less satisfactory but are still gold mines of information—and footnotes.

In article literature, the 1920s are still very much the forgotten decade. The classic article by J. B. Brebner, "Canada, the Anglo-Japanese Alliance and the Washington Conference" (*Political Science Quarterly*, 1935), was an early analysis of Arthur Meighen's triumph in helping to persuade the British not to renew their links with Japan. This should now be supplemented by Graham's work, by Fry's and by J. S. Galbraith, "The Imperial Conference of 1921 and the Washington Conference" (*CHR*, 1948). Ramsay Cook's two articles, "J. W. Dafoe at the Imperial Conference of 1923" (*CHR*, 1960) and "A Canadian Account of the 1926 Imperial Conference" (*Journal of Commonwealth Political Studies*, 1965), are useful primary sources with inside information on Canadian policy and planning. Finally, Donald Page's 'The Development of a Western Canadian Peace Movement" in Susan Trofimenkoff, *The Twenties in Western Canada* (Ottawa, National Museum, 1972), is a unique attempt to analyze public opinion through analysis of varied (and massive) sources, while Norman Hillmer's "A British High Commissioner for Canada 1927-28" (*Journal of Imperial and Commonwealth History*, 1973) and "Anglo-Canadian Relations 1927-34" in *The Dominions Between the Wars* (L., Institute of Commonwealth Studies, 1972) use British and Canadian documents to explore the pressures in Ottawa and London that led to British diplomatic representation in Ottawa.

The 1930s have received somewhat more attention from scholars. Kenneth McNaught's "Canadian Foreign Policy and the Whig Interpretation: 1936-1939" (*CHAR*, 1957) was the first attempt to suggest that Mackenzie King wanted to go to war in the late 1930s and manoeuvred so as to make it possible. Blair Neatby's fine article, "Mackenzie King and National Unity," in H. L. Dyck and H. P. Krosby, *Empire and Nations* (T., UTP, 1969), worked something of the same ground and clearly demonstrated that King saw his task as keeping the country together—and getting it into the war "at Britain's side." Neatby's argument is carried further by J. L. Granatstein and R. Bothwell in "'A Self Evident National Duty': Canadian Foreign Policy 1935-9" (*Journal of Imperial and Commonwealth History*, 1975). For the (in)famous "Riddell" incident at the League of Nations during the Italo-Ethiopian War the most recent source is Bothwell and John English, " 'Dirty Work at the Crossroads': New Perspectives on the Riddell Incident"

(*CHAR*, 1972). These last two articles make extensive use of British, American and Canadian primary sources, almost the first articles that do so. Almost unique in Canadian intellectual history is Lawrence Stokes' essay "Canada and an Academic Refugee from Nazi Germany: The Case of Gerhard Hertzberg." (*CHR*, 1976). Stokes studies one refugee's efforts to become accepted in Canada—and eventually to win a Nobel Prize. A good documents collection on the period is R. Bothwell and G. N. Hillmer, *"The In-Between Time": Canadian External Policy in the 1930s* (T., Copp Clark, 1975). Hillmer has also written a basic article on O. D. Skelton, the key figure in interwar Canadian foreign policy. This article, along with a brilliant piece by James Eayrs on Anglo-Canadian relations, is in Peter Lyon, ed., *Britain and Canada* (L., Cass, 1976).

In the 1930s there was for the first time a substantial body of contemporary opinion and argument on foreign policy. A few references are all that can be ventured here. One such is *Canada, the Empire and the League* (T., Nelson, 1938), a collection of speeches made at the 1938 Couchiching conference. Most of the views were quite conventional. Less so is the section on foreign policy in Frank Scott's *Canada Today* (T., OUP, 1938), still probably the best analysis of depression-ridden Canada. Scott's articles were regularly featured in the *Canadian Forum* during the 1930s, along with those of Frank Underhill, G. M. A. Grube and other left-wing intellectuals. They made the *Forum* into one of the best sources for anti-British and pacifistic articles; surprisingly, perhaps, other such articles can be found in *Dalhousie Review* and *Quee₁'s Quarterly* as well.

A few books on the Pacific area need mention. William Strange's *Canada the Pacific and War* (T., Nelson, 1937) tried to explore Canada's interests in the Pacific and her possible military involvement there. More historically oriented is Charles Woodsworth's *Canada and the Orient* (T., Mac., 1941), a detailed, academic survey of relations with the East dating back to the mid-nineteenth century. One book that must be cited here, out of chronology, is Forrest LaViolette, *The Canadian Japanese and World War II* (T., UTP, 1948), a socio-psychological account of the way Canadian Nisei withstood persecution and internment in

Canada during the war. La Violette should now be supplemented with Ken Adachi's *The Enemy that Never Was* (T., M&S, 1976), a well-written account of the Canadian-Japanese but one that inexplicably fails to use some valuable primary sources. A useful essay, based on solid primary source research is W. P. Ward's "British Columbia and the Japanese Evacuation," (*CHR*, 1976).

This is also the place to refer again to the Canadian Institute of International Affairs. The CIIA has published a wide range of books and journals on foreign policy over the last forty years—three of the four titles cited in the last paragraph, for example, were sponsored by the Institute. In 1941, the CIIA launched its series *Canada and World Affairs* with the publication of F. H. Soward, *et. al., Canada and World Affairs: The Pre-War Years* (OUP). Thereafter, volumes have been issued to cover two-year periods, and the series as a whole, now numbering a dozen volumes, is the best generally available source on Canadian policy since the 1930s. The CIIA's pamphlet series, *Behind the Headlines,* is also very valuable, and since 1940 at least six titles have been issued each year. After the war, *International Journal,* the first scholarly journal of foreign policy in Canada, was started. The debt scholars owe the CIIA is immense. For a historical study on the "Antecedents and Origins of the Canadian Institute of International Affairs," the article by Edward Greathed in Dyck and Krosby, *Empire and Nations,* is available.

THE SECOND WORLD WAR

The basic and best source for the Second World War is J. W. Pickersgill's *The Mackenzie King Record* (T., UTP, 1960-70). Skillfully edited from the massive King diaries, the *Record* is an absolutely unique document giving the Prime Minister's views on people and events. Here, there is Mackenzie King's view on conscription, on the political tactics of elections, on foreign policy and social welfare. The *Record* is in four volumes, with Vol. I covering the period from 1939 to 1944, Vol. II from 1944 to 1945, and Vols. III-IV taking the story to 1948 and through the beginnings of the Cold War. This is the place to begin for all wartime topics.

Other biographies of value include Pearson's *Mike*, Vol. I, Roger Graham's *Arthur Meighen*, Vol. III: *No Surrender* (T., Clarke Irwin, 1965), Chubby Power's *A Party Politician*, and Vincent Massey's memoirs. John Swettenham's *McNaughton*, Vols. II-III (T., Ryerson, 1969) is extremely good on the conscription crisis of 1944 but much less valuable—and more partial—on the reason why General McNaughton was removed from command of the Army overseas. The biography of *Louis St. Laurent: Canadian* (T., Mac., 1967) by Dale Thomson is only lightly referenced and adds little for the war period. Robert Speaight, *Vanier: Soldier Diplomat and Governor General* (T., Collins, 1970), is rather naive and uninformed but has some useful material on Vanier's diplomatic life before and during the war. The despatches and memos of a very shrewd American diplomat, J. Pierrepont Moffat, the U.S. Minister in Ottawa from 1940 to 1943, are collected in Nancy Hooker, ed., *The Moffat Papers 1919-1943* (Cambridge, Harvard Univ. Press, 1956). A soldier's autobiography is E. L. M. Burns' *General Mud* (T., Clarke Irwin, 1970), an account by a good general who ran into hard luck in the war. Another general's autobiography is Maurice Pope's *Soldiers and Politicians: The Memoirs of Lt.-Gen. Maurice A. Pope* (T., UTP, 1962), which is very useful in its treatment of politico-military questions.

There are numerous official military histories for the war. The Navy has two: G. N. Tucker's *The Naval Service of Canada*, Vol. II, which treats service on shore, and the more popular account of operations by Joseph Schull, *The Far Distant Ships* (Ottawa, KP, 1950). There is as yet no air force history. The official army history is in three volumes: C. P. Stacey's *Six Years of War* (Ottawa, QP, 1955), G. W. L. Nicholson's *The Canadians in Italy* (1957), and Stacey's *The Victory Campaign* (1960). All three are models of what official history should be: judicious, colorful, well illustrated with photographs and first-rate maps.

The very best official book on the war is Stacey's *Arms, Men and Governments: The War Policies of Canada, 1939-1945* (Ottawa, Information Canada, 1970). This is Stacey's finest work, a brilliant and detailed analysis of Canadian policy in alliance warfare, a study of the homefront and of conscription, of supply and development. The view of

Mackenzie King is occasionally very critical, but the assessment of policy is always fair and balanced. Stacey's work is the finest synthesis of the war period we are ever likely to get. With *The Mackenzie King Record*, this is indispensable.

One other official volume, not wholly satisfactory, is J. de N. Kennedy, *History of the Department of Munitions and Supply* (Ottawa, KP, 1950). There is much material here on the great Canadian production effort that C. D. Howe mobilized during the war, but the book's organization foils the reader every time. Kennedy's charts, however, are useful. One American official history deserves note. S. W. Dziuban, *Military Relations Between the United States and Canada 1939-1945* (Washington, Office of the Chief of Military History, 1959), has some useful material and serves to supplement the Canadian accounts.

The conscription crisis has received substantial attention, as might be expected, particularly in the Swettenham and Stacey books cited above. R. MacGregor Dawson, one of the King biographers, was the posthumous author of *The Conscription Crisis of 1944* (T., UTP, 1961), an incomplete account based on the King papers, and one that should have been revised before publication. There is a good account in James Eayrs, *The Art of the Possible* (T., UTP, 1961), a study of government and foreign policy-making with a good section on the role of the military. There are long chapters on conscription in J. L. Granatstein's *Canada's War: The Politics of the Mackenzie King Government 1939-1945* (T., OUP, 1975), and the interpretation here clashes with Stacey's on several crucial points. Material on the Conservatives can be found in Granatstein's *The Politics of Survival: The Conservative Party 1939-45* (T., UTP, 1967), and in his *Conscription in the Second World War: A Study in Political Management* (T., Ryerson, 1969). Granatstein's articles, "The Conservative Party and Conscription in the Second World War" (*CHAR*, 1967) and "Le Québec et le plebiscite de 1942 sur la conscription" (*RHAF*, 1973), have additional new material. Another article that should be consulted is R. H. Roy's "Major-General G. R. Pearkes and the Conscription Crisis in British Columbia 1944," (*BC Studies*, Winter 1975-6) a spirited defence of Pearkes' activities while he was in command of the military area that had the most difficulties both in recruiting NRMA men for active service and in containing the conscripts after partial compulsion was imposed.

For Quebec and the war, the student should use Robert Rumilly's *Histoire de la province de Québec*, tomes XXXVIII-XLI (M., Fides, 1968-9) and his massive two-volume biography of *Maurice Duplessis et son temps* (M., Fides, 1973), although there is little new in the later work. Very evocative and very useful is André Laurendeau's *La Crise de la conscription 1942* (M., Editions du Jour, 1962), an account of the brilliantly successful campaign against the plebiscite on conscription in Quebec in 1942. This work is translated in its entirety in Philip Stratford, ed., *André Laurendeau: Witness for Quebec* (T., Mac., 1973). Jean-Yves Gravel has written two articles on Quebec and the war, both surveys that put the case for Quebec's disinterest in the war as consequences of military discrimination. One is in Gravel's collection *Le Québec et la Guerre* (M., Boréal Express, 1974); the other is in a special Canadian edition of the *Revue d' Histoire de la Deuxième Guerre Mondiale* (octobre, 1976), a French journal. Two very useful surveys of Quebec press opinion were published by the CIIA in 1940 and 1941. These are Florent Lefebvre's *The French Canadian Press and the War*, an analysis of attitudes prior to and just after the declaration of war, and Elizabeth Armstrong's *French Canadian Opinion and the War*, a similar survey covering the period from January, 1940 to June, 1941. Another, more personal, look at Quebec opinion can be found in Jacques Gouin, *Lettres de Guerre d'un Québécois, 1942-45* (M., Editions du Jour, 1975), a collection of letters sent from training camps in Canada and overseas by a young artillery officer.

For strictly foreign policy subjects the literature is largely in article form. One book that is extremely informative and detailed is R. W. James' *Wartime Economic Cooperation* (T., Ryerson, 1949), a thorough-going study of Canadian American economic relations during the war years. In the same vein is J. L. Granatstein and R. D. Cuff, "The Hyde Park Agreement, 1941" (*CHR*, 1974), an article that the authors have collected along with others on wartime economic history in *Canadian-American Relations in War-*

time: From the Great War to the Cold War (T., Hakkert, 1974). Other articles on Canadian-American relations include Granatstein's "The Conservative Party and the Ogdensburg Agreement" (*International Journal*, 1966-7), Charles Stacey's "The Turning Point: Canadian-American Relations During the Roosevelt-King Era" (*Canada: an Historical Quarterly*, 1973), and the unconsciously revealing article by S. D. Pierce and A. F. W. Plumptre, "Canada's Relations with Wartime Agencies in Washington" (*CJEPS*, 1945). Donald Creighton's "The Ogdensburg Agreement and F. H. Underhill," in Carl Berger and Ramsay Cook, *The West and the Nation* (T., M&S, 1976) captures the virulence with which critics of the status quo and the place of Canada in the Empire could be attacked in 1940 and 1976.

The war produced an enormous outpouring of contemporary literature about the prospects for the postwar world. Some that deserve mention are Grant Dexter's *Canada and the Building of Peace* (T., CIIA, 1944) and two collections edited by Violet Anderson, *The United Nations Today and Tomorrow* (T., Ryerson, 1943), and *This is the Peace* (T., Ryerson, 1945). Among valuable articles are Alexander Brady, "Dominion Nationalism and the Commonwealth" (*CJEPS*, 1944), R. A. MacKay, "Canada and the Balance of World Power" (*CJEPS*, 1941), and Brooke Claxton, M.P., "The Place of Canada in Post-War World Organization" (*CJEPS*, 1944). There are many, many more.

THE POSTWAR YEARS

The literature on this period is massive, although the number of scholarly studies is still small. For material after 1960, the best guide to events is to be found in the yearly volumes of John Saywell, ed., *The Canadian Annual Review* (T., UTP, 1961-). The *Canada and World Affairs* series is indispensable, as is the CIIA's *Monthly Report on Canadian External Relations*.

As might be expected, the biographies are sketchy and largely journalistic. *The Mackenzie King Record*, Vols. III-IV, is essential, as is Lester B. Pearson, *Mike: The Memoirs of the Rt. Hon. Lester B. Pearson*, Vol. II: 1948-57 (T., UTP, 1973) and J. G. Diefenbaker's *One Canada: Memoirs of the Rt. Hon. John G. Diefenbaker* (T., Mac., 1975, 1976).

Pearson's speeches are collected with interesting commentary in his *Words and Occasions* (T., UTP, 1970). Less useful are the disappointing memoirs by Arnold Heeney, *The Things that are Caesar's* (T., UTP, 1972), and Dana Wilgress, *Memoirs* (T., Ryerson, 1967). The ingrained diplomatic habit of discretion could not be overcome. One first-class essay by a former diplomat is Escott Reid's study of "Canada and the Creation of the North Atlantic Alliance, 1948-1949," in M. G. Fry, ed., *Freedom and Change* (T., M&S, 1975). This Fry volume, a *festschrift* in honour of Lester Pearson, also has good essays on Pearson's academic career and his role as a diplomat in post-1956 Suez. There is also material in Massey's memoirs, in General Pope's, in the St. Laurent biography and in the studies of McNaughton and Vanier.

Denis Smith's *Gentle Patriot: A Political Biography of Walter Gordon* (Edmonton, Hurtig, 1973) has very good material on Canada-United States relations in the 1960s, and the spate of books about John Diefenbaker should be examined, particularly for information on the nuclear arms debate of the 1960s. Peter Newman's *Renegade in Power* (T., M&S, 1963) is still the best, although Peter Stursberg's *Diefenbaker 1956-62* and *Diefenbaker 1962-67* (T., UTP, 1975, 1976) are close seconds, despite their total reliance on oral history sources. Two biographies of Pierre Trudeau can be cited: Walter Stewart, *Shrug: Trudeau in Power* (T., New Press, 1971), and Anthony Westell, *Paradox: Trudeau as Prime Minister* (T., Prentice-Hall, 1972). Neither is satisfactory.

There are two official histories of the Korean War, one each for the army and the navy. H. F. Wood's *Strange Battleground* (Ottawa, QP, 1966) is very well done if discreet. Somewhat less satisfactory is T. Thorgrimsson and E. C. Russell, *Canadian Naval Operations in Korean Waters 1950-55* (Ottawa, QP, 1965). Col. Wood's book should be supplemented with his funny, flawed novel on Korea, *The Private War of Jacket Coates* (T., Longman, 1966). Everything that official discretion prevented from appearing in the official history is in the novel. Another official document, the *Report of the Royal Commission on Bilingualism and Biculturalism*, Vol. 3A (Ottawa, QP, 1969), has a long study of the linguistic problems of the armed forces that is revealing of the difficulties that still face French-speaking Canadians interested in a military career.

The best study of post-war foreign policy is James Eayrs, *In Defence of Canada*, Vol. III: *Peacemaking and Deterrence* (T., UTP, 1972). Eayrs' style and research are as always superb, and his vignettes of the policy-makers are brilliant in every respect. But the volume is flawed by a lack of continuity somewhat more annoying than that in its predecessors. Eayrs' *The Commonwealth and Suez* (T., OUP, 1964) is a model documents book on the 1956 crisis, and his provocative essay collections are also splendid. *Northern Approaches* (T., Mac., 1961) and *Minutes of the Sixties* are probably his best, while *Diplomacy and its Discontents* (T., UTP, 1971) is the toughest. *Greenpeace and Her Enemies* (T., Anansi, 1973) collects Eayrs' more recent newspaper columns.

Another very solid academic work is Denis Stairs' *The Diplomacy of Constraint: Canada, The Korean War and the United States* (T., UTP, 1974), a brilliant analysis of Canadian policy in the Korean War. Stairs' article, "The Military as an Instrument of Foreign Policy," is the only redeeming feature in Hector Massey, ed., *The Canadian Military: A Profile* (T., Copp Clark, 1972). A unique study, virtually the only serious work on Canadian-Latin American relations, is *Gringos from the Far North: Essays in Canadian-Latin American Relations 1867-1967* (T., Mac., 1976) by J. C. M. Oglesby. Some of the essays are very informative on business and religious links, but a few are uneven. Another very fine book is Jon McLin's *Canada's Changing Defence Policy 1957-63* (Baltimore, Johns Hopkins Univ. Press, 1967), an examination of the difficulties alliance politics posed for the Diefenbaker government. One article is J. L. Granatstein's "Strictly on its Merits': The Conscription Issue in Canada After 1945" (*QQ*, 1972), a demonstration that conscription did not disappear as an issue after 1945. Granatstein has also edited a documents collection, *Canadian Foreign Policy Since 1945* (T., Copp Clark, 1973), and with Alastair Taylor and David Cox he is the author of *Peacekeeping: International Challenge and Canadian Response* (T., CIIA, 1968), the best study of peacekeeping in a Canadian context.

There are several important essay collections. John W. Holmes, a long-time senior official in the Department of External Affairs and then in the CIIA, collected two volumes of his voluminous and excellent essays on foreign policy under the title *The Better Part of Valour* (T., M&S, 1970) and *Canada: A Middle-Aged Power* (T., M&S, 1975). The essays cover virtually all aspects of Canadian policy. Holmes' boss was Lester Pearson, and the *International Journal* devoted its Winter 1973-4 issue to essays about Mr. Pearson. The *Journal's* Summer 1967 issue is also worthy of note, being devoted entirely to retrospective looks at Canadian policy. Another useful book is King Gordon, ed., *Canada's Role as a Middle Power* (T., CIIA, 1966), an examination of the concept that is usually claimed as Canada's own. Much more argumentative and reflective of the tenor of the debate in the mid-1960s is Stephen Clarkson, ed., *An Independent Foreign Policy for Canada?* (T., M&S, 1968). The question mark says it all. Some of the essays in this book are very good.

The Clarkson collection is revisionist in tenor. The only other books that take a similar tack are Cuff and Granatstein, *Canadian-American Relations in Wartime*, and John Warnock, *Partner to Behemoth* (T., New Press, 1970), a roundhouse attack on Canada's links with the U.S. war machine. Warnock tries hard but he doesn't quite carry it off, although nascent Canadian revisionism will probably survive even this.

Three books by General E. L. M. Burns mark him as one of that rare breed of literate and compassionate military men. The first, and best, is *Between Arab and Israeli* (T., Clarke Irwin, 1962), a fine and revealing account of his service for the United Nations in the Middle East. *Megamurder* (T., Clarke Irwin, 1966) is a hard-hitting attack on nuclear madness and includes a sketch history of aerial bombing. His third book, *A Seat at the Table: The Struggle for Disarmament* (T., Clarke Irwin, 1972), is an account of his role as Canada's chief disarmament negotiator from 1960 to 1968.

There are three good studies of Pierre Trudeau's foreign policy and of the changes in policy that have taken place since 1968. The best is Bruce Thordarson, *Trudeau and Foreign Policy* (T., UTP, 1972), an excellent analysis of the policy-making process during the much-heralded foreign policy review. Also valuable is the book by the former diplomat, Peter Dobell, *Canada's Search for New Roles* (L., OUP, 1972), a book that suffers somewhat from being pitched at British readers. Finally, Colin Gray, *Canadian Defence Priorities* (T., Clarke Irwin, 1972) is a very well done, tough-minded and realistic examination of the way equipment on hand has shaped government defence planning in the Trudeau period.

Finally, three texts might be mentioned, none of them entirely satisfactory. R. B. Farrell, *The Making of Canadian Foreign Policy* (T., Prentice-Hall, 1969), is valuable only for its exposition of the mechanical aspects of Canadian diplomacy. The skim survey, D. C. Thomson and Roger Swanson, *Canadian Foreign Policy: Options and Perspectives* (T., McGraw Hill-Ryerson, 1971), tries to do much and is unfortunately somewhat full of errors, typographical and otherwise. And the collection of documents by H. A. Leeson and W. Vanderelst, *External Affairs and Canadian Federalism* (T., Holt Rinehart & Winston, 1973), brings together some good evidence, but much of it is in recent primary sources that every library will have.

The remainder of the postwar literature must go uncited. Students should refer to the bibliographies cited above for further guidance, and they should also check the government publications listed. There is much to be done, new techniques to be exploited, and old ikons to be shattered. No area has more room for good students than the history of Canadian foreign and defence policy.

Economic, Business, and Labour History

Michael Bliss

I. ECONOMIC AND BUSINESS HISTORY

Many historians are dissatisfied with the state of our knowledge of post-Confederation economic and business history. In the 1930s and early 1940s much of the best writing about Canada was in the field of economic history, by such economists as W. A. Mackintosh and H. A. Innis and historians like Donald Creighton and A. R. M. Lower. After the Second World War, however, the study of economics in Canada became less historically-oriented and more influenced by theoretical and statistical analysis. Many economists neglected traditional economic history; many of those still interested in economic history produced quantitative studies that are difficult for the layman to understand. On their part, Canadian historians tended to concentrate on political subjects, perhaps partly discouraged by the complexity and sophistication of the new economics. Business history, long recognized in other countries as a field of study in its own right, languished in Canada until the 1970s from lack of interest by historians and businessmen. Consequently a survey of what needs to be done in Canadian economic and business history—there is no history of Canadian manufacturing, no satisfactory survey of post-Confederation economic history, no readable work on a wide range of industries and companies, etc., etc.—might be as long as or longer than an article on the existing literature.

But professorial complaints about the inadequacies of the field will not impress the beginning student of Canadian history, who in this as in every other field finds that historians have already written more than anyone can (or should) read. The older generation of economic historians produced a massive amount of valuable writing, most of which has stood up remarkably well over time. A few outstanding economists and historians continued to develop themes in economic and business history through the 1950s and 1960s. It seems that many younger Canadian historians are once again becoming interested in economic and business topics and, as well, the quantitative approach of the new economic historians is beginning to pay off in important studies challenging key aspects of the older interpretations. Despite the gaps in the literature, then, the existing work is already far too extensive to be more than touched upon in a short essay. Challenging new studies are appearing in increasing numbers, and there is every prospect of a renewed emphasis on economics and business in the writing and teaching of Canadian history. The titles mentioned in the following sections are only a small fraction of the existing literature. The bias in selection is towards introductory and standard works and, taking account of the problem most history students have with advanced economics, slightly away from some of the more technical studies.

SURVEYS AND INTERPRETATIONS

For many years the standard textbook has been W. T. Easterbrook and Hugh G. J. Aitken, *Canadian Economic History* (T., Mac., 1956). Heavily reflecting the traditional "staples approach" to Canadian economic history (in which the exploitation of a succession of staple products is seen as providing the basic framework of Canadian economic development), it is strongest in its treatment of primary industries and transportation, weakest on manufacturing, business-government relations, and the period after approximately 1930. Two older and less substantial general textbooks, M. Q. Innis, *Economic History of Canada* (*T., Ryerson*, second ed., 1954), and A. W. Currie, *Canadian Economic Development* (T., Nelson, 1942), reflect similar strengths and weakness. The best single volume on post-Confederation economic history is Book I of the *Report of the Royal Commission on Dominion-Provincial Relations*

(Ottawa, KP, 1940), readily available in a 1963 Carleton Library paperback edition edited by Donald V. Smiley and entitled *The Rowell/Sirois Report, Book I.* Alternatively, W. A. Mackintosh, *The Economic Background of Dominion-Provincial Relations* (Ottawa, KP, 1939, reprinted in the Carleton Library, 1964), was the special study for the Rowell-Sirois Commission upon which much of the economic history in Book I was based. Both volumes give special attention to the regional impact of national economic policies as well as to their effects upon Dominion-provincial relations.

O. J. Firestone's *Canada's Economic Development, 1867-1953* (L., Bowes & Bowes, 1958) is not so much a survey of Canadian economic development as a pioneering reconstruction of statistical series. Much of Firestone's data has been incorporated in the more comprehensive, indeed indispensable, *Historical Statistics of Canada* (T., Mac., 1965), edited by M. C. Urquhart and K. A. H. Buckley. It can usefully be supplemented by Warren E. Kalbach and Wayne W. McVey, *The Demographic Bases of Canadian Society* (T., McGraw-Hill, 1971).

The most useful general anthology of articles, several of which reconsider the staples approach, is W. T. Easterbrook and M. H. Watkins, eds., *Approaches to Canadian Economic History* (T., M&S, Carleton Library, 1967). A necessary supplement to it, however, is the very important article by Peter J. George and Ernest H. Oksanen, "Recent Developments in the Quantification of Canadian Economic History" *(Histoire Sociale/Social History,* 1969), which shows how recent work is challenging older interpretations. Two anthologies, David S. Macmillan, ed., *Canadian Business History: Selected Studies, 1497-1971* (T., M&S, 1971), and Glenn Porter and Robert Cuff, eds., *Enterprise and National Development: Essays in Canadian Business and Economic History* (T., Hakkert, 1972), illustrate the strengths and weaknesses (much too often the weaknesses in the Macmillan volume) of current work in Canadian business history. All of these titles contain good bibliographies or bibliographical articles as guides for further reading. Although some of the articles and theoretical assumptions in H. A. Innis, *Essays in Canadian Economic History* (T., UTP, 1956), are dated, it is still an indispensable collection of the shorter writings of Canada's greatest economic historian. The one collection of documents substantially devoted to post-Confederation economic history is Kevin H. Burley, ed., *The Development of Canada's Staples, 1867-1939* (T., M&S, Carleton Library, 1972). Tom Naylor's two volume work, *The History of Canadian Business, 1867-1914* (T., Lorimer, 1975), is eclectically radical, and factually unreliable. Some reviewers have found it brilliant, others judge it useless.

The period since 1940 has not, for the most part, been treated as an historical era. One good source of material on economic developments through the mid-1950s, as well as a brilliant reconstruction of the whole pattern of Canadian economic history, is R. E. Caves and R. H. Holton, *The Canadian Economy: Prospect & Retrospect* (Cambridge, Harvard Univ. Press, 1959). A particularly useful guide to the main themes of government management of the economy through the early 1960s is the collection of essays, *Canadian Economic Policy Since the War*, published in 1965 by the Canadian Trade Committee of the Private Planning Association of Canada. The essays in W. D. Wood and Pradeep Kumar, eds., *Canadian Perspectives on Wage-Price Guidelines: A Book of Readings* (Kingston, Industrial Relations Centre, 1975) supply background for understanding the wage-price controls issue in the 1970s.

There are few surveys or syntheses of the economic history of specific time periods of post-confederation history or of the regions of the country. An important exception to the vacuum in chronological studies is A. E. Safarian, *The Canadian Economy in the Great Depression* (T., UTP, 1959; reprinted in the Carleton Library, 1970), a fairly technical study, but essential to the understanding of that decade. More technical but also important is Edward Marcus, *Canada and the International Business Cycle, 1927-1939* (N.Y., Bookman Associates, 1954). Although the better provincial histories devote some space to economic developments, the only general economic history of a region is S. A. Saunders, *The Economic History of the Maritimes* (Ottawa, KP, 1939). The North and mid-north are also treated extremely well in Morris Zaslow, *The Opening of the Canadian North, 1870-1914* (T., M&S, 1971), which is also generally useful for Canadian resource policy as a whole in that period. Dealing with the years just before Confederation, Michael B. Katz has a most suggestive chapter on "The Entrepreneurial Class" in his trail-breaking study, *The People of Hamilton, Canada West* (Cambridge, Harvard University Press, 1975). Another stimulating thesis about the role of businessmen in urban life is contained in Alan F. J. Artibise, *Winnipeg, A Social History of Urban Growth, 1874-1914* (M., McGill-Queen's, 1975).

Not surprisingly, the province of Quebec has been the region most singled out for special attention, particularly by French-Canadian economic historians. The best short introduction to Quebec's post-confederation economic history is still the essay by A. Faucher and M. Lamontagne, "History of Industrial Development," most readily available in Marcel Rioux and Yves Martin, eds., *French-Canadian Society*, volume I (T., M&S, Carleton Library, 1964). Jean Hamelin and Yves Roby, *Histoire Economique du Québec, 1851-1896* (M., Fides, 1971), is an important synthesis for the second half of the nineteenth century; and the collection of articles edited by Robert Comeau, *Economie Québécoise* (M., Les Presses de l'université du Québec, 1969), contains several pertaining to twentieth century economic development and French-Canadian economic thought. A good general introduction to the problem of French-Canadian economic "backwardness" is René Durocher and Paul-André Linteau, eds., *Le "retard" du Québec et l'infériorité économique des Canadiens-français* (Trois Rivières, Editions Boréal Express, 1971). There is an excellent chapter on French Canada and the new industrialism in Robert Craig Brown and Ramsay Cook, *Canada 1896-1921: A Nation Transformed* (T., M&S, 1974). William F. Ryan, *The Clergy and Economic Growth in Quebec (1896-1914)* (Québec, Les Presses de l'Université Laval, 1966), has been the single most important study suggesting a reconsideration of the belief that the Church deliberately retarded industrial development.

THE STAPLE INDUSTRIES

Although of diminishing importance by the time of Confederation, Canada's first two great staple industries were still significant to the economy. Their post-Confederation history is outlined in the later chapters of H. A. Innis's two classic studies, *The Fur Trade in Canada: An Introduction to Canadian Economic History* (New Haven, Yale Univ. Press, 1930; revised edition, T., UTP, 1956) and *The Cod Fisheries: The History of an International Economy* (New Haven, Yale Univ. Press, 1940). The replacement of the square timber trade by that in lumber as the chief forest industry is treated in detail in A. R. M. Lower, *The North American Assault on the Canadian Forest: A History of the Lumber Trade Between Canada and the United States* (T., Ryerson, 1938). The best study of the later development of pulp and paper as the dominant forest industry is J. A. Guthrie, *The Newsprint Paper Industry* (Cambridge, Harvard Univ. Press, 1941). A few histories of individual lumbering and pulp companies can be found in the bibliographies mentioned above. But special attention might be given to Richard S. Lambert, with Paul Pross, *Renewing Nature's Wealth* (T., Department of Lands & Forests, 1967), a history of the Department of Lands and Forests in Ontario which is also one of the few studies stressing the development of conservation.

There is no complete history of Canadian mining. H. A. Innis, *Settlement and the Mining Frontier* (T., Mac., 1936), is still the best introduction to the development of mineral resources. It can be supplemented by E. S. Moore, *American Influence on Canadian Mining* (T., UTP, 1941), and two popular histories: D. M. LeBourdais, *Metals and Men* (T., M&S, 1957), and Arnold Hoffman, *Free Gold: The Story of Canadian Mining* (N.Y., Rinehart & Company, 1946). O. W. Main's *The Canadian Nickel Industry* (T., UTP, 1955) is a particularly good study of problems of monopoly and marketing in that industry. The later development of uranium is discussed in W. D. G. Hunter, "The Development of the Canadian Uranium Industry: An Experiment in Public Enterprise" (*CJEPS*, 1962).

Studies of post-Confederation agricultural history should begin with Chester Martin, *"Dominion Lands" Policy* (T., Mac., 1938), the definitive study of federal land policy, reprinted in the Carleton Library series in 1973 with an introduction by L. H. Thomas. Two of the better studies of the settlement of the prairies are A. S. Morton, *A History of Prairie Settlement* (T., Mac., 1938), and, with special emphasis on ethnic groups, Robert England, *The Colonization of Western Canada* (L., P. S. King, 1936). Canada's finest agricultural historian was Vernon C. Fowke. His *National Policy and the Wheat Economy* (T., UTP, 1957) is one of the great works in Canadian economic history, a sweeping study of agricultural development in the context of national development policies. Fowke's earlier work, *Canadian Agricultural Policy, The Historical Pattern* (T., UTP, 1946), is also essential, particularly for the role of government in the stimulation of agricultural research. The leading historian of the development of the wheat economy was D. A. MacGibbon in his two volumes, *The Canadian Grain Trade* (T., Mac., 1932), and *The Canadian Grain Trade, 1931-1951* (T., UTP, 1952). In "The North Atlantic Triangle and Changes in the Wheat Trade before the Great War" (*Dalhousie Review*, 1975), Bruce Richard sets the rise of prairie grain exports in a useful comparative perspective with the United States. A great deal can be learned about the economic and social patterns of Western agriculture from G. E. Britnell's *The Wheat Economy* (T., UTP, 1939).

More than any other industry, agriculture has been characterized by political action to remedy real and fancied grievances. Louis Aubrey Wood, *A History of Farmers Movements in Canada* (orig. pub. 1924, reprinted T., UTP, 1975), is still the best introduction to the history of agrarian protest. Among the most useful of the many other accounts of farmer unrest are Paul F. Sharp, *The Agrarian Revolt in Western Canada* (Minneapolis, Univ. of Minnesota Press, 1948), and W. L. Morton, *The Progressive Party in Canada* (T., UTP, 1950). An example of the most recent scholarship exploring the social and economic foundations of rural discontent is W. R. Young, "Conscription, Rural Depopulation, and the Farmers of Ontario, 1917-1919" (*CHR*, 1972). J. A. Irving, *The Social Credit Movement in Alberta* (T., UTP, 1959), and C. B. Macpherson, *Democracy in Alberta: Social Credit and the Party System* (T., UTP, 1953) are the usual introductions to the Social Credit variation of agrarian protest.

Perhaps the energy problems of the 1970s will lead economic historians to correct their neglect of the history of energy resources. The one fine historical study of the utilization of an energy resource is John H. Dales' model economic history, *Hydroelectricity and Industrial Development: Quebec, 1898-1940* (Cambridge, Harvard Univ. Press, 1957). Merrill Denison's *The People's Power: The History of Ontario Hydro* (T., M&S, 1960) is the most recent of several works on Ontario Hydro. The early history of petroleum is sketched in Victor Ross, *Petroleum in Canada* (T., Southam Press, 1917). A popular history, Eric J. Hanson's *Dynamic Decade* (T., M&S, 1958), describes the explosion of the oil and gas industry in Alberta after the Second World War. A pioneering and very useful study of coal resources in the context of national energy policy is A. A. den Otter, "Railways and Alberta's Coal Problem, 1880-1960," in Anthony Rasporich, ed., *Western Canada Past and Present* (Calgary, M&S West, 1975). As background to current Canadian-American energy problems it is useful to consult Alan R. Plotnick, *Petroleum, Canadian Markets and United States Foreign Trade Policy* (Seattle, Univ. of Washington Press, 1964), and John T. Miller, *Foreign Trade in Gas and Electricity in North America* (N. Y., Praeger, 1970). William Kilbourn's history of TransCanada Pipelines, *Pipeline* (T., Clarke Irwin, 1970), is a good introduction to the economic and political problems of gas transportation in the 1950s.

TRANSPORTATION

The standard introduction is still G. P. de T. Glazebrook, *History of Transportation in Canada* (T., Ryerson, 1938; reissued in two volumes in the Carleton Library series, 1964). Its concentration on railways accurately reflects the overwhelmingly central role these have played in Canadian transportation history. Some of the reasons for this emerge from the remarkable writings of T. C. Keefer, recently republished as *Philosophy of Railroads and Other Essays* (T., UTP, 1972), with a particularly fine introduction by H. V. Nelles. Canadians' continuing fascination with railways has been shown by the extraordinary popularity of Pierre Berton's two-volume history of the building of the Canadian Pacific Railway, *The National Dream* and *The Last Spike* (T., M&S, 1970 and 1971). These are immensely colourful narrative histories containing a good deal of material on aspects of the CPR little noticed in the more scholarly histories, such as surveying and land speculation, and have been reasonably well received by professional historians. On the C.P.R., though, it is still useful to consult H. A. Innis, *A History of the Canadian Pacific Railway* (1923; reissued T., UTP, 1971), particularly the 1971 reissue which contains a foreword by Peter J. George raising important questions about profitability and the subsidies given to the corporation. It is also both useful and entertaining to consult an important critical review of Berton's first volume by H. V. Nelles in the November-December 1970 issue of the *Canadian Forum* and the resulting exchange between Nelles and Berton in the February 1971 issue.

The Canadian National Railway system has been well served by G. R. Stevens, whose two-volume *Canadian National Railways* (T., Clarke Irwin, 1960 and 1962) is a complete history of all of the railways that had become the CNR by 1921, including the Grand Trunk, Canadian Northern, Grand Trunk Pacific, and National Transcontinental. With the publication of T. D. Regehr's *The Canadian Northern Railway: Pioneer Road of the Northern Prairies 1895-1915* (T., Macmillan, 1976) we now have both a definitive study of a magnificent failure as well as a model of first-class scholarship in business history. It supersedes Regehr's earlier article, "The Canadian Northern Railway: The West's Own Product" (*CHR*, 1970). Of the many other studies of major or minor railways in Canada two worth consulting are A. W. Currie, *The Grand Trunk Railway of Canada* (T., UTP, 1957), and Howard Fleming, *Canada's Arctic Outlet: A History of the Hudson Bay Railway* (Berkeley and Los Angeles, Univ. of California Press, 1957). A valuable study of railway systems in a continental perspective is William J. Wilgus, *The Railway Interrelations of the United States and Canada* (T., Ryerson, 1937). There are a number of biographies, varying greatly in quality, of railway leaders. The best of these both deal with C.P.R. presidents: Heather Gilbert, *Awakening Continent: The Life of Lord Mount Stephen: Volume I, 1824-1891* (Aberdeen, Univ. of Aberdeen Press, 1965), and Walter Vaughan, *The Life and Work of Sir William Van Horne* (L., OUP, 1926). Railway leaders are among the chief targets of Gustavus Myers' muckraking *A History of Canadian Wealth* (1914; first Canadian edition, T., James Lewis & Samuel, 1972).

Other forms of transportation in the post-Confederation years have been generally neglected by economic historians, John F., Due, *The Intercity Electric Railway Industry in Canada* (T., UTP, 1966), contains a mass of factual data on the golden age of electric street railways. The best introductions to the history of aviation in Canada are Frank H. Ellis, *Canada's Flying Heritage* (T., UTP, second ed., 1961), and C. A. Ashley, *The First Twenty-Five Years: A Study of Trans-Canada Air Lines* (T., Mac., 1963). William Willoughby's *The St. Lawrence Seaway: A Study in Politics and Diplomacy* (Madison, Univ. of Wisconsin Press, 1961) is a study of the most recent attempt to recreate the empire of the St. Lawrence.

FINANCE

Canadian financial institutions and policy have, on the whole, been well studied by economists and historians. R. Craig McIvor's *Canadian Monetary, Banking and Fiscal Development* (T., Mac., 1958) is a comprehensive introduction to almost all aspects of Canadian financial history. Indispensable reference volumes on the history of taxation in Canada are J. Harvey Perry's, *Taxes, Tariffs and Subsidies: A History of Canadian Fiscal Development* (T., UTP, 2 volumes, 1955). They are up-dated in A. Milton Moore, J. Harvey Perry and Donald I. Beach, *The Financing of Canadian Federation: The First Hundred Years* (T., Canadian Tax Foundation, 1966). For the earlier period of Dominion-Provincial financial relations J. A. Maxwell, *Federal Subsidies to the Provincial Governments in Canada* (Cambridge, Harvard Univ. Press, 1937), is the best guide. The often hilarious history of Parliament's attempts to control government spending is recounted in Norman Ward, *The Public Purse, A Study in Canadian Democracy* (T., UTP, 1962). Irving Brecher, *Monetary and Fiscal Thought and Policy in Canada, 1919-1939* (T., UTP, 1957), is a helpful study of the problems of monetary policy in those transitional years.

The best introduction to the history of banking in Canada is a documentary collection edited by E. P. Neufeld, *Money and Banking in Canada: Historical Documents and*

Commentary (T., M&S, Carleton Library, 1954). Neufeld's own most recent book, *The Financial System of Canada: Its Growth and Development* (T., Mac, 1972), is a masterly study of the growth of all forms of financial intermediaries, like Perry an indispensable reference work. Few of the company-sponsored histories of banks and insurance companies are noteworthy. The best of these is Victor Ross and A. St. L. Trigge, *A History of the Canadian Bank of Commerce* (T., OUP, 3 volumes, 1920-34).

THE TARIFF AND SECONDARY INDUSTRY

The history of Canadian manufacturing is inseparable from that of the government policy which was designed to stimulate and protect the manufacturing sector of the economy. The National Policy of tariff protection became the single most controversial economic policy adopted by a Canadian government. In recent years historical judgement on the protective tariff has been harsh, very strongly influenced by John H. Dales' *Protective Tariff in Canadian Development* (T., UTP, 1966). Because of the heavy reliance on economic theory in that work the beginning student might consult Dales' article, "Protection, Immigration and Canadian Nationalism," in Peter Russell, ed., *Nationalism in Canada* (T., McGraw-Hill, 1966). In the same volume, Craig Brown's "The Nationalism of the National Policy" is a good explanation of the assumptions held by the politicians who established the National Policy. O. J. McDiarmid, *Commercial Policy in the Canadian Economy* (Cambridge, Harvard Univ. Press, 1946), is a good, detached, survey of commercial policy to 1939. An older, very hostile, but still useful history of protection in Canada is Edward Porritt, *Sixty Years of Protection in Canada* (Winnipeg, Grain Growers Guide, 1913).

A good starting point for the history of Canadian-American tariff negotiations is D. C. Masters, *Reciprocity, 1846-1911* (Ottawa, Canadian Historical Association, Booklet No. 12, 1961). The movement for commercial union, along with other economic problems in Canadian-American relations, is dealt with in R. Craig Brown, *Canada's National Policy, 1883-1900* (Princeton, Princeton Univ. Press, 1964). L. E. Ellis, *Reciprocity 1911: A Study in Canadian-*

American Relations (New Haven, Yale Univ. Press, 1939), is still the best account of that critical election. The sometimes neglected history of Canadian tariff policy in the 1930s is most easily approached through Richard N. Kottman, *Reciprocity and the North Atlantic Triangle, 1932-1938* (Ithaca, Cornell Univ. Press, 1968). Douglas H. Arnett, *British Preferences in Canadian Commercial Policy* (T., Ryerson, 1948) is also useful.

There is still no single work on the history of manufacturing industries. The best study of the regional growth and national integration of manufacturing in the late nineteenth and early twentieth centuries is an unpublished doctoral thesis by T. W. Acheson, "The Social Origins of Canadian Industrialism: A Study in the Structure of Entrepreneurship" (University of Toronto, 1971). The chapter of the thesis published as "The National Policy and the Industrialization of the Maritimes, 1880-1910" (*Acadiensis*, 1972) is a particularly valuable study of manufacturing in that region. There is a fine chapter on the rise of manufacturing in Jacob Spelt's *Urban Development of South-Central Ontario* (1955; reissued T., M&S, Carleton Library, 1972). For Quebec the works cited in section I should be consulted. An important statistical overview is Gordon W. Bertram, "Historical Statistics on Growth and Structure in Manufacturing in Canada. 1870-1957," Canadian Political Science Association, *Conference on Statistics, Papers, 1962-3* (T., UTP, 1963).

The secondary literature on specific manufacturing industries is particularly sporadic. Works by Main and Guthrie on the nickel and newsprint paper industries have already been mentioned. William G. Phillips, *The Agricultural Implement Industry of Canada* (T., UTP, 1956), is a solid economic study. Within that industry, Merrill Denison has written a popular history of Massey-Ferguson, *Harvest Triumphant* (T., M&S, 1948), and E. P. Neufeld has produced a model contemporary history of a multinational corporation in *A Global Corporation: A History of the International Development of Massey-Ferguson Limited* (T., UTP, 1969). William Kilbourn's history of The Steel Company of Canada, *The Elements Combined* (T., Clarke Irwin, 1960), is one of the few other first-class histories of a manufacturing enterprise. For further information on the nineteenth and early twentieth century iron and steel industries W. J. Donald's older study, *The Canadian Iron and Steel Industry* (Boston and N.Y., Houghton Mifflin, 1915), is still useful.

Very little has been written about the marketing of goods and services in post-Confederation Canada. There is no account of the Hudson's Bay Company's transition from fur trading to retailing, for example, or of the rise of chain and department stores in the early twentieth century. C. L. Burton's *A Sense of Urgency* (T., Clarke Irwin, 1952) is the best autobiography written by a Canadian businessman and contains much useful material on Simpson's (which Burton headed after 1929) and on the philanthropic activities of Toronto businessmen. Another good biography of a retailer, written by a professional historian, is Alan Wilson, *John Northway: A Blue-Serge Canadian* (T., Burns & McEachern, 1965).

THE STATE AND ECONOMIC LIFE

The interaction of businessmen and governments in the development and regulation of Canadian economic activity, particularly during the transformation to an urban, industrialized society, is a subject of growing interest to business historians and to Canadian historians generally. For introductory surveys of the role of Canadian governments in economic life two articles by Hugh G. J. Aitken should be consulted: "Defensive Expansion: The State and Economic Growth in Canada," in Easterbrook and Watkins, eds., *Approaches to Canadian Economic History*; and "Government and Business in Canada: An Interpretation" (*Business History Review*, 1964). In addition, J. A. Corry, *The Growth of Government Activities Since Confederation* (Ottawa, KP, 1939), is a straightforward survey of the growth of government involvement in the economy, weak on the period before 1914, but containing much useful factual information. The recent publication of H. V. Nelles, *The Politics of Development: Forests, Mines, and Hydro-Electric Power in Ontario, 1849-1941* (T., Mac., 1974), makes available a superb analysis of the interaction of political and business groups in the shaping and development of resources policy in Ontario. Nelles' work challenges a number of traditional assumptions about the uses of state power in Canada, is a mine of information on the industries discussed, and should be a model and stimulant for similar studies of other provinces.

Aside from Nelles, historians are only beginning to produce case studies of the relations of businessmen, corporations, and governments. A good example of an attempt to generalize about business-government relations in the Laurier period, in conscious comparison with recent American historiography, is Christopher Armstrong and H. V. Nelles, "Private Property in Peril: Ontario Businessmen and the Federal System, 1898-1911," in Porter and Cuff, eds., *Enterprise and National Development*. Patricia Roy, who has written several fine articles on the British Columbia Electric Railway, discusses its lobbying tactics in "The Fine Arts of Lobbying and Persuading: The Case of the B. C. Electric Railway," in Macmillan, ed., *Canadian Business History*, and discusses state regulation of its activities in "Regulating the British Columbia Electric Railway: The First Public Utilities Commission in British Columbia" (*B.C. Studies*, 1971). Also in the Porter and Cuff volume, Michael Bliss discusses the early years of Canadian competition policy in "Another Anti-Trust Tradition: Canadian Anti-Combines Policy, 1889-1910." For the general theme of competition and consolidation in the Canadian economy, however, students should consult Lloyd G. Reynolds, *The Control of Competition in Canada* (Cambridge, Harvard Univ. Press, 1940), and, with emphasis on the more recent period, L. A. Skeoch, ed., *Restrictive Trade Practices in Canada* (T., M&S, 1966).

Historians are also beginning to appreciate the immense importance of business-government relations in wartime. An article like Robert Cuff's "Organizing for War: Canada and the United States During World War I" (*CHAR*, 1969) is very suggestive of the themes to be developed in future studies. At present, however there is still limited material on the Canadian economy in the two world wars. The chapter on the war economy in Brown and Cook, *A Nation Transformed*, is an excellent introduction to economic organization in the War of 1914-1918. The much more complex World War II economy still awaits similar treatment. R. W. James, *Wartime Economic Cooperation: A Study of Relations Between Canada and the United States* (T., Ryerson, 1949), stands almost alone as a detailed and suggestive study. Current discussions of wage and price controls should lead to more study of the wartime experience; at the moment K. W. Taylor, "Canadian War-Time Price Controls, 1941-46" (*CJEPS*, 1946) is the best introduction. Some idea of the critical role of C. D. Howe in the management of the war economy can be gleaned from Leslie Roberts' popular biography, *C.D., The Life and Times of Clarence Decatur Howe* (T., Clarke Irwin, 1957).

FOREIGN OWNERSHIP

The emergence of a new Canadian economic nationalism in the 1960s has sparked a continuing interest in the role of foreign capital, technology, and enterprise in Canadian economic development. Although much has been written about French and English involvement in the British North American economy before Confederation, the material on the post-Confederation years, particularly on American investment in Canada, is still limited and uneven in quality. Hugh G. J. Aitken's *American Capital and Canadian Resources* (Cambridge, Harvard Univ. Press, 1961) is the best survey of the situation as it had developed through the 1950s. It can usefully be supplemented by the essays in Hugh G. J. Aitken, ed., *The American Economic Impact on Canada* (Durham, Duke Univ. Press, 1959). An older study which is still a standard source for the period before 1940 is Herbert Marshall, Frank A. Southard Jr., and Kenneth W. Taylor, *Canadian-American Industry: A Study in International Investment* (orig. pub. 1936, repub. T., Carleton Library, 1976).

Among the more recent attempts to explore the growth of American influence in Canadian manufacturing are Stephen Scheinberg's provocative article, "Invitation to Empire: Tariffs and American Economic Expansion," in Cuff and Porter, eds., *Enterprise and National Development*, and Michael Bliss's comment on the ironies of the National Policy, "Canadianizing American Business: the Roots of the Branch Plant," in Ian Lumsden, ed., *Close the*

49th Parallel, Etc. The Americanization of Canada (T., UTP, 1970). Mira Wilkins sets the American spillover into Canada in a much wider context in *The Emergence of Multinational Enterprise: American Business Abroad from the Colonial Era to 1914* (Cambridge, Harvard Univ. Press, 1970) and *The Maturing of Multinational Enterprise: American Business Abroad from 1914 to 1970* (Cambridge, Harvard University Press, 1974). For American involvement in resource industries and the tensions between nationalism and continentalism in development policy Nelles' *The Politics of Development* is invaluable. The most commented upon of the socialist/nationalist attempts at an historical explanation of the foreign ownership problem is R. T. Naylor's long essay, "The rise and fall of the third commercial empire of the St. Lawrence," in Teeple, ed., *Capitalism and the National Question in Canada*. Naylor refines and somewhat alters his thesis in *The History of Canadian Business, 1867-1914*. L. R. MacDonald directly challenges Naylor's basic conceptualization in "Merchants against Industry: an Idea and its Origins" (*CHR*, 1975).

As the debate on foreign ownership developed in the 1960s it produced an extraordinary volume of analysis and polemic, much of it directed against the free-trade, antinationalist views held by most Canadian economists in the 1950s and early 1960s and set out most clearly in several of the articles in Harry G. Johnson's *The Canadian Quandary* (T., McGraw-Hill, 1963). One of the first and most articulate of the new nationalists was Abraham Rotstein, whose articles have been collected in *The Precarious Homestead: Essays on Economics, Technology and Nationalism* (T., New Press, 1973). Denis Smith's biography of Walter Gordon, *Gentle Patriot* (Edmonton, Hurtig, 1973), is an outstanding source of information on Gordon's attempts to convert the Liberal Party to economic nationalism. Kari Levitt's *Silent Surrender: The Multinational Corporation in Canada* (T., Mac., 1970) was the most widely-read attack on foreign ownership. The most prominent of the economists with grave doubts about the new economic nationalism was A. E. Safarian, whose position is set out briefly and lucidly in "Foreign Investment in Canada: Some Myths" (*JCS*, 1971).

II. LABOUR AND INDUSTRIAL RELATIONS

This is one of the most rapidly expanding, vital, and exciting areas of Canadian studies. The new labour history, now being produced faster than it can be catalogued in essays like this, combines sound scholarship with new conceptualization drawn from British, American, and French work in labour and social history. The articles in the first issue of the journal of Canadian labour history, *Labour/Le Travailleur*, (vol. 1, No. 1, 1976) are an appropriate sampling of the best of the new work. In particular, the review essay "To the Dartmouth Station: A Worker's Eye View of Labour History" by Michael S. Cross, is not only an excellent critical guide to recent work, but a brilliant satire succeeding on several levels. The other essential anthology of recent articles is Gregory S. Kealey and Peter Warrian, eds., *Essays in Canadian Working Class History* (T., M&S, 1976), which also has a comprehensive bibliographic essay. A much more extensive guide to primary sources—union records, pamphlets, and newspapers—is Russell Hahn, *et. al, Primary Sources in Canadian Working Class History, 1860-1930* (Kitchener, Dumont Press, 1973). The standard bibliographic guide to labour in Quebec is André E. Leblanc and James D. Thwaites, *Le monde ouvrier au Québec: bibliographie rétrospective* (M., Les Presses de l'université du Québec, 1973).

TRADE UNIONS

Traditional working class history has concerned itself almost exclusively with the development of trade unions in Canada. Two Canadian Historical Association booklets, *The Canadian Labour Movement, 1812-1902* (Ottawa, CHA, 1974) by Eugene Forsey, and *The Canadian Labour Movement, 1902-1960* (Ottawa, CHA, 1975) by Irving Abella, are handy surveys of trade union history. H. A. Logan's *Trade Unions in Canada: Their Development and Functioning* (T., Macmillan, 1948) is excessively factual, dull, and sometimes erroneous, but still the best one-volume source on Canadian labour organizations. A leftist-nationalist survey of trade union history is Charles Lipton, *The Trade Union Movement of Canada, 1827-1959* (M., Canadian Social Publications Limited, 1967). In *No Power Greater: A Century of Labour in British Columbia* (Vancouver, B.C., Federation of Labour and Boag Foundation, 1967), Paul A. Phillips has surveyed trade union activity in the province where labour has been most militant. Fernand Harvey, ed., *Aspects Historiques du mouvement ouvrier au Québec* (M., Boréal Express, 1973), is an uneven collection of essays surveying labour and union history in Quebec. The same field is also covered, somewhat sketchily, in Richard Desrosiers and Denis Heroux, *Le Travailleur Québécois et le syndicalisme* (M., Les Presses de l'université du Québec, 1973). Pierre Elliott Trudeau, ed., *The Asbestos Strike* (orig. pub. 1956, translation T., James Lewis and Samuel, 1974) contains useful background essays on Quebec labour as well as analyses of the famous strike.

Steven Langdon, "The Emergence of the Canadian Working Class Movement" (*JCS*, May, Aug. 1973) reprinted as a pamphlet by New Hogtown Press, T., 1975) has been well received by other labour historians as an attempt to set trade union development in the general context of working class history. Two articles by Bernard Ostry, "Conservatives, Liberals and Labour in the 1870s" (*CHR*, 1960), and "Conservatives, Liberals and Labour in the 1880s" (*CJEPS*, 1961), are still the best introduction to trade unions and federal politics in the nineteenth century. Although badly dated and apt to be superseded at any time, Douglas R. Kennedy, *The Knights of Labor in Canada* (London, University of Western Ontario, 1956) is still the only monograph on that organization's penetration into Canada. There is an excellent account of strikes and the development of trade unions in late nineteenth century Quebec in Hamelin and Roby, *Histoire Economique du Québec, 1851-1896*. Noel Belander, *et. al*, *Les Travailleurs Québécois, 1851-1896* (M., Les Presses de l'université du Québec, 1973), attempts, like the Langdon essays, to set trade unions into a conceptual framework involving the worker's role in the changing capitalist economy.

Robert Babcock, *Gompers in Canada: A Study in American Continentalism Before the First World War* (T., UTP, 1974), is the best single study of the early twentieth century entrance of international unions. It is mildly controversial because of the author's nationalist position. Another still helpful study of the growth of labour organizations on a continental scale is Norman J. Ware and H. A. Logan, *Labour in Canadian-AmericanRelations* (T., Ryerson, 1937).

The history of industrial disputes in the early twentieth century is surveyed extremely well in Stuart Jamieson, *Times of Trouble: Labour Unrest and Industrial Conflict in Canada, 1900-1966* (Study No. 22 of the Task Force on Labour Relations, O., 1971). Irving Abella, ed., *On Strike: Six Key Labor Struggles in Canada* (T., James Lewis and Samuel, 1974) is also a useful introduction to twentieth century disputes. The Winnipeg general strike of 1919 has, of course, received intensive study by historians. David J. Bercuson's *Confrontation at Winnipeg* (M., McGill-Queen's Press, 1974) is now the most comprehensive monograph on the background to the strike, although D. C. Masters, *The Winnipeg General Strike* (T., UTP, 1950), should still be read along with it. The essential primary source on Winnipeg is Norman Penner, ed., *Winnipeg, 1919: The Strikers' Own History of the Winnipeg General Strike* (rev. ed. T., Lorimer, 1975). David J. Bercuson's "Western Labour Radicalism and the One Big Union: myths and realities" (*JCS*, May, 1974) is an important and controversial interpretation of the role of Canada's most famous radical labour organization.

The rise of industrial unionism in Canada and its impact on older labour organizations is thoroughly described in Irving Abella, *Nationalism, Communism and Canadian Labour: The C.I.O., the Communist Party, and the Canadian Congress of Labour, 1935-56* (T., UTP, 1973). It is described in the Cross review article as "the best damned book on labour history yet. It would be even better, though, if it had some social history in it.... But, hell, let's not kick a gift horse in the nuts—it's a real good book." Two introductions to the political activities of organized labour are Martin Robin, *Radical Politics and Canadian Labour, 1880-1930* (Kingston, Industrial Relations Centre, Queen's University, 1968), a book which is flawed by excessive detail; and for the later period Gad Horowitz, *Canadian Labour in Politics* (T., UTP, 1968). A more specialized study of the recent past is David Kwavnick, *Organized Labour and Pressure Politics: The CLC 1955-1968* (M., McGill-Queen's, 1972).

It is necessary to re-emphasize that many more articles have recently been published on individual strikes, regional aspects of the union movement, and various incidents in organized labour's development. Many of these are listed in the bibliography in Kealey and Warrian, eds., *Essays in Canadian Working Class History*.

WORKING CLASS LIFE

The first step in developing an historical understanding of the lives and culture of ordinary working Canadians has been the publication or republication of essential primary sources. Michael Cross, ed., *The Workingman in the Nineteenth Century* (T., OUP, 1974) is the only comprehensive source book for the earlier period, an excellent introduction to the real world of the working classes. There is a mass of detail on all aspects of working and living conditions, industrial relations, and social problems in the 1880s in Greg Kealey, ed., *Canada Investigates Industrialism: The Royal Commission on the Relations of Labour and Capital, 1889* (T., UTP, 1973). Herbert B. Ames, *The City Below the Hill* (orig. pub. 1897, repub. T., UTP, 1972) was a pioneering study of wages and living conditions among Montreal workers. Written from first-hand observation, Edmund Bradwin's *The Bunkhouse Man: A Study of Work and Pay in the Camps of Canada, 1903-1914* (orig. pub. 1928, repub. T., UTP, 1972) is still the best book on any group in the Canadian labour force, the frontier workers whose importance in Canadian labour history is too often neglected by students concentrating on urban industrial workers.

The new labour historians are concerned with showing how older patterns of work and values were altered by the development of Canadian industrialism in the second half of the nineteenth century. Most of their work is still in article form and is most accessible in *Labour/Le Travailleur* and *Essays in Canadian Working Class History*. Three recent books, however, are indispensable for an understanding of what has been done and the likely course of future studies. Jacques Rouillard, *Les travailleurs du coton au Québec, 1900-1915* (M., Les Presses de l'université du Québec, 1974) is the first study of a group of workers in the context of the development of their industry and its relation to the general society. T. J. Copp's *Anatomy of Poverty: The*

Condition of the Working Class in Montreal, 1897-1929 (T., M&S, 1974) is an ambitious study of work, wages, and living conditions for an important section of the urban proletariat. Finally, *Women at Work: Ontario, 1850-1930* (T., Canadian Women's Educational Press, 1974) is a collection of essays written from a radical/feminist perspective which shows how much can be achieved and how much there is to be done when women set out to rediscover the working class dimension of their past.

Labour history as a distinct field of Canadian historical studies was not mentioned when this volume was originally conceived, about 1973. The expanded discussion in this edition does not adequately cover the area. I have suggested that working class and trade union history be given a separate chapter in the next edition of this guide.

Social and Intellectual History

Carl Berger

Social and Intellectual history are not highly developed aspects of Canadian historical writing and any description of the works in these areas must necessarily be rather fragmentary. The following analysis is highly selective and intended only to suggest some of the major issues and themes.

SOCIOLOGICAL STUDIES

The pioneer work in Canadian social history was inaugurated by sociologists. In an introductory, documentary survey, *The Social Development of Canada* (T., UTP, 1942), S. D. Clark focussed on the problems of social dislocation that occurred in frontier areas throughout the country's past. His *Church and Sect in Canada* (T., UTP, 1948) illustrates how staple exploitation in new areas led to dissatisfaction with formal and traditional religious organizations and services and ultimately to religious movements of protest. This analysis extends from the mid-18th century to 1900 and the discussions of the Methodist Church and the urban scene in the late 19th century are extremely valuable. Clark also edited a nine-volume series (T., UTP) that explored the background and traced the development of the Social Credit movement in Alberta. Political scientists, sociologists and historians investigated a wide-range of subjects but the most substantial contributions from the point of view of social history were Jean Burnet's *Next-Year Country* (1951), a detailed examination of standards of living, family and ethnic relations in the district of Hanna, Alberta, and W. E. Mann's *Sect, Cult, and Church in Alberta* (1955), which depicts the aberrant and fundamentalist religious groups in the province.

A series of studies under the general title, Canadian Frontiers of Settlement, (T., Mac.), edited by W. A. Mackintosh and W. L. G. Joerg, also centred on prairie society. Two volumes by the sociologist Carl A. Dawson are still of considerable interest: *Pioneering in the Prairie Provinces: The Social Side of the Settlement Process* (1940), and *Group Settlement: Ethnic Communities in Western Canada* (1936), which stresses the assimilation of Doukhobors, Mennonites, Mormons, German Catholics, and French Canadians.

The major developments and issues involved in the evolution of French Canada from a rural to a predominantly industrial and urban society are set out in two excellent collections of articles, *French-Canadian Society* (T., M& S, 1964), eds. Marcel Rioux and Yves Martin, and *Essais sur le Québec contemporain/ Essays on Contemporary Quebec* (Quebec, Laval, 1953), ed. Jean C. Falardeau. There is a good listing of additional literature in René Durocher and Paul-Andre Linteau, *Histoire du Québec: bibliographie sélective (1867-1970)* (Trois Rivières, Editions Boréal Express, 1970).

Another sociological study but of a different character, John Porter, *The Vertical Mosaic: An Analysis of Social Class and Power in Canada* (T., UTP, 1965), is an examination of class structure and elite groups. Though it describes the situation in the mid-twentieth century, the work is seminal for the range of questions it suggests about the past as well as for the richness of its historical illustrative material.

SOCIAL HISTORIES

Compared to these sociological studies the social histories written by historians often seem to equate social history with the more colorful incidents in the lives of people rather than with general interpretations of social movements and forces. *Canadians in the Making* (T., Longmans, 1958), by A. R. M. Lower is a personal, opinionated and eccentric general survey of social development. Lower's concern is with the impediments to the formation of a genuine sense of community and his narrative is an extended disquisition of the bad effects of Calvinism, colonialism and unselective immigration. A more informative, though still rather conventional and descriptive study, is G. P. de T. Glazebrook,

Life in Ontario: A Social History (T., UTP, 1968). Two collections of essays that mirror the more recent concern with demography, social class, group consciousness and protest, are *Studies in Canadian Social History*, eds. Michiel Horn and Ronald Sabourin (T., M&S, 1974) and *Prophecy and Protest: Social Movements in Twentieth-Century Canada*, eds. Samuel D. Clark, J. Paul Grayson, and Linda M. Grayson (T., Gage, 1975). J. L. Finlay, *Canada in the North Atlantic Triangle: Two Centuries of Social Change* (T., OUP, 1975) is an introductory survey of some broad themes of social development—including industrialism, populism, and socialism—set into a comparative framework of British, American, and Canadian experience.

SOCIAL DEVELOPMENTS

The conclusions of a recent effort to analyze the social realities of mid-nineteenth century Hamilton, Ontario, through the statistical analysis of patterns of class and social structure is presented in Michael Katz, "Social Structure in Hamilton, Ontario," in Stephen Thernstrom and Richard Sennett, eds., *Nineteenth-Century Cities: Essays in the New Urban History* (New Haven, Yale Univ. Press, 1969), his "The People of a Canadian City: 1851-2" (*CHR*, 1972), and his *The People of Hamilton, Canada West. Family and Class in a Mid-Nineteenth-Century City* (Cambridge, Harvard U. Press, 1975). Some of the implications of these conclusions relating to education, literacy, and school attendance are traced through in several articles in *History of Education Quarterly* (1972), a special issue on education and social change in English-speaking Canada, and in Harvey J. Graff, "Literacy and Social Structure in Elgin County, Canada West: 1861" (*Social History*, 1973). A similar approach to a rural area which also stresses the extraordinary degree of the transiency of population is David Gagan and Herbert Mays, "Historical Demography and Canadian Social History: Families and Land in Peel County, Ontario" (*CHR*, 1973).

Three major developments that were intensified in the period between Confederation and the Great War were urbanization, immigration, and the growth of industry, and these have been subjected to some examination. The programmatic statement of the metropolitan approach which called attention to the need to trace the relationship between urban communities and their hinterlands is J. M. S. Careless, "Frontierism, Metropolitanism, and Canadian History," in C. Berger, ed., *Approaches to Canadian History* (T., UTP, 1967). Jacob Spelt, *Urban Development of South-Central Ontario* (first ed., 1955; T., M&S, 1973), analyses the political, geographic and economic factors behind Toronto's dominance over the region; a more limited but still useful survey is D. C. Masters, *The Rise of Toronto, 1850-1890* (T., UTP, 1947). Though a rather difficult book, *Victorian Toronto, 1850 to 1900: Pattern and Process of Growth* (Chicago, Univ. of Chicago Press, 1970) by Peter Goheen is especially notable for its explanation of class segregation within the city. A balanced and informative but all too brief account of the relations of classes and ethnic groups within another metropolis is given in J. I. Cooper, *Montreal* (M., McGill-Queen's, 1969). A. F. J. Artibise, *Winnipeg, A Social History of Urban Growth, 1874-1914* (M., McGill-Queen's, 1975) provides an excellent survey of the processes of growth, class and ethnic segregation, and urban politics of that prairie centre. A more disconnected—but still illuminating—picture of another prairie city emerges from the essays in *Frontier Calgary. Town, City, and Region, 1875-1914* (Calgary, M&S West, 1975) eds. Anthony W. Rasporich and Henry Klassen. *Cities in the West*, eds. A. R. McCormack and Ian Macpherson (Ottawa, National Museum of Man, Mercury Series, 1975) contains both general papers on the urban frontier as well as research on such subjects as municipal politics, sport, and businessmen and reform. A listing of additional literature on urbanization and cities may be found in Gil Stelter, *Canadian Urban History: A Selected Bibliography* (Sudbury, Laurentian Univ., 1972).

The literature on immigration and particularly the history of specific ethnic groups other than French or British is extensive, as may be seen even in such a limited listing as Andrew Gregorovich, *Canadian Ethnic Groups Bibliography* (T., Ontario Dept. of the Provincial Secretary, 1972). A few of the more adequate studies of individual groups written with a greater awareness of the social and political milieu than is generally the case with this type of history are George Woodcock and Ivan Avakumovic, *The Doukhobors* (T., OUP, 1968), Robin Winks, *The Blacks in Canada* (New Haven, Yale Univ. Press, 1971), J. G. MacGregor, *Vilni Zemli (Free Lands): the Ukrainian Settlement of Alberta* (T., M&S, 1969), John Norris, *Strangers Entertained: A History of the Ethnic Groups of British Columbia* (Vancouver, B.C. Centennial Committee, 1971), Frank H. Epp, *Mennonites in Canada, 1786-1920. The History of a Separate People* (T., Mac., 1974), and Howard Palmer, *Land of the Second Chance: A History of Ethnic Groups in Southern Alberta* (Lethbridge, *Lethbridge Herald*, 1972). In a rather different category but still useful for factual information about certain groups are: Wilhelm Kristjanson, *The Icelandic People in Manitoba* (Winnipeg, Wallingford Press, 1965); Victor Peters, *All Things Common: The Hutterian Way of Life* (Minneapolis, U. of Minnesota Press, 1965); B. G. Sack, *History of the Jews in Canada* (Montreal, Harvest House, 1965); Mykhailo Marunchak, *The Ukrainian Canadians. A History* (Winnipeg, Ukrainian Free Academy of Sciences, 1970); Wiktor Turek, *The Poles in Manitoba* (T., Polish Research Institute of Canada, 1967); John Gellner and John Smerk, *The Czechs and Slovaks in Canada* (T., UTP, 1968). Additionally the first three volumes of "Generations A History of Canada's Peoples" have been published (1976) by McClelland and Stewart for the Multiculturalism Program of the Department of the Secretary of State. These are Grace Anderson and David Higgs, *A Future to Inherit: Portuguese Communities in Canada*; Henry Radecki with Benedykt Heydenkorn, *A Member of a Distinguished Family: The Polish Group in Canada*; and W. S. Reid, ed., *The Scottish Tradition in Canada*.

While most histories of ethnic groups have tended to concentrate on agricultural settlement, R. F. Harney and Harold Troper, *The Immigrants: A Portrait of the Urban Experience, 1890-1930* (T., Van Nostrand, 1975), a richly illustrated document book, focusses on another milieu. Donald Avery, "Canadian Immigration Policy and the Foreign Navvy, 1896-1914," (CHA *Historical Papers*, 1972), argues that while policy at the turn of the century aimed mainly at recruiting farmer settlers, it increasingly also sought to import an industrial proletariat.

Two speculative and provocative articles dealing with the general question of the degree to which ethnic groups were compelled to assimilate to a single pattern are J. E. Rea, "The Roots of Prairie Society," in D. Gagan, ed., *Prairie Perspectives* (T., Holt, Rinehart & Winston, 1970), and Allan Smith, "Metaphor and Nationality in North America" (*CHR*, 1970). David E. Smith, *Prairie Liberalism: The Liberal Party in Saskatchewan, 1905-71* (T., UTP, 1975) examines a concrete case of the integration of immigrant voters into a provincial political machine and the defeat of that party by an outburst of nativism and prejudice in the election of 1929. There is no better source for understanding the emotional and human dimensions of the experience of a young boy from an immigrant background accommodating himself to the dominant Anglo-Saxon culture than John Marlyn's novel, *Under the Ribs of Death* (T., M&S, 1957).

There are few social studies of the working class or business during Canada's age of industrialism. Books and articles on the trade union movement contain very little on the standards of living of workers or working class culture. Three exceptions are *Canada Investigates Industrialism* (T., UTP, 1973), ed. Greg Kealey, which contains selections from the testimony of industrialists, government officials, and working people on conditions of labour in factories and mines given before the Royal Commission on the Relations of Labour and Capital in the later 1880s, Edmund Bradwin, *The Bunkhouse Man* (T., UTP, 1972), a fine study of the life of men in the railway camps in the decade before the Great War and Terry Copp, *The Anatomy of Poverty: The Condition of the Working Class in Montreal, 1897-1929* (T., M&S, 1974) which attributes the problems of labour to structural rather than cultural peculiarities of that city. F. W. Watt, "The National Policy, the Workingman, and Proletarian Ideas in Victorian Canada" (*CHR*, 1959), analyses the attitudes of the more radical fringe of labour spokesmen toward capitalism in the same period. The representative writings of one such figure have been collected in *The Politics of Labor* by T. Phillips Thompson (1887; T., UTP, 1975). Two fine studies in business history are T. W. Acheson, "Changing Social Origins of the Canadian Industrial Elite, 1880-1910," in Glen Porter and Robert D. Cuff, eds., *Enter-*

prise and National Development: Essays in Canadian Business and Economic History (T., Hakkert, 1973), and M. Bliss, *A Living Profit: Studies in the Social History of Canadian Business, 1883-1911* (T., M&S, 1974) which is especially informative on the self-images of businessmen and the formation of self-protective associations in the late nineteenth century.

Intellectual history of the half-century after Confederation has been examined mainly in terms of nationalist thought and social criticism and reform movements. The ideology of imperialism has been analyzed in C. Berger, *The Sense of Power: Studies in the Ideas of Canadian Imperialism, 1867-1914* (T., UTP, 1970), which suggests how English-Canadian nationalism fused a loyalty to Canada with a deep commitment to the British Empire, and in Robert Page, "Canada and the Imperial Idea in the Boer War Years" (*JCS*, 1970). The life and ideas of the leading critic of imperialism in Canada and an advocate of continental unity are lucidly analyzed in Elizabeth Wallace, *Goldwin Smith: Victorian Liberal* (T., UTP, 1957). The best source of Smith's thought is his *Canada and the Canadian Question* (1891; T., UTP, 1972). In *The Image of Confederation* (T., CBC, 1964) F. H. Underhill sought to depict the various ways in which English and French Canadian intellectuals have understood the nature of confederation. An illuminating assessment of traditional Canadian views of American political institutions in the nineteenth century is S. F. Wise and R. C. Brown, *Canada Views the United States* (T., Mac., 1967).

S. E. D. Shortt, *The Search for an Ideal: Six Canadian Intellectuals and their Convictions in an age of Transition 1890-1930* (T., UTP, 1976) analyzes the thought of six university figures, not only on national and social issues but also on culture and, above all, religion. The sustained effort of one Canadian scientist's attempt to reconcile religious faith and evolution is assessed in Charles F. O'Brien, *Sir William Dawson, A Life in Science and Religion* (Philadelphia, American Philosophical Society, 1971).

PROGRESSIVE THOUGHT AND SOCIAL CRITICISM

Canadian development in the period after 1880 gener-

ated a considerable volume of social criticism and a middle-
class, moralistic, reform movement which reached its climax
during World War I. This general progressive impulse included urban reform, temperance and female suffrage but
its common denominator was a revival of social concern
among the Protestant denominations. Historians of religious institutions have not generally paid much attention to
the influence of religious conviction in the broad social
sense but a survey, *The Christian Church in Canada* (T.,
Ryerson, 1956), by H. H. Walsh, does describe the problems
faced by the churches and the major religious developments
in a lucid, summary fashion. John Moir, *Enduring Witness:
A History of the Presbyterian Church in Canada* (T., Presbyterian Church in Canada official history, 1974) deals very
effectively with one denomination's contributions to social
service and missions and contains a lucid account of the
church union movement. The crucial work for understanding the "social gospel" is Richard Allen's *The Social Pas-
sion: Religion and Social Reform in Canada, 1914-28* (T.,
UTP, 1971), in which the desire to create the kingdom of
God on earth is seen as the master impulse behind the reform movements, and an attempt is made not to analyze its
ideology abstractly but to trace its impact in concrete action
relating to the labour churches, church union, prohibition,
social work, the Winnipeg General Strike and the Progressive Party. One major figure in the movement, J. S. Woodsworth, is the subject of a sympathetic biography, *A Prophet
in Politics* (T., UTP, 1959), by Kenneth McNaught, and two
of his works have been recently reprinted; *Strangers Within
Our Gates* (1909; T., UTP, 1972) deals with the challenge of
massive immigration, and *My Neighbor* (1911; T., UTP,
1972) with conditions in the growing cities and the need for
urban reform. A general overview of the latter subject is
given in Paul Rutherford, "Tomorrow's Metropolis: the
Urban Reform Movement in Canada, 1880-1920" (*CHAR*,
1971).

Another dominant strand of the progressive movement has been chronicled in *The Woman Suffrage Movement in Canada* (1950; T., UTP, 1974) by C. Cleverdon.
Nellie McClung's *In Times Like These* (1915; T., UTP,
1972) is an illuminating statement by an early feminist,

especially interesting for her view of female character and the relationship between female suffrage and general social reformation. One of the few attempts to understand the role of females in the labour force, as distinct from the leaders of middle class reformers, is offered in *Women at Work: Ontario, 1850-1930*, edited by Janice Acton, Penny Goldsmith, and Bonnie Shepard (T., Canadian Women's Education Press, 1974). A very comprehensive bibliography of literature relating to the subject has been compiled by V. Strong-Boag in *Women in Canada* (T., New Press, 1973), ed. Marylee Stephenson.

Gerald Hallowell, *Prohibition in Ontario, 1919-1923* (T., Ontario Historical Society, 1972) is a detailed appraisal of the success of prohibition, the difficulties in enforcing it, and its eventual repudiation. Graeme Decarie, "Something Old, Something New....: Aspects of Prohibitionism in Ontario in the 1890s," in *Oliver Mowat's Ontario* (T., Mac., 1972), ed. D. Swainson, is a sardonic analysis of the motives behind the campaign for the abolition of the use of liquor. The abuse of alcohol and the prohibition movement in another region has been colorfully examined in James Gray, *Booze: The Impact of Whiskey on the Prairie West* (T., Mac., 1972), and its connection with another "social evil" is developed in his equally sensationalist study of prostitution, *Red Lights on the Prairies* (T., Mac., 1971). E. Forbes, "Prohibition and the Social Gospel in Nova Scotia" (*Acadiensis*, 1971), is a very fine study of the abandonment of the prohibition experiment in favor of government control. The later chapters of R. C. Brown and R. Cook, *Canada, 1896-1921: A Nation Transformed* (T., M&S, 1974), contain an excellent interpretation of the prohibition movement, millenial reform, and the atmosphere of the Great War. John H. Thompson, "The Harvests of War: The Prairie West, 1914-1918" (Ph.D. thesis, Queen's University, 1975) examines the impact of the conflict on prairie society generally.

An ancillary dimension of moral reform was the concern with social welfare and education. A background study, stressing the administrative aspect, Richard B. Splane, *Social Welfare in Ontario, 1791-1893* (T., UTP, 1965), should be supplemented by Terrance Morrison, "The Child and Urban Social Reform in Late Nineteenth Century Ontario,

1875-1900" (Ph.D. thesis, University of Toronto, 1970), which deals with the awakening of concern among middle class professionals—women, educators, clergymen, social workers—for the child in the industrial-urban society and the beginnings of "Progressive" education. Neil Sutherland, *Children in English-Canadian Society, 1880-1920* (T., UTP, 1976) carries the story forward and details the beginning of the public health movement, the institution of juvenile courts, and the restructuring of school curricula to reflect the new perceptions of the child.

A critical survey of the development of public school systems and educational thought and practice which attempts—sometimes successfully—to relate the history of education to the social context is J. Donald Wilson, Robert M. Stamp, and Louis-Philippe Audet, *Canadian Education: A History* (Scarborough, Prentice-Hall, 1970).

The social roots and ideas of farmer protest during the first three decades of the century have been treated in such essentially political studies as W. L. Morton, *The Progressive Party in Canada* (T., UTP, 1950), and Paul Sharp, *The Agrarian Revolt in Western Canada* (Minneapolis, Univ. of Minnesota Press, 1948). C. B. Macpherson, *Democracy in Alberta* (T., UTP, 1953), contains an excellent analysis of the political philosophy of the United Farmers of Alberta based on the writings of Henry Wise Wood and William Irvine as well as a convincing explanation of how their ideas of government based on economic groups was a rationalization of the peculiar features of the prairie economy. W. L. Morton, "Social and Political Philosophy of Henry Wise Wood" (*Agricultural History*, 1948), is a useful assessment. W. R. Young, "Conscription, Rural Depopulation, and the Farmers of Ontario, 1917-19" (*CHR*, 1972), is a good study of the social background of the surge of farmer protest in the province at the end of the First World War. W. C. Good's autobiography, *Farmer Citizen* (T., Ryerson, 1958), is an honest and illuminating statement of the farmers' case seen in retrospect.

FRENCH CANADA

The reaction of French Canada to the problems of the age of industrialism has not received as much attention as is the case with English Canada. One important and revisionist work, William F. Ryan, *The Clergy and Economic Growth in Quebec, (1896-1914)* (Québec, Laval, 1966), challenges the view that the Church impeded economic growth by analyzing the encouragement that the clergy gave to various industrial enterprises in an effort to retain French Canadians within the province. The general conclusion is that there were no ascertainable theological barriers to economic growth but rather that the failure of French Canadians to control their own economic development arose from accidental circumstances. This is but one aspect of a complex debate over the question of the "economic inferiority" of French Canada, a debate which involves not only questions of economics but also of culture and social values generally. A collection of articles representing a variety of approaches to this problem is René Durocher and Paul-André Linteau, eds., *Le "Retard" du Québec et l'infériorité économique des Canadiens français* (Trois Rivières, Editions Boréal Express, 1971). Michel Brunet, "Trois dominantes de la pensée canadienne-française: l'agriculturisme, l'anti-étatisme et le messianisme," in his *Présence anglaise et les Canadiens* (M., Beauchemin, 1958), is a classic dissection of the elements of the traditional French-Canadian outlook which are held to have impeded that society's ability to control its own economic life. Jean Hulliger, *L'Enseignement social des évêques Canadiens de 1891-1950* (M., Fides, 1950), is a useful but not profound analysis of the social pronouncements of the clergy based on their public statements. Louis-Philippe Audet, *Histoire de l'Enseignement du Québec* (T., Holt, Rinehart & Winston, 2 vols., 1971), is an able summary of the development of the educational system which has often been seen as an additional barrier to French-Canadian participation in economic life. Two volumes of essays that elucidate the variety of responses in Quebec to the emergent industrial and urban society are *Idéologies au Canada français, 1850-1900*, dir. Fernand Dumont, Jean-Paul Montminy et Jean Hamelin (Québec, Laval, 1971), and *Idéologies au Canada Français, 1900-1929*, dir. Fernand Dumont, Jean Hamelin, Fernand Harvey, et Jean-Paul Montminy (Québec, Laval, 1974). Much has been written about the exodus of French Canadians to the United

States and A. Faucher, "L'émigration des Canadiens français au XIXe siècle: position du problème et perspectives"
(*Recherches sociographiques*, 1964), is a good introduction
to this literature and the problems of the topic.

The social thought of the French-Canadian nationalist
movement which centred on Henri Bourassa in the two decades after 1900 has been analyzed in Joseph Levitt, *Henri
Bourassa and the Golden Calf: The Social Program of the
Nationalists of Quebec, 1900-1914* (Ottawa, Univ. of Ottawa
Press, 1969), which finds that Bourassa's attempt to come to
terms with economic changes was moulded by his moralism
and above all by his fear that any enhancement of the power
of the secular state would decrease that of the Church to
which he gave his primary allegiance. The other two main
subjects of the nationalist programme are generously represented in *Henri Bourassa on Imperialism and Bi-culturalism 1900-1918* (T., Copp Clark, 1970), ed. Joseph Levitt.
Ramsay Cook, ed., *French-Canadian Nationalism* (T., Mac.,
1969), is a very useful anthology of nationalist advocacy and
analysis ranging from the mid-nineteenth century to the
quiet revolution of the 1960s. An indispensible older work
by a foreign observer, André Siegfried, *The Race Question
in Canada* (1907; T., M&S, 1966), offers a penetrating analysis of the different outlooks of the two peoples and is effective in isolating the religious bases of these outlooks.

The standard account of the nationalist movement in
the inter-war period is Michael Oliver, "The Social and Political ideas of French Canadian Nationalists, 1920-1945"
(Ph.D. thesis, McGill University, 1956). Susan M. Trofimenkoff, ed., *Abbé Groulx: Variations on a Nationalist Theme*
(T., Copp Clark, 1973), is an introduction to the thought of
the major figure, and her *Action Française: French Canadian Nationalism in the Twenties* (T., UTP, 1975) offers a
lucid account of the organization which he founded. His
autobiography, *Mes Mémoires* (3 vols., M., Fides, 1970,
1972), and J.-P. Gaboury, *Le Nationalisme de Lionel Groulx*
(Ottawa, Univ. of Ottawa Press, 1970), are helpful for an
understanding of the historical mythology underpinning his
outlook.

DEPRESSION

There is a substantial and growing body of work on

the depression of the 1930's and much of it tends to focus on the prairies where the effects of the economic breakdown were catastrophic. James Gray, *The Winter Years: The Depression on the Prairies* (T., Mac., 1966), is a memoir of that period illuminating life in Winnipeg, the relief system and make-work projects, and, to a lesser extent, revealing conditions of life in rural areas. A more systematic economic study of the effects of the depression on income and expenditure, provincial and municipal institutions, standards of living, and rehabilitation in Saskatchewan is George Britnell, *The Wheat Economy* (T., UTP, 1939). A fine article which describes the relief system is Blair Neatby, "The Saskatchewan Relief Commission, 1931-1934," in D. Swainson, ed., *Historical Essays on the Prairie Provinces* (T., M&S, 1970). Barry Broadfoot's *Ten Lost Years, 1929-1939: Memoirs of Canadians who Survived the Depression* (T., Doubleday, 1973) contains transcripts of segments of interviews with over six hundred people who experienced the depression in various walks of life. A documentary collection of broader scope, Michael Horn, ed., *The Dirty Thirties: Canadians in the Great Depression* (T., Copp Clark, 1972), illustrates governmental policy at all levels. *Recollections of the On-to-Ottawa Trek by Ronald Liversedge with Documents Related to the Vancouver Strike and the On to Ottawa Trek* (T., M&S, 1973), ed. Victor Hoar, contains a radical's description of conditions in the camps for the single unemployed and the Regina riot. Lita-Rose Betcherman, *The Swastika and the Maple Leaf: Fascist Movements in Canada in the Thirties* (T., Fitzhenry and Whiteside, 1975) concentrates on anti-semitic groups—some insignificant; others, like Adrien Arcand's National Social Christian Party, of more than passing curiosity.

The political protest movements of the 1930's—particularly the Co-operative Commonwealth Federation and the Social Credit Movement—have been studied in numerous works, two of which, S. M. Lipset's *Agrarian Socialism: The Co-operative Commonwealth Federation in Saskatchewan: A Study in Political Sociology* (N.Y., Anchor, 1968, and John A. Irving, *The Social Credit Movement in Alberta* (T., UTP, 1959), are fine examples of social-intellectual history. M. Horn, "The League for Social Reconstruction" (Ph.D. thesis, University of Toronto, 1969) is a comprehensive analysis of this association of radical intellectuals and their role in formulating the ideology of the national C.C.F.

Some of these figures, like Graham Spry, were also members of a pressure group that advocated a national broadcasting system for Canada. M. Prang, "The Origins of Public Broadcasting in Canada" (*CHR*, 1965), examines the activities of the Canadian Radio League and other interests. Frank Peers, *The Politics of Canadian Broadcasting, 1920-1951* (T., UTP, 1969), offers a detailed history of the creation of the Canadian Broadcasting Corporation, the interests and groups both opposed to and in favour of it, and the gradual abandonment of early commitments.

ASPECTS

Much of the best literature on Canadian politics has been in the form of political biographies, and these must necessarily provide the basis for any assessment of Canadian political thought and traditions. George P. de T. Glazebrook, *A History of Canadian Political Thought* (T., UTP, 1966), is not a systematic examination of political ideas but a series of extended reflections on Canadian political problems. There are, however, a relatively large number of essays, written by and large by political biographers, which attempt to summarize in a general fashion the major convictions and beliefs of their subjects. J. M. S. Careless, the biographer of the Liberal George Brown, for example, has examined the impact of British Manchester liberalism and its modifications in the colonial environment in "Mid-Victorianism in Central Canadian Newspapers, 1850-67" (*CHR*, 1950) and "The Toronto *Globe* and Agrarian Radicalism, 1850-67" (*CHR*, 1948), and gave a short assessment of his subject in "George Brown" in *Our Living Tradition*, Second and Third Series, ed. Robert L. McDougall (T., UTP, 1959). F. H. Underhill analyzed Canadian liberalism in the generation after Confederation in a number of essays, among them "Political Ideas of the Upper Canadian Reformers, 1867-1878," in his *In Search of Canadian Liberalism* (T., Mac., 1960), and "Edward Blake and Liberal Nationalism," in *Essays in Canadian History* (T., UTP, 1939), ed. R. Flenley. J. D. Livermore, "The Personal Agonies of Edward Blake" (*CHR*, 1975) is a brilliant examination of his psychology and mental agonies. D. G. Creighton, "Sir John A. Macdonald," in *Our Living Tradition: Seven Canadians* (T., UTP, 1957), ed. C. T. Bissell, is a forceful defence of the Conservative leader's conviction that Canadian survival could only be ensured by a centralized federation and the alliance with Britain.

A rather uneven collection, *Les idées politiques des premiers ministres du Canada/The Political Ideas of the Prime Ministers of Canada* (Ottawa, Univ. of Ottawa Press, 1968), ed. Marcel Hamelin, contains short assessments of Sir Robert Borden by R. C. Brown, Arthur Meighen by Roger Graham and W. L. M. King by Blair Neatby. Perhaps the most revealing source for Mackenzie King's convictions about the nature of society, politics and unseen forces is his *Industry and Humanity* (1919; T., UTP, 1973). J. H. R. Wilbur, "R. B. Bennett as a Reformer" (*CHR*, 1969), deals with the question of the seriousness of that conservative Prime Minister's belated commitment to reform. In a provocative essay at the beginning of his *Canadian Labour in Politics* (T., UTP, 1968), Gad Horowitz advanced the notion that Canadian political culture possessed a "tory touch" which explained not only why socialism appeared stronger in Canada than in the United States but also why conservatives like Bennett sometimes resorted, without any serious inhibitions, to the use of state power to ensure national ends.

Histories of institutions of higher learning are rigidly factual and generally make little effort systematically to relate the role of a particular university to the social and intellectual context. Still, among those works that do convey the feeling for the unique tradition and institutional milieu of specific universities, are D. D. Calvin, *Queen's University at Kingston, 1841-1941* (Kingston, Queen's Univ. Press, 1941), C. MacMillan, *McGill and its Story, 1821-1921* (T., OUP, 1921), and W. S. Wallace, *A History of the University of Toronto, 1827-1926* (T., UTP, 1927). R. S. Harris and A. Tremblay have compiled *A Bibliography of Higher Education in Canada* (T., UTP, 1960, Supplement 1971), a comprehensive list of works relating to universities and areas of study.

Two such disciplines of immediate interest here are

history and economics. The major forces which have shaped historical writing on Canada are examined in Carl Berger, *The Writing of Canadian History: Aspects of English Canadian Historical Literature and Thought* (T., OUP, 1976), and in two essays by Ramsay Cook on the theme of survival in English and French-Canadian history in his *The Maple Leaf Forever* (T., Mac., 1971). A unique and peppery record of reminiscences of one major historian is A. R. M. Lower, *My First Seventy-Five Years* (T., Mac., 1967).

Canadian economic history has been dominated by the staples thesis of H. A. Innis whose life has been sympathetically recorded by D. G. Creighton in *H. A. Innis: Portrait of a Scholar* (T., UTP, 1957), and whose work has been assessed by Robin Neill in *A New Theory of Value: The Canadian Economics of H. A. Innis* (T., UTP, 1972).

The relationship between social and intellectual history, and imaginative literature and painting, is an extremely complex one and though there are numerous descriptive histories of literature and the arts there have been few systematic attempts to relate them in a general cultural history. The two standard guides to literature are Carl F. Klinck, ed., *Literary History of Canada* (T., UTP, 1976), and Pierre de Grandpré, dir., *Histoire de la Littérature française du Québec* (4 vols., M., Beauchmin, 1967-70). Russell Harper, *Painting in Canada* (T., UTP, 1966), is a good introduction to both the main developments and additional writing in the field.

General attempts to relate the themes that writers of fiction have dealt with to the culture of the country have been more notable for their boldness than for their general acceptance. Margaret Atwood, *Survival: A Thematic Guide to Canadian Literature* (T., Anansi, 1972) stresses the defeatist preoccupation with mere existence in some Canadian fiction and poetry; a more convincing as well as more limited study, Ronald Sutherland, *Second Image: Comparative Studies in Quebec/Canadian Literature* (T., New Press, 1971), suggests, for example, the pattern of puritanism in both literatures. Outstanding examples of occasional essays collected by two interpreters of Canadian culture are Jean-Charles Falardeau, *Notre Société et son roman* (M., Beauchemin, 1962), and Northrop Frye, *The Bush Garden: Essays on the Canadian Imagination* (T., Anansi, 1971).

The West

Hartwell Bowsfield

There is no general history covering the prairie provinces and British Columbia in the post-Confederation period. The one attempt to treat the West as a unit, A. S. Morton's classic study, *A History of the Canadian West to 1870-71* (1939; T., UTP, 1973), ends with the entry of the two regions into Confederation. Similarly Douglas Hill's *The Opening of the Canadian West* (L., Heinemann, 1967), a lively, readable account, covers the story of the West only to the formation of the provinces of Saskatchewan and Alberta in 1905.

Each of the western provinces has at present a periodical devoted to its area of interest, and each deals with both the pre- and post-Confederation periods. The oldest of these periodicals is the *Transactions of the Historical and Scientific Society of Manitoba*, first issued in 1882. Publication, however, was not continuous, and the first series ended in 1906; a second was published between 1926 and 1930. Since the third series began in 1944-45 *Transactions* has appeared annually. The Saskatchewan Archives Board has issued *Saskatchewan History* since 1944, while the *Alberta Historical Review*, published by the Alberta Historical Society, first appeared in 1953. *The British Columbia Historical Quarterly* was published between 1937 and 1958, but no comparable publication appeared until *B.C. Studies* was started in 1968. Each issue of this periodical contains a bibliography of items related to the province.

Bruce Peel's revised *A Bibliography of the Prairie Provinces to 1953* (T., UTP, 2nd. ed., 1973) contains some items written in the post-1953 period. The volume includes an author and title index and short biographical notes on the authors. Two useful bibliographies on British Columbia are Frances Woodward's compilation, *Theses on British Columbia History and Related Subjects in the Library of the University of British Columbia* (Vancouver, University of British Columbia Library, revised and enlarged edition, 1971), and Barbara J. Lowther, *A Bibliography of British Columbia*, Vol. 1: *Laying the Foundations 1849-1899* (Victoria, University of Victoria, 1968).

INTERPRETATION

Throughout much of his writing, W. L. Morton, the West's foremost historian, has assigned to the Canadian prairies a decisive role in the Confederation movement and in the interpretation of Canadian history. A summary account of Canadian and American interest in the West and how the prairies and British Columbia were brought into Confederation is his *The West and Confederation 1857-1871* (Ottawa, Canadian Historical Association, 1965). In his article "Clio in Canada: The Interpretation of Canadian History" (*University of Toronto Quarterly*, 1946), Morton stated that the West could not accept the Laurentian interpretation which was based on the economic subordination of the West. He asserted that the key factors or "decisive" sections in Canadian history were French survival, the domination of Ontario, and the subordination of the West. The Maritimes and British Columbia did not rank so high because they had always possessed destinies alternative to that of incorporation in Canada. Without them there might have been a Canada, Morton claimed, but there could have been no Canada without the decisive sections. The theme of the subordination of the West is further expanded in his article "The Bias of Prairie Politics" (*TRSC*, 1955) where the process of resistance to central Canada is divided into three periods: the struggle for political equality; the agrarian protest movement; and the attempt to build a political utopia through Social Credit and the CCF.

A number of Canadian historians have considered the applicability of Frederick Jackson Turner's frontier thesis to Canada. A survey of some of their writings is found in Morris Zaslow, "The Frontier Hypothesis in Recent Historiography" (*CHR*, 1948), in Michael Cross, ed., *The Frontier Thesis and the Canadas: The Debate on the Impact of the*

Canadian Environment (T., Copp Clark, 1970), and in
Maurice Careless' historiographical article "Frontierism,
Metropolitanism, and Canadian History" (*CHR*, 1965). A
more general but related treatment of the role of the frontier in shaping social and institutional life is found in S. D.
Clark, *The Developing Canadian Community* (T., UTP, 2nd
ed., 1968), and Russell Ward, "Frontierism and National
Stereotypes" (*CHAR*, 1964). Turner advanced the proposition that the frontier promoted the formation of a composite
nationality, developed the powers of the national government, and fostered democracy and individualism. A systematic study of the application of this proposition to the Canadian West has to date not been undertaken.

COLLECTIONS

Since 1969, the University of Calgary has sponsored
annually the Western Canada Studies Conference. The
papers presented at this conference have been published
under a variety of titles: David Gagan (ed.), *Prairie
Perspectives* (T., Holt, Rinehart & Winston, 1970); A. W.
Rasporich & Henry C. Klassen (eds.), *Prairie Perspectives
2* (T., Holt, Rinehart & Winston, 1973); S. M. Trofimenkoff
(ed.), *The Twenties in Western Canada* (Ottawa, National
Museum, 1972); David Bercuson (ed.), *Western Perspectives 1* (T., Holt, Rinehart & Winston, 1974); A. W. Raspor-
itch (ed.), *Western Canada Past and Present* (Calgary,
Univ. of Calgary & M&S West, 1975). The stated purpose of
the conference is to present the research of established and
younger scholars, and, as J. E. Rea says in *Western Perspectives 1*, to provide a corrective to the emphasis on the history of the West as an agrarian experience and to explore
the urban, labour, and immigrant "fact" in western development. The papers published cover a wide variety of subjects:
the urban and labour scene, native peoples, religion, education, the physical landscape, the West in fiction. A similar
interdisciplinary approach is taken in the publications of
the Canadian Plains Studies Centre of the University of
Regina, notably the collection of papers *A Region of the
Mind, Interpreting the Western Plains*, Richard Allen (ed.),
1973, and *Religion and Society in the Prairie West*, Richard
Allen (ed.), 1974. The most recent collection of papers on

the west is Carl Berger and Ramsay Cook (eds.), *The West and the Nation* (T., M&S, 1976). Carl Berger's essay in this collection analyzing the writings of W. L. Morton should be required reading for any student of the history of the west.

The theme of western alienation is covered in John J. Barr and Owen Anderson, eds., *The Unfinished Revolt, Some Views on Western Independence* (T., M&S, 1971), a collection of articles by Albertans. The tone expressed is strident and angry, raising the question of western economic independence and separation. *Proceedings of One Prairie Province, A Question for Canada*, edited by David K. Elton (Lethbridge, University of Lethbridge & Lethbridge Herald, 1970), is a selection of papers presented at a 1970 conference in Lethbridge considering the feasibility and implications of a merger of the three prairie provinces, while Donald Swainson, ed., *Historical Essays on the Prairie Provinces* (T., M&S, 1970), brings together excerpts from some nineteenth century historians of the West and diverse articles from western historical journals.

MANITOBA

No history of a province can compare with the achievement of W. L. Morton's *Manitoba, A History* (T., UTP, 1957, 1967). Morton's work is both a narrative and an analysis of the political, economic, social and cultural life of a distinct provincial society, yet it is never parochial. "With this volume," said a reviewer in 1957, "provincial history has come of age, both as a subject of study itself and as a field where a most striking contribution can be made to Canada as a whole." James A. Jackson, *The Centennial History of Manitoba* (T., M&S, 1970), is a sound, readable volume, while Murray Donnelly's *The Government of Manitoba* (T., UTP, 1963), a study of the province's political institutions, is the only such study to date on any of the western provinces.

Documents relating to Manitoba's entry into Confederation in 1870 have been collected in W. L. Morton, ed., *Manitoba: The Birth of a Province* (Altona, Manitoba Record Society, 1965). Included in the volume are excerpts from the House of Commons debate on the Manitoba Bill, the Journal of Rev. N. J. Ritchot, one of the delegates appointed to negotiate the terms of Manitoba's entry into Confederation, and three of the four "Lists of Rights" drawn up in the Red River Settlement. American interest in the Canadian West at the time of the first Riel rebellion may be followed in Alvin C. Glueck Jr., *Minnesota and the Manifest Destiny of the Canadian Northwest* (T., UTP, 1965), and in Hartwell Bowsfield, ed., *James Wickes Taylor Correspondence 1859-1870* (Altona, Manitoba Record Society, 1968). Taylor was the special agent of the American State Department appointed to report on Red River affairs; he became American Consul at Winnipeg in 1870.

The Manitoba Act of 1870 guaranteed a system of denominational schools and French as a legal language in the province. To what extent this was the recognition of a bicultural compact made at the time of Confederation in 1867 has been a matter of dispute. Donald Creighton, in "John A. Macdonald, Confederation, and the Canadian West," in R. C. Brown, ed., *Minorities, Schools and Politics* (T., UTP, 1969), argues that the bicultural nature of the Manitoba Act resulted from Riel's "dictatorship" and the need for a quick resolution of the difficulties at Red River. This interpretation, as well as Creighton's view regarding the establishment of denominational schools and the recognition of French in the North West Territories, is challenged in a harsh rebuttal by Ralph Heintzman, "The Spirit of Confederation: Professor Creighton, Biculturalism and the Use of History" (*CHR*, 1971). Heintzman suggests that the bicultural institutions established in the West were not, as Creighton characterized them, the result of accident and improvisation. The decisions made, he asserts, were made with deliberate intent and with the implications clearly in mind.

BRITISH COLUMBIA

The general history of British Columbia since its discovery has been the subject of a number of writers, including the distinguished American historian H. H. Bancroft. The most comprehensive and balanced of the general histories, Margaret Ormsby's *British Columbia, A History* (T., Mac., 1958), is based on extensive research and covers the social and economic background of the province as well as the political events. The most recent and certainly the most controversial history of the province is Martin Robin's two-volume *The Rush for Spoils: The Company Province, 1871-1933* (T., M&S, 1972), and *Pillars of Profit: The Company Province, 1934-1972* (1973). The emphasis in Robin's work is on British Columbia in the post-Confederation period and specifically on political history which, as a socialist historian, he defines as the struggle "between classes for shares of the wealth, disputes between parties over the course of development, [and] the ways and means used by politicians to purchase allegiance." His theme, the exploitation of the province's resources by the "companies" and the class struggle between worker and capitalist is advanced also in his articles "The Social Basis of Party Politics in British Columbia," (*QQ*, 1965-66) and "British Columbia, The Politics of Class Conflict" in Martin Robin, ed., *Canadian Provincial Politics, The Party Systems of the Ten Provinces* (Scarborough, Prentice-Hall, 1972).

The question of annexation to the United States or union with Canada is treated by Hugh L. Keenleyside, "British Columbia Annexation or Confederation" (*CHAR*, 1928), and Willard Ireland, "The Annexation Petition of 1869" (*British Columbia Historical Quarterly*, 1940). Margaret Ormsby in "Canada and the New British Columbia" (*CHAR*, 1948) notes the internal and external pressures which overcame opposition to Confederation and the beginnings of the Canadianization process. A collection of essays on British Columbia personalities and the province's economy and society at the time of union with Canada is found in W. George Shelton, ed., *British Columbia & Confederation* (Victoria, University of Victoria, 1967).

The crisis between British Columbia and the federal government in the 1870's over the delay in the building of the transcontinental railway promised British Columbia at the time of its entry into Confederation is dealt with by W. Kaye Lamb, "A Bent Twig in British Columbia History" (*CHAR*, 1948); J. A. Maxwell, "Lord Dufferin and the Difficulties with British Columbia, 1873-1877" (*CHR*, 1931); and Margaret Ormsby, "Prime Minister Mackenzie, the Liberal Party and the Bargain with British Columbia" (*CHR*, 1945). It can, of course, be followed in national political studies, too, including Dale Thomson's biography of *Alexander Mackenzie, Clear Grit.*

The way British Columbia was integrated with the nation and the federal party system extended to the province is examined in a number of articles: in W. N. Sage, "British Columbia becomes Canadian (1871-1901)" (*QQ*, 1945); in Edith Dobie's articles, "Some Aspects of Party History in British Columbia, 1871-1903" (*Pacific Historical Review*, 1932), and "Party History in British Columbia, 1903-1933" (*Pacific North West Quarterly*, 1936); in W. N. Sage, "Federal Parties and Provincial Political Groups in British Columbia, 1871-1903" (*British Columbia Historical Quarterly*, 1948); and in K. A. MacKirdy, "Conflicting Loyalties: The Problem of Assimilating the Far Wests into the Canadian and Australian Federations" (*CHR*, 1951). Some of the above articles, other papers, and excerpts from histories of British Columbia have been brought together in J. Friesen & H.K. Ralston (eds.), *Historical Essays on British Columbia* (T., M&S, 1976). The editors have included a useful bibliographical essay.

B.C. Studies (Spring 1972) includes a number of articles on British Columbia attitudes to national economic questions. In the introduction to these articles, ("Notes on a Western Viewpoint") A. D. Scott points out the incompatibilities with eastern Canada on questions such as labour unions, tariffs, foreign ownership, energy, and health and welfare systems. British Columbia cannot, he argues, be as concerned as eastern economic nationalists over foreign ownership since it has never had much local control of large industries. He notes also the fact that compared to the prairie provinces British Columbia has received little attention from the economists and economic historians.

ALBERTA AND SASKATCHEWAN

There is no scholarly history of Alberta or Saskatchewan comparable to that done for Manitoba and British Columbia by W. L. Morton and Margaret Ormsby. Robert Kroetsch in *Alberta* (T., Mac., 1968) and Edward McCourt in *Saskatchewan* (T., Mac., 1968) convey admirably the spirit of these two provinces in books that are combinations of history and travelogue. The most recent general history of Alberta is James G. MacGregor's *A History of Alberta* (Edmonton, Hurtig, 1972), a narrative account intended for Albertans with only a limited attempt to see provincial developments within the national context.

The scholarly treatment of the territorial period of Alberta and Saskatchewan history is L. H. Thomas, *The Struggle for Responsible Government in the North West Territories, 1870-1897* (T., UTP, 1956), and C. C. Lingard, *Territorial Government in Canada: The Autonomy Question in the Old North West Territories* (T., UTP, 1946). This period and the struggle for provincial status are covered in summary form in L. H. Thomas, *The North West Territories 1870-1905* (Ottawa, Canadian Historical Association, 1970). Documentary source material will be found in Volume 2 of E. H. Oliver, *The Canadian North West: Its Early Development and Legislative Records* (2 vols., Ottawa, KP, 1915).

In *The Liberal Party in Alberta, A History of Politics in the Province of Alberta* (T., UTP, 1959), L. G. Thomas refers to Alberta as a province with a reputation for "political eccentricity." For fifty years (1921-1971) Alberta was ruled by the United Farmers of Alberta and Social Credit. Thomas examines the Liberal dominance from 1905-1921 as a characteristic of Alberta politics and relates this both to a non-party tradition and to the failure of opposition parties to provide an acceptable alternative to the government in power.

The best analysis of the political scene in Saskatchewan is *Politics in Saskatchewan*, a collection of articles edited by Norman Ward and Douglas Spafford (T., Longmans, 1968), a collection that deserves imitators for every province in Canada. The most recent volume on the political life of the province is David E. Smith, *Prairie Liberalism: The Liberal Party in Saskatchewan 1905-71* (T., UTP, 1975).

LOUIS RIEL

The life of Louis Riel and the rebellions of 1869-70 and 1885 have received profuse attention. The scholarly biography is George Stanley, *Louis Riel* (T., Ryerson, 1963). It is, and is likely to remain for some time, the definitive work. Joseph Kinsey Howard, in *Strange Empire, A Narrative of the Northwest* (N.Y., William Morrow, 1952), presents Riel as a symbol of the North American frontier, doomed, as were the *métis* and Indian people, by the advance of white society. Other biographies of Riel include W. M. Davidson, *Louis Riel, 1844-1885* (Calgary, Albertan Publishing Co., 1955), E. B. Osler, *The Man Who Had to Hang, Louis Riel* (T., Longmans Green, 1961), and Hartwell Bowsfield, *Louis Riel, The Rebel and the Hero* (T., OUP, 1971).

George Stanley, in *The Birth of Western Canada, A History of the Riel Rebellions* (L., Longmans Green, 1936), treats the rebellions in terms of cultural conflict, the clash between a primitive and a civilized society. The value of this pioneering study is enhanced by Stanley's analysis of the years between the two rebellions and the development of Indian, *métis* and white grievances against the federal government. The 1880's are seen within the context of cultural conflict and the beginnings of a western agrarian protest movement. The theme of cultural conflict is found also in Stanley's booklet *Louis Riel: Patriot or Rebel?* (Ottawa, Canadian Historical Association, 1954).

W. L. Morton has rejected Stanley's cultural conflict interpretation as related to the 1869-70 rebellion, arguing that the Red River Settlement by 1869 was not a primitive but rather a civilized society. He interprets Riel's resistance to the Canadian government in 1869 as an extension of the traditional racial and religious tension of eastern Canada to the West. Morton's discerning analysis of the situation at Red River in 1869-70 is found in his introduction to *Alexander Begg's Red River Journal and Other Papers Relative to the Red River Resistance of 1869-1870* (T., Champlain Society, 1960).

Among contemporary accounts of the two rebellions are Alexander Begg, *The Creation of Manitoba: or a History of the Red River Troubles* (T., 1871), Charles A. Boulton, *Reminiscences of the North West Rebellions* (T., 1886), and C. P. Mulvaney, *The History of the North West Rebellion of 1885* (T., 1885). A recent account of the 1885 rebellion by Desmond Morton, *The Last War Drum: The North West Campaign of 1885* (T., Hakkert, 1972), deals with the campaign itself in detail.

R. E. Lamb's *Thunder in the North* (N.Y., Pageant

Press, 1957), while lacking analysis, presents an abundant selection of contemporary reactions to Riel—excerpts from the newspapers and the political debate. A collection of contemporary accounts, documents and recent interpretations has been brought together in Hartwell Bowsfield, *Louis Riel, Rebel of the Western Frontier or Victim of Politics and Prejudice?* (T., Copp Clark, 1969). The report of the House of Commons committee investigating the rebellion of 1869-70 and the promise of an amnesty to Riel is in *Journals of the House of Commons*, Vol. 8, Appendix 6, 1874. The trial of Riel is found in *Canada Sessional Papers*, 1886, Vol. 19, No. 43, and reprinted in Desmond Morton (ed.), *The Queen versus Louis Riel* (T., UTP, 1974).

There are two histories of the *métis* people: Marcel Giraud, a French historian and sociologist, *Le Métis Canadien* (Paris, Université de Paris, Institut d'Ethnologie, 1945), and A. H. de Trémaudan, *Histoire de la Nation Métisse dans l'Ouest Canadien* (M., Editions Albert Lévesque, 1936). George Woodcock in *Gabriel Dumont, the Métis Chief and His Lost World* (Edmonton, Hurtig, 1975) asks why Canadians chose to celebrate the martyr Riel and not the hero Dumont. The choice, he says, reflects the complexities of the Canadian inner feeling. Riel symbolizes Canadian alienation and defeat as a people. Canadians see themselves as a besieged minority. His biography of Dumont is an effective piece of writing outlining the social, political and economic decline of the métis people.

THE NATIONAL POLICY

The combination of railway, settlement and tariff programmes called the National Policy which were intended to develop a viable transcontinental economy but which provoked western protest is the subject of V. C. Fowke's *The National Policy and the Wheat Economy* (T., UTP, 1957). Fowke's brilliant study traces also the grain marketing problems of the West and the development of the wheat pool system. In "The National Policy—Old and New" (*CJEPS*, 1952) he provides a good summary of the role of the National Policy in integrating the West in the Canadian economy. Similar studies are W. A. Mackintosh's 1939 work for the Rowell-Sirois Commission on Dominion-Provincial

Relations, *The Economic Background of Dominion-Provincial Relations* (reprinted T., M&S, 1964), and R. C. Brown, "The Nationalism of the National Policy," in Peter Russell, ed., *Nationalism in Canada* (T., McGraw-Hill, 1966). The same volume contains John Dales' "Protection, Immigration and Canadian Nationalism," which effectively questions some of the traditional interpretations of the value of the National Policy.

A comparison between the National Policies of Canada and the United States is found in Melville H. Watkins, "The 'American System' and Canada's National Policy" (*Bulletin of the Canadian Association for American Studies*, 1967). A similar but more probing comparison is V. C. Fowke, "National Policy and Western Development in North America" (*Journal of Economic History*, 1956).

The best theoretical approach to the controversy between protectionism and free trade in Canadian economic development is J. H. Dales, "Some Historical and Theoretical Comment on Canada's National Policies" (*QQ*, 1964), and his suggestive *The Protective Tariff in Canada's Development* (T., UTP, 1966). Western attitudes toward the National Policy can be found in Edward Porritt, *The Revolt in Canada Against the New Feudalism: Tariff History from the Revision of 1907 to the Uprising in the West in 1910* (L., Cassell, 1911). Criticism of national economic policies, not entirely dissimilar to Porritt's, remains part of the current western attitude towards Confederation. A number of the readings referred to above reflect these attitudes.

IMMIGRATION, SETTLEMENT AND RAILWAYS

Towards the end of the 19th century and as part of the National Policy, the Canadian government embarked upon an aggressive immigration programme directed toward the settlement of the prairies. The result was a phenomenal growth in population, western development, and an increase in the number of immigrants from southern and eastern Europe. An excellent general account of this period is R. C. Brown and Ramsay Cook, *Canada 1896-1921, A Nation Transformed* (T., M&S, 1974).

D. C. Corbett, *Canada's Immigration Policy, A Critique* (T., UTP, 1957), while emphasizing Canadian immi-

gration policies in the post-1945 period when immigration
was urban, not agriculturally oriented, has background on
the earlier periods. Corbett's specific interest is in the economic effects of immigration. Another general history, Norman Macdonald, *Canada, Immigration and Colonization:
1841-1903* (T., Mac., 1966), has extended coverage of immigration to the West and provides information on specific
ethnic groups. An older but still valuable study, with helpful statistical tables, is W. G. Smith, *A Study in Canadian
Immigration* (T., Ryerson, 1920). Smith deals with specific
immigrant groups, and notes the problem of assimilation
which had been first brought to the attention of the Canadian public in 1909 by J. S. Woodsworth in *Strangers
Within Our Gates: or, Coming Canadians* (1909; T., UTP,
1972). The attempted assimilation of European groups in
Saskatchewan is covered by Robert England, *The Central
European Immigrant in Canada* (T., Mac., 1929). England's
*The Colonization of Western Canada; A Study of Contempo-
rary Land Settlement (1869-1934)* (L., P. S. King, 1936) is
the story of the adaptation of individuals and group communities to the environment from 1870 to the depression
years of the 1930s.

The movement of hundreds of thousands of Americans, one of the largest immigrant groups, into the prairie
provinces is covered by Karel Bicha, *The American Farmer
and the Canadian West 1896-1914* (Lawrence, Kansas, Co-
ronado Press, 1972) and by Harold Troper, *Only Farmers
Need Apply* (T., Griffin House, 1972).

A number of the volumes of the "Canadian Frontiers
of Settlement" (T., Mac.,) series are of fundamental importance to the study of immigration and settlement. Especially
valuable are: W. A. Mackintosh, *Prairie Settlement, the Geographical Setting* (1934), which covers the land, climate,
railways, and the spread of settlement; C. A. Dawson, *Group
Settlement, Ethnic Communities in Western Canada* (1936),
which deals with specific groups (Doukhobors, Mennonites,
Mormons, German Catholics, French Canadians), referring
to them as "cultural islands" inhibiting the process of assimilation; and C. A. Dawson & E. R. Yonge, *Pioneering in
the Prairie Provinces, The Social Side of the Settlement Process* (1940), which covers the western economy, agricultural

practices and the establishment of educational and religious institutions. Originally published with A. S. Morton, *A History of Prairie Settlement* (T., Mac., 1938) as one volume in the series, Chester Martin's *Dominion Lands' Policy* analyzes federal regulations and the administration of public lands. An abridged edition of Martin's work was published (T., M&S) in 1973.

The periodical *Canadian Ethnic Studies* (University of Calgary, 1969-) has extensive bibliographical data on ethnic groups in Canada. Other bibliographical sources are Andrew Gregorovich, ed., *Canadian Ethnic Groups Bibliography* (T., Ontario Department of the Provincial Secretary & Citizenship, 1972), and a series of bibliographies covering both published and unpublished sources issued by the federal Department of Citizenship and Immigration and its successor department, Manpower and Immigration.

The policy of railway land grants and the administration of lands granted to the Canadian Pacific Railway is traced in J. B. Hedges, *The Federal Railway Land Subsidy Policy of Canada* (Cambridge, Harvard Univ. Press, 1934), and in his *Building the Canadian West, the Land and Colonization Policies of the Canadian Pacific Railway* (N.Y., Mac., 1939).

The romance and high drama of the building of the transcontinental railway abounds in Pierre Berton's two volumes, *The National Dream, The Great Railway 1871-1881* (T., M&S, 1970), and *The Last Spike, The Great Railway 1881-1885* (1971). The serious student of the Canadian Pacific Railway should not miss, in addition, the more prosaic but fundamental study by Harold Innis, *A History of the Canadian Pacific Railway* (1923; T., UTP, 1970), or L. B. Irwin, *Pacific Railways and Nationalism in the Canadian-American Northwest 1845-1873* (1939; N.Y., Greenwood Press, 1968). A recent attempt at debunking the "national dream" school of Berton and criticizing the relationship between the CPR and the federal government is Robert Chodos, *The CPR, A Century of Corporate Welfare* (T., James Lewis & Samuel, 1973).

Myth-making has also been the rule in much that has been written about the Royal Canadian Mounted Police. The centenary of the organization of the force in 1973 saw reprints of a number of earlier titles. J. P. Turner's, *The North-West Mounted Police 1873-1893* (2 vols., Ottawa, Department of Justice, 1950) is basically a chronology. Ronald Atkin, *Maintain the Right, The Early History of the North West Mounted Police, 1873-1900* (L., Mac., 1973), covers familiar ground well, and provides many human touches. Nora and William Kelly, *The Royal Canadian Mounted Police, A Century of History 1873-1973* (Edmonton, Hurtig, 1973), is too defensive toward the force and so uncritical that Lorne and Caroline Brown's, *An Unauthorized History of the RCMP* (T., James Lewis & Samuel, 1973), in which the Mounties are seen as strike-breakers and persecutors of radicals and immigrants, is almost welcome. The only balanced and analytical study to date is R. G. Macleod, *The North West Mounted Police and Law Enforcement 1873-1905* (T., UTP, 1976) which places the police within the framework of politics and political ideology.

MANITOBA SCHOOL QUESTION

In 1890 the Manitoba legislature withdrew financial support from denominational schools thought to have been guaranteed under the Manitoba Act of 1870. An introduction to the complex religious and racial problem which resulted and which bedevilled Canadian political life throughout the 1890s is Lovell Clark, ed., *The Manitoba School Question: Majority Rule or Minority Rights?* (T., Copp Clark, 1968). This compilation provides a sampling of contemporary opinion as well as both legal and historical interpretations. Clark's personal approach is that the controversy was not inherent in the local situation but resulted from the actions of a "demagogue and bigot," D'Alton McCarthy from Ontario, who succeeded in arousing the prejudices of Anglo-Saxon, Protestant Manitoba. In his history of Manitoba, W. L. Morton suggests that Manitoba could have settled the school question "quietly" had outside forces and events not intervened. Why Manitoba responded so readily to McCarthy and why Manitoba, usually spoken of as an extension of Ontario society, refused to accept the separate school system established in Ontario are questions which still need exploration.

John S. Ewart's *The Manitoba School Question* (T.,

Copp Clark, 1894) is a compilation of the legislation and legal proceedings related to the school question. A lawyer, Ewart was a participant in the controversy and argued cases on behalf of the Roman Catholic minority in Manitoba. His role is analyzed in W. T. Shaw, *The Role of John S. Ewart in the Manitoba School Question* (M. A. thesis, University of Manitoba, 1959).

The attack on the denominational school system in Manitoba in the 1870's and the disappearance of the issue in the 1880's is dealt with by R. E. Clague, *The Political Aspects of the Manitoba School Question, 1890-1896* (M.A. thesis, University of Manitoba, 1939). The convulsive effect of the question on national political parties and its place in the 1896 federal election is examined in most of the studies on Wilfrid Laurier, the latest being H. Blair Neatby, *Laurier and a Liberal Quebec* (T., M&S, 1973). See also: John Saywell, ed., *The Canadian Journal of Lady Aberdeen, 1893-1898* (T., Champlain Society, 1960); Ellen Cooke, *The Federal Election of 1896 in Manitoba* (M.A. thesis, University of Manitoba, 1943); and Lovell Clark, "The Conservative Party in the 1890's (*CHAR*, 1961). The most comprehensive study is Paul Crunican, *Priests and Politicians: Manitoba Schools and the Election of 1896* (T., UTP, 1974).

WINNIPEG GENERAL STRIKE 1919

D. C. Masters, *The Winnipeg General Strike* (T., UTP, 1950), remains the standard and perhaps the most objective account of the origins of the great strike of 1919. Masters concludes that despite "wild talk" by some radicals the strike was exactly what it purported to be, an effort to secure collective bargaining, not a seditious conspiracy or a Bolshevik plot. A contemporary interpretation of the strike as a conspiracy is in the *Canadian Annual Review 1919*. In this interpretation the strike was a deliberate attempt by labour to capture the government of Winnipeg and eventually "overthrow the existing system of National government and replace it by one of workmen only." The strike as part of Canadian labour history is covered in H. A. Logan, *Trade Unions in Canada* (T., Mac., 1948) and by Eugene Forsey, "History of the Labour Movement in Canada" (*Canada Year Book 1957-58*). The strike in terms of class conflict is dealt with by Kenneth McNaught in his biography of J. S. Woodsworth, *A Prophet in Politics* (T., UTP, 1959), by Martin Robin in *Radical Politics and Canadian Labour, 1880-1930* (Kingston, Queen's Univ., 1968), and by H. C. Pentland, "Fifty Years After," (*Canadian Dimension*, 1969). The workers' account of the events is in Norman Penner, ed., *Winnipeg 1919: The Strikers' Own History of the Winnipeg General Strike* (T., James Lewis & Samuel, 1973). David Bercuson, *Confrontation at Winnipeg* (M., McGill-Queen's, 1974) focuses on the industrial background of the strike examining labour-management relations in Winnipeg from the turn of the century to 1919. Kenneth McNaught & David Bercuson, *The Winnipeg General Strike 1919* (T., Longman, 1974) provide a short, general survey and a helpful chapter on "pivotal" interpretations. Two Royal Commission reports on the strike were made, one by the federal government (Mathers Report), the other by the government of Manitoba (Robson Report).

THIRD PARTIES

The West has been the birthplace for a succession of new political movements. Regional politics and third parties are covered in: Hugh Thorburn, ed., *Party Politics in Canada* (Scarborough, Prentice-Hall, 1972); John C. Courtney, *Voting in Canada* (Scarborough, Prentice-Hall, 1967); Paul Fox, *Politics in Canada*, (T., McGraw-Hill, 1966); and F. C. Engelmann & Mildred Schwartz, *Political Parties and the Canadian Social Structure* (Scarborough, Prentice-Hall, 1967). Desmond Morton's *NDP: The Dream of Power* (T., Hakkert, 1974) treats the NDP governments in the West as well as the national party. Martin Robin's *Canadian Provincial Politics, The Party Systems of the Ten Provinces* has a chapter on each of the prairie provinces and British Columbia. In *Democracy and Discontent* (T., Ryerson, 1969), Walter D. Young looks at the Progressive, Social Credit, and CCF parties.

The basic study of Canada's first "third" party is W. L. Morton, *The Progressive Party in Canada* (T., UTP, 1950), which was issued as the first of a ten-volume series designed to cover the background and development of Social Credit in Alberta. The Progressives' electoral triumph of

1921 is represented as the culmination of western agrarian discontent. Morton's study includes coverage of the western provincial political scene, the conflicting rivalries within the Progressive Party, and its decline in the 1920's. Paul Sharp, in *The Agrarian Revolt in Western Canada* (Minneapolis, Univ. of Minnesota Press, 1948), makes a comparison between the American and Canadian agrarian protest movements, while Louis Aubrey Wood, *A History of Farmers' Movements in Canada* (T., UTP, 1975), presents an historical survey of the agrarian movement covering the establishment of the Grange in Ontario in 1872, the Patrons of Industry, the grain growers' associations on the prairies, the struggle against the tariff 1896-1911, and the Progressive Party.

The populist background of the American-born Alberta agrarian leader Henry Wise Wood and his theory of occupational representation and group government is analyzed in W. L. Morton, "The Social Philosophy of Henry Wise Wood, the Canadian Agrarian Leader" (*Agricultural History*, 1948). The attempt to put Wood's theory into practice by Alberta Progressives in the 1920's and the problem faced by third parties in the parliamentary system is covered by the prolific Morton in "The Western Progressive Movement and Cabinet Domination" (*CJEPS*, 1946). The origins of the Progressive movement and the conflict between Wood's followers and those of the Manitoban Thomas Crerar who preferred traditional party practices and sought to avoid "class" politics is looked at in his "The Western Progressive Movement, 1919-1921" (*CHAR*, 1950). W. K. Rolph's biography, *Henry Wise Wood of Alberta* (T., UTP, 1950), includes the story of Wood's leadership of the United Farmers of Alberta and his organization of wheat pools. There is no biography of Crerar as yet.

Indispensable to the study of Social Credit in Alberta are John A. Irving, *The Social Credit Movement in Alberta* (T., UTP, 1959), and C. B. Macpherson, *Democracy in Alberta* (T., UTP, 1953, 1962). Irving's narrative approach covers the years from 1932 when William Aberhart embraced the monetary theories of Major C. H. Douglas to the Social Credit electoral victory of 1935. Since the success of the movement was so largely dependent on the personality of one man, Irving devotes considerable attention to Aberhart's career as a school teacher, fundamentalist, and radio evangelist. He investigates the background of a number of secondary leaders and, based on interviews, provides a psychologist's picture of the response of followers to Aberhart and his teachings. To Irving, the rise of Social Credit can be attributed to the failure of the United Farmers of Alberta government to cope with the depression of the 1930's and to Aberhart's personal appeal and organizational abilities. An article-length study of the rise of Social Credit is his "The Evolution of the Social Credit Movement" (*CJEPS*, 1948). John J. Barr, *The Dynasty, The Rise and Fall of Social Credit in Alberta* (T., M&S, 1974) carries the story of the party to the electoral victory of Peter Lougheed and the Conservatives in 1971.

In Macpherson's book the reader will find an extended analysis of Social Credit monetary theory and a theoretical approach to the reasons Alberta turned from the traditional two-party system, first to the United Farmers of Alberta in 1921 and to Social Credit in 1935. Macpherson dismissed the UFA and Social Credit as third parties and characterized Alberta as having a "quasi-party" system in which the dominance of one party was the result of a homogeneous electorate. The electorate acted as it did because Alberta was a petit-bourgeois, quasi-colonial society in rebellion against the political and economic power of central Canada. In "The Political Theory of Social Credit" (*CJEPS*, 1949), Macpherson considers the relationship of Social Credit theory to parliamentary democracy and class politics. Although concentrating on the Social Credit movement in Quebec, Maurice Pinard, in *The Rise of a Third Party, A Study in Crisis Politics* (Englewood Cliffs, Prentice-Hall, 1971), puts forward a general hypothesis regarding the rise of third parties which is relevant to the Alberta situation. He rejects Macpherson's quasi-party thesis and argues that Alberta has always been an area of one party dominance.

Denis Smith, "Prairie Revolt, Federalism and the Party System," printed in Hugh Thorburn's *Party Politics*, also challenges Macpherson's theory. Macpherson's suggestion that the alternate party system never took firm root in western Canada must be modified, he says, since the dominance of one party as reflected in the number of seats in a provincial legislature is not reflected in the popular vote: "No prairie party has received more than fifty-eight percent of the popular vote in a provincial election since 1917." In the same article, Smith also challenges Frank Underhill's thesis in *Canadian Political Parties* (Ottawa, Canadian Historical Association, 1957) that third parties at the provincial level constitute the real centre of political opposition to the federal government. In "Liberals and Conservatives on the Prairies, 1917-1968" in David Gagan, ed., *Prairie Perspectives*, he contends that the two traditional national parties have always maintained "a substantial presence" in western Canada.

J. R. Mallory's study, *Social Credit and the Federal Power in Canada* (T., UTP, 1954), covers the Alberta scene from 1935-1945 but goes beyond the details of the disallowance of Alberta's Social Credit legislation. He includes an historical survey of the federal disallowance power from 1867 to 1936 and places the struggle between Alberta and the federal government within the context of a revival of federal control over the provinces. The disallowance of the 1937 Social Credit legislation is dealt with by Mallory in "Alberta Social Credit Legislation of 1937" (*CJEPS*, 1948).

W. E. Mann, *Sect, Cult, and Church in Alberta* (T., UTP, 1955), looks at the religious background of the Alberta community. The relationship between the evangelical religious movement and Social Credit is examined by S. D. Clark in "The Religious Sect in Canadian Politics" (*American Journal of Sociology*, 1945), and in his *The Developing Canadian Community*.

A number of "radicals" or "left wing" leaders in the 1920's and 1930's, for example, E. A. Partridge, in *A War On Poverty* (Winnipeg, c1925), argued that farmers and workers, both victims of the capitalist, free enterprise system should join in establishing a cooperative society. The role of such leaders in moving the farm organizations in Saskatchewan toward the cooperative and socialist goal is examined by Duff Spafford, "The Left Wing 1921-1931," in *Politics in Saskatchewan*. S. M. Lipset, in *Agrarian Socialism, The Cooperative Commonwealth Federation in Saskatchewan, A Study in Political Sociology* (Berkeley, Univ. of California

Press, 1950), identified the agrarian protest and cooperative movement as a socialist movement. He makes it clear, however, that as the CCF approached success in 1944 it was not a doctrinaire socialist party. A second edition of Lipset's work (N.Y., Doubleday, 1968) contains several articles which examine the CCF movement after the electoral victory of 1944 in Saskatchewan. These cover an analysis of class voting behaviour, the doctors' strike of 1962 and the medicare programme. In one of these articles, "Agrarian Pragmatism and Radical Politics," John W. Bennett and Cynthia Drueger challenge Lipset's interpretation of the leftward swing in the agrarian movement and claim that evidence of collective action should not be equated with socialism. They point out that the grass roots support of the CCF in Saskatchewan was interested primarily in remedying specific economic grievances and that by 1944 the socialist ideology of the party had been much diluted. Dean E. McHenry, in *The Third Force in Canada, The Cooperative Commonwealth Federation, 1932-1948* (Berkeley, Univ. of California Press, 1950), notes the relationship between the British and Canadian socialist movement. The emphasis in his work is on party organization and structure. The meaning of the "Third Force" in his title is his belief that the CCF was a middle way between the extremes of reaction and revolution.

In "The League for Social Reconstruction and the Development of a Canadian Socialism, 1932-1936" (*JCS*, 1972) Michiel Horn argues that the Regina Manifesto of 1933 was in large part worked out by eastern intellectuals and that Canadian socialism, though British in origin, had its unique Canadian content. Useful on the background of the socialist movement in Canada to 1920 is Paul Fox, "Early Socialism in Canada," in J. H. Aitchison, ed., *The Political Process in Canada* (T., UTP, 1963). Gad Horowitz, *Canadian Labour in Politics* (T., UTP, 1968), offers a study of Louis Hartz' thesis of fragment cultures applied to Canada and of the role of socialism in Canada and its relationship to organized labour.

The CCF movement in Saskatchewan is covered also by Walter D. Young in his excellent history of the national party, *The Anatomy of a Party: The National CCF 1932-1961* (T., UTP, 1969). The only scholarly biography of the "father" of the CCF is McNaught's *A Prophet in Politics*, which covers Woodsworth's various careers as preacher, social worker, Winnipeg striker, pacifist, and socialist politician. A personal account of Woodsworth's life is that by his daughter, Grace McInnis, *J. S. Woodsworth, A Man to Remember* (T., Mac., 1953). A collection of Woodsworth's writings has been put together in Edith Fowke, ed., *Towards Socialism, Selections from the Writings of J. S. Woodsworth* (T., Ontario Woodsworth Memorial Foundation, 1948). A useful compilation reflecting the changes in the party's political philosophy is found in *The Decline and Fall of a Good Idea, CCF-NDP Manifestoes 1932 to 1969*, introd. by Michael Cross (T., New Hogtown Press, 1974).

DEPRESSION 1930's

Undiversified economy plus a series of drought years made the prairies tragically vulnerable to the depression of the 1930's. Comprehensive examinations of the period are: A. E. Safarian, *The Canadian Economy in the Great Depression* (T., UTP, 1959); W. A. Mackintosh, *Economic Problems of the Prairie Provinces* (T., Mac., 1935); and the *Report of the Royal Commission on Dominion-Provincial Relations* (Ottawa, KP, 1940). H. Blair Neatby, *The Politics of Chaos, Canada in the Thirties* (T., Mac., 1972), and Ramsay Cook, ed., *Politics of Discontent* (T., UTP, 1967), have articles on Woodsworth, Aberhart, and T. Dufferin Pattullo of British Columbia. Victor Hoar has edited a collection of articles and reminiscences, *The Great Depression* (T., Copp Clark, 1969), as well as *The On-To-Ottawa Trek* (T., Copp Clark, 1970), which deals with the relief camp strike in British Columbia and the Regina riot of 1935. *Recollections of the On-To-Ottawa Trek* (T., M&S, 1973) is a personal account by a participant, Ronald Liversedge. James Gray, in *The Winter Years, The Depression on the Prairies* (T., Mac., 1966), captures brilliantly the essence of the depression years in human and social terms.

SUMMARY

Writing on the Canadian West is dominated by studies in political and economic history, by the east-west relationship, and western political dissent. Despite this em-

phasis a recent observer suggested that there was a need for
more primary research in prairie politics. David Smith
makes this comment in "Interpreting Prairie Politics" (*JCS*,
1972), a survey of the political literature on the prairie
provinces with extensive bibliographic references. There
are, Smith argues, many gaps in the study of political culture and institutions. The most obvious gap is in the field of
biography. Few full-length studies on political and other
figures have been undertaken. The absence of a serious
biography of William Aberhart perhaps epitomizes this gap.
One of the themes in writings on the West is that the West
was invaded by an eastern culture. Studies of the cultural
carriers—the newspaper editors, the clergymen, the teach-
ers, the professional class, the agrarian and political leaders
—are needed to represent both the process of Canadianization of the West as well as the regionalization of its people.

The political and economic "domination" of the West
by central Canada has been treated extensively within the
context of the Laurentian and Metropolitan interpretations
of Canada history. The Metropolitan thesis outlines how
such centres as Montreal and Toronto attached an economic, political and cultural hinterland to their respective
metropolitan bases. In the hinterland a sub-metropolis, Winnipeg or Vancouver, attached sub-hinterlands. The analysis
of this secondary process has begun but remains a fertile
field for investigation. The suggestion by Maurice Careless
in "'Limited Identities' in Canada" (*CHR*, 1969) that the
true Canadian experience has been regional rather than national should prompt not only further studies of regionalism
in Canada, but also an examination of the economic, political and cultural relationships between urban and rural
areas in the Canadian West. Inquiry might be made into the
influence and role of urban newspapers or educational institutions. There has been to date no study of a western city
comparable to D. C. Masters' examination of Toronto. The
contribution such research might make is manifest in such
articles as Professor Careless' "Aspects of Urban Life in the
West, 1870-1914" in *Prairie Perspectives 2*, and "Development of the Winnipeg Business Community, 1870-1890"
(*TRSC*, 1970), or Karl Lenz, "Large Urban Places in the
Prairie Provinces—Their Development and Location" in R.

L. Gentilcore, *Canada's Changing Geography* (T., Prentice Hall, 1967). The best published study of a western city is Alan Artibise, *Winnipeg, A Social History of Urban Growth, 1874-1914* (M., McGill-Queen's, 1975).

In his "Clio in Canada," W. L. Morton commented that Frederick Jackson Turner's sectional interpretation of American history was relevant to Canada and argued that western sectionalism "in different terms" was as justified as Quebec nationalism or the British nationalism of Ontario. No study comparing the political minority position of the West and the racial minority of Quebec has been made. Studies on the West still seek to discover a western mystique based on a different geography and economy or to isolate the characteristics which make the West a unique society. There is much to be done.

Ontario

Peter Oliver

There has been very little effort by Canadian historians consciously to write the regional history of Ontario. As a result, while there has been much history written by Ontario historians and while there is much about Ontario in that work, there does not at the moment exist a historical literature devoted to Ontario in the sense that such may be said to exist for other Canadian regions. This is not intended to signify that there are not studies of the development of education, of political systems, of business interests and other facets of Ontario life which are comparable to those done elsewhere but merely that in contrast to the spirit and method of work done, say about the West or Quebec, that which has taken Ontario for its subject has not always had Ontario as its theme. Put simply, there seems to have been a tacit, almost unthinking, assumption that no regional history of this province is required or even appropriate.

In explanation of this phenomenon, Morris Zaslow, a past president of the Ontario Historical Society, has commented that "the regionalism of Ontario is often so closely identified with Canadian nationalism that many Ontarians fail to regard Ontario as a region at all and equate the larger Dominion with the purposes of Ontario." Witness, for example, the role played by Ontario writers in the general development of Canadian historical scholarship. From the day of Wrong, Kennedy and Skelton to that of Innis, Creighton and Careless, the major concern of Ontario scholars, on the face of it at least, was not the province but the nation. Let the westerners write about their wheat economy and the French Canadians their nationalism; any study of the work of Ontario historians will show that they took all Canada for their subject.

Yet while national politics, the federal government, and the Canadian economy provided them with subjects, such interests could not disguise the fact that many of the assumptions and values on which their analysis rested, or to which their interpretations pointed, attested to the Ontario origins of their authors. They were products of the same society which produced politicians determined that "Ontario must lead the way" and churchmen bent on the "Canadianization" of the West. Seldom do they seem to have recognized that the work they were doing might reflect a regional bias just as surely as did that whose subject matter was explicitly regional, but nonetheless theirs was a brand of national history with which those living elsewhere than in Ontario must have had some difficulty in identifying. The Manitoba historian, W. L. Morton, perceived this when he noted of the influential Laurentian interpretation propounded by Innis and Creighton that "its implications cannot be but misleading both to those brought up in the metropolitan area and those brought up in the hinterlands. Teaching inspired by the historical experience of metropolitan Canada cannot but deceive, and deceive cruelly, children of the outlying sections."

Eventually, the historian of ideas will draw upon the rich lode of national historical scholarship produced by Ontarians to explain many of that society's values and prejudices. This does not, however, provide adequate compensation for that which other Canadian regions already have in somewhat greater measure, that is, a respectable brand of regional history. That most historical scholarship produced here has been directed towards national themes has meant that in a very real way Ontario, so far as written history is concerned, must be classified as a have-not province. There is no recent general history of Ontario, no really satisfactory published biography of a single Premier, and little by way of economic history in comparison, for example, with Quebec. Deficiencies in the educational, cultural, intellectual and general social history of the province are as great if not greater. There has, in short, been no sustained effort to delineate and explain Ontario's regional characteristics.

Of course the preoccupation of Ontario Historians with "national history," together with the major role played by Ontarians in that history, means that the student may turn to such general works and find much enlightenment about Ontario themes. Yet the focus of such works must be always on the broader context and their treatment of the regional and the local often will be blurred. Furthermore, the lack of work on post-Confederation Ontario has had a negative effect on efforts to arrive at a national synthesis. If Canada is a country of regions, it makes little sense to attempt to achieve such a synthesis before one of the country's major regions has been the subject of conscious and thoroughly scholarly investigation. As well, if national history has been one preoccupation of Ontario historians, the pre-Confederation period has been another. While much work undeniably remains to be done on Upper Canada and Canada West, on that period has been lavished the attention of some of the province's most distinguished historians. That some of that fascination remains is attested to by the high proportion of articles in *Ontario History (OH)* still devoted to the pre-Confederation years. No one wishing to understand modern Ontario can afford to ignore the extent to which the province's social and institutional structures and ideological outlook were in place by Confederation. One cannot begin the study of Ontario society with Confederation.

Finally there is the fact, as true in scholarship as in other fields of endeavour, that it is a sense of grievance, a protest against existing conditions, which attracts attention like a magnet. Ontario, wealthy, politically stable, sure of its role in Confederation, could, perhaps, be taken for granted. Many Ontario academics have studied the phenomenon of sectional unrest in the West and the fascinating nationalism of French Canada while ignoring the society in which they themselves lived and taught. It would not be far off the mark to conclude that the colour and turbulence of regional protest movements motivated those studies rather than any theoretical commitment to the validity of regional approaches to Canadian history. The problem and not the region proved the drawing card. In a more limited way, this applied as well to the work of those who were not professional historians but who took pen in hand and provided sometimes interesting, sometimes abysmal, records of local events and colour. These writers, frequently dismissed as "mere antiquarians" but often faithful and acute recorders of the past, were motivated by the need to proclaim the virtues of the regions with which they identified most closely. In Ontario the need was less urgent as the society in its post-Confederation phase became more established and in turn less threatened.

Indeed Ontario, in the period after the old Grit crusade for provincial rights passed into history, in the view of one scholar became so bland as to cause him to raise the question, "Ontario—Does It Exist?" (*OH*, 1968). Professor A. R. M. Lower answered his question with a ringing "no." Once, he wrote, in the day of the crusaders for "rep by pop" and provincial rights and the struggle over separate schools, the province thrilled to the election cry, "The Traitor's hand is on thy throat, Ontario!" and everyone knew who the traitor was and what he was betraying. But the very size of the province, its own internal regional diversification and, most of all, the eroding power of unchecked urbanization and industrialization, destroyed that sense of identity more completely than anywhere else in Canada until Lower could conclude that no more are there Ontarians but merely people who happen to live in Ontario.

Perhaps that is why the editors of *OH* in an editorial in their December, 1962 issue found it necessary to lament the lack of work being done on the post-Confederation period—and why in provocative essays in *OH* (June, 1963) and in *Profiles of a Province* (Ontario Historical Society, T., 1967), Professor W. H. Magee has argued that "Ontario is the most curiously neglected subject in modern Canadian literature. For more than a generation," Professor Magee continued, "since the First World War, Canadian poets and novelists have almost ignored the existence of this, the dynamic centre of Canadian civilization." Creative writers, the argument goes, have had no difficulty capturing the uniqueness of the West or the Maritimes or Quebec; when they turn to Ontario their pens freeze, their minds are immobilized. A Margaret Atwood might find that there is too much success, not enough glorious failure and too few victims for

Ontario to provide an entirely satisfactory setting for Canadian fiction, while Professor Magee writes that, in the failure of the creative artists, it has been given to the writers of the *Financial Post* to catch the pulsating spirit of industry and commerce and "to react dynamically to a civilization which is dynamic." Although the argument falls short of total conviction, most observers may agree that the lamentable shortage of "victims" has combined with a certain lack of definition in Ontario society to present a challenge to which both creative writers and historians have failed to respond adequately.

In history, at least, the picture is changing rapidly, and the last five years have seen more good work than the previous quarter of a century. The next decade promises a real flowering of Ontario studies. One sign of the times is that several universities, and not only in Ontario, now offer courses in Ontario history. The pace of development may also be gauged by the fact that in all likelihood the reading lists used in those courses will be composed almost exclusively of articles, theses and books completed no earlier than about 1960. Many young scholars have made Ontario their field, and if they go about their work properly, a productive future lies ahead.

In large measure, the new interest in Ontario studies merely reflects the recognition of the extent to which the region previously was neglected. Since so much remains to be done, and since the province has, after all, played a considerable role in Confederation, it is not surprising that there should be efforts to correct past deficiencies. As well, modern scholarship increasingly is as interested in analysing and explaining such phenomena as economic concentration and growth and political stability as it is in the converse. In any case, it is quite possible that when the Ontario community is probed more fully, traditional assumptions about that society will be discredited and such factors as class conflict, intra-provincial economic disparities and urban-rural tensions will assume a larger place in the pattern of development.

One explanation of the quickening of interest in Ontario history relates to trends in national and international historiography. The technical proficiency and interpretive success achieved by some of the newer forms of social history in France, the United States and the United Kingdom, for example, stirred a new if belated interest among Canadian historians in the possibilities of such approaches. Increasingly in the 1960's historians came to realize that the organizing concepts and historiographical schools such as frontierism, Laurentianism and metropolitanism, however useful they might continue to be, were no longer adequate to the needs of Canadian history. Not only did no satisfactory national synthesis seem likely to emerge, but through such approaches too much of the Canadian past remained unexplained and unexplainable. Such "national" interpretations distorted the story of the West and omitted almost entirely that of the Maritimes; in any case "macrohistory" was almost always political, constitutional and sometimes economic in its emphasis. It was not an appropriate vehicle for studying the history of the family, for example, or the growth of schools and churches, or the problems of sewage disposal and public health. In a 1968 essay on "Canadian Historical Writing" published for the Royal Society, Ramsay Cook argued that "we have seriously overworked the national approach to Canadian history" and insisted that to understand our development, "we shall have to forego to a considerable extent history . . . which takes the nation as its central focus." In the *CHR* (1969) Maurice Careless applauded this view and argued that the Canadian reality can be understood only by an approach which comes to terms with regional realities.

Thus regional studies have become intellectually respectable. More than that, they are regarded as a principal vehicle of the new social history which is so much in vogue. Ontario history, more than that of any other region, needed such conceptual justification. It may, therefore, benefit most of all from the new dispensation.

BIBLIOGRAPHICAL WORKS

The most comprehensive bibliography of Ontario history, *Ontario Since 1867, A Bibliography*, appeared in 1973 under the auspices of the Ontario Historical Studies Series. Organized topically, it includes books, periodical articles, government reports and Royal Commissions. Loraine Spencer and Susan Holland compiled *Northern Ontario, a bibli-*

ography (T., UTP, 1968). In 1972 Laurentian University
Press published *Community Development in Northeastern
Ontario, A Selected Bibliography*, compiled by Gilbert A.
Stelter and John Rowan. As well Professor Stelter's *Canadian Urban History, A Selected Bibliography* (Sudbury,
Laurentian Univ. Press, 1972) contains a useful section on
Ontario. Benjamin Fortin and Jean-Pierre Gaboury have
prepared a *Bibliographie analytique de l'Ontario français*
(Cahiers du Centre de Recherche en Civilisation Canadienne-Française, l'Université d'Ottawa, 1975). A guide to
current work in Franco-Ontarian history is the volume, *Situation de la recherche sur la vie française en Ontario* published in 1975 by the Association Canadienne-Français pour
l'avancement des sciences, and the Centre de Recherche en
Civilisation Canadienne-Française de l'Université d'Ottawa.
Andrew Gregorovich's *Canadian Ethnic Groups Bibliography, A selected bibliography of ethno-cultural groups in
Canada and the Province of Ontario* appeared in 1972 under
the auspices of the Ontario Dept. of the Provincial Secretary and Citizenship. *Ontario Ethno-Cultural Newspapers,
1835-1972*, an annotated checklist, was compiled by Duncan
McLaren (T., UTP, 1973). A large number of county and
local histories have been written in Ontario, with the late
nineteenth century and the recent centenary period representing the years of peak production. Although these vary
enormously in quality, there is no critical guide to assist the
reader but Mrs. Barbara B. Aitken's *Local Histories of Ontario Municipalities Published In The Years 1957-1972* (revised and enlarged edition, Kingston, Public Library Board,
1972) provides one convenient listing. Also useful is the
register of theses on microfilm published by the National
Library. Finally, Hazel I. MacTaggart has provided two invaluable guides to government documents in her *Publications of the Government of Ontario 1901-1955* (T., UTP,
1964) and *Publications of the Government of Ontario 1956-
1971* (T., Ministry of Government Services, 1975). Dr. Olga
Bishop's *Publications of the Government of Ontario 1867-
1900* (T., Ministry of Government Services, 1976) successfully completes the cycle. The *Directory and Guide to the
Services of the Government of Ontario* (Department of
Tourism and Information, 1967) and *The Ontario Govern-*

ment Directory and Guide (1971) contain useful information on government publications.

PERIODICALS

There is no scholarly period devoted to historical work in Ontario which quite comes up to the standard set in Quebec by the *Revue d'Histoire de l'Amérique Française.* Perhaps *OH*, the quarterly journal of the Ontario Historical Society, comes closest, but many Ontario scholars seem to prefer to publish their best work in journals with a national audience. While it cannot be denied that some of the articles published here should never have seen the light of day, much of value does appear and in recent years the quality has improved substantially. The journal preserves the useful tradition of publishing the work not only of university-based historians and graduate students but of those for whom history is an avocation. Pre-Confederation studies still have primacy in its pages and in the twelve numbers issued between 1971 and 1973, such articles out-distanced those devoted to the modern period by more than two to one. An *Index To The Publications of the Ontario Historical Society, 1899-1972* was compiled by Hilary Bates and Robert Sherman and published by the Society in 1974.

In a category by themselves are the sixty-odd publications of La Société Historique du Nouvel-Ontario. Under the guiding genius of Lorenzo Cadieux, S. J., of Laurentian University, these include studies of community life, educational development, church history, economic and mining affairs, folk music, biographical portraits and other themes. Although the quality varies greatly, they are indispensable to the study of Northern Ontario in general and Franco-Ontarian history in particular.

Several periodicals devoted to more local studies should also be noted, including *Wentworth Bygones, Historic Kingston*, and *Western Ontario Historical Notes* and *Western Ontario History Nuggets* started by Fred Landon of that university. A list of articles published in the latter two between 1942 and 1972 was prepared at the D. B. Weldon Library of the University of Western Ontario. Some of the province's local historical societies (their names and addresses are conviently listed on the back cover of *OH*) from time to time publish notes and transactions but there is no general guide to these.

Among the official and semi-official periodicals which are of value are the *Ontario Economic Review*, a bi-monthly publication edited in the Ministry of Treasury, Economics and Intergovernmental Affairs, the *Ontario Statistical Review* published annually by the same Ministry, the *Bulletin* of the Hydro Electric Power Commission, and the *Ontario Northland Quarterly*, a publication of the Ontario Northland Railway Commission. Only the first two of these continue to be published in their original form.

GENERAL WORKS

Only a few chapters of Alexander Fraser's *A History of Ontario* (2 vols., T., The Canada History Company, 1907) deal with the post-Confederation period and their approach is that of an uncritical political narrative. The series *Canada And Its Provinces* recognized that there is more to history than past politics and the two volumes dealing with Ontario, prepared by such scholars as W. S. Wallace, James Mavor, Adam Shortt and B. E. Fernow, included discussions of education, the municipal and judicial systems, and economic development as well. Although aimed at the general reader and somewhat lacking in original research and critical analysis, they often repay rereading today. In 1927 two distinguished students of Ontario history, Fred Landon of the University of Western Ontario and J. E. Middleton, whose particular interest was municipal history, published in four volumes their *Province of Ontario, A History* (T., Dominion Publishing Company). A well balanced description of social, economic and political developments organized thematically, it includes separate essays on the provincial Liberal and Conservative parties, on trade, education banking, transportation, the churches and even on journalism, the courts and the medical profession. Some attention is paid to particular regions within the province and a large section, "An Historical Gazetteer of the Counties and Districts in the Province of Ontario," uses census and assessment data plus many of the thirty-five-odd Ontario County Atlases which appeared in the late nineteenth century to provide brief descriptions of Ontario municipalities. In common with Fraser's *History*, much space, in this case over two volumes, is devoted to brief biographical essays on prominent citizens. Since the pre-Confederation period is also dealt with, the time spent on the more recent years is cut down drastically. Still, there is much of value in Middleton and Landon and they do not hesitate to take a critical approach, as in their judgment that Mowat Liberalism gradually "petrified into a complete Toryism." There is also some discussion of post-Confederation developments in Professor Landon's fine volume on *Western Ontario And The American Frontier*, which was first published in 1941 by Ryerson Press and Yale University Press in the Carnegie Endowment Series and reprinted in paperback in 1967 in the Carleton Library. No major general history has been published since Middleton and Landon in 1927. G. P. de T. Glazebrook, *Life in Ontario, A Social History* (T., UTP, 1968) is a bland narrative which contains some interesting material but generally confirms the impression that much additional monograph research must be done before a successful synthesis can be achieved.

There are several other items of a general nature that it would be useful to mention at this point. Since J. E. Hodgett's invaluable *Pioneer Public Service* (T., UTP, 1955) stops with Confederation, there is no administrative study of the provincial government but F. F. Schindeler's *Responsible Government in Ontario* (T., UTP, 1969), which carefully examines the executive and the legislative branches and concludes that executive encroachments have so transformed the province's governmental system that parliamentary government may remain only as a myth. Schindeler's indictment provides a carefully documented study of the evolution of government in terms of his central thesis, but a volume broader in scope, less polemical and devoting more attention to the pre-1945 period is still very much needed. There is an important geographical study, *Ontario*, edited by Louis Gentilcore, (T., UTP, 1972).

Two collections of essays available in paperback provide an introduction to Ontario history and an indication of recent trends in research. *Profiles of a Province*, a centennial project commissioned by the Ontario Historical Society and which appeared in 1967, includes sections on the formative years, the political scene, the economy and the Ontario outlook. Very much a mixed bag, the volume was a reflection of weakness rather than strength, relieved principally by S. F. Wise's perceptive study of Upper Canadian Toryism, several suggestive essays on modern politicians and W. H. Magee's thoughts on the literary scene. *Oliver Mowat's Ontario*, edited by Donald Swainson, (T., Mac., 1972), more restricted in its chronological scope, showed a higher standard of scholarship, and essays by Graeme Decarie on prohibition, Michael Bliss on the collective impulse in the business community and H. V. Nelles on the political economy of the resource sector are among the better contributions. *Aspects of Nineteenth Century Ontario* (T., UTP, 1974) edited by F. H. Armstrong, H. A. Stevenson and J. D. Wilson is a *festschrift* in honour of Dr. J. J. Talman, one of the province's pioneer social historians.

Ontario governments have been as adept as any in Canada at the art of Royal Commissioning, and some of the most important material relating to Ontario history is contained in the reports and in the transcripts of evidence, some of which were not available. The several guides to government publications conveniently list the Royal Commissions and commissions of inquiry; and there is also an excellent unpublished preliminary inventory, *Records of Commissions and Committees* (1969), which is available for use at the Ontario Archives. McTaggart usefully indicates which of the reports in her period (1901-1955) were published in the Sessional Papers while Sessional Paper No. 6, 1894, lists Royal Commissions which appeared between 1867 and 1894. Another guide is R. P. Smith, *Royal Commissions of the Province of Ontario, 1867 to 1950* (Kingston, Queen's Univ. Press, 1950).

There are several other resources which might best be described in this catch-all section. Every student of Ontario history soon discovers to his regret that too often historical statistics are unavailable on a provincial basis and even when Urquhart and Buckley's *Historical Statistics of Canada* does deal with provincial matters, it usually presents them in terms of national aggregates. A guide to regional sources of statistical information is Dean Tudor, *Sources of Statistical Data for Ontario* (Ottawa, Canada Library Association, 1972). The Province has also produced a constituency by constituency history of election results compiled by Roderick Lewis, the chief election officer. The most recent edition is the *Centennial Edition Of A History Of The Electoral Districts, Legislatures and Ministries Of The Province Of Ontario 1867-1968* (T., Queen's Printer, n.d.). Most provinces have not had Hansards until fairly recently and Ontario is no exception, with regular recording of debates beginning only during the Drew administration of the 1940's. Fortunately, except for two brief periods, newspaper clippings from the holdings of the Ontario Archives and the Legislative Library have been microfilmed and this *Newspaper Hansard,* drawn very largely from the Toronto *Globe,* is available from 1867 in the Provincial Archives and in some university libraries. Finally, the old *Canadian Annual Review of Public Affairs* which appeared between 1901 and 1938 and the new version which commenced publication in 1960 contain essays on Ontario affairs.

PROVINCIAL POLITICS, 1867-1896

In provincial politics as in all other aspects of Ontario history, the volume of published material is less than overwhelming, and it is frequently necessary to turn to M.A. and Ph.D. theses which are usually available on interlibrary loan or on microfilm. For the same reason, it is perhaps premature to attempt to place what material does exist in any historiographical tradition and in most cases all that is really in order is to say a word or two about its general merit, or lack thereof.

Only two chapters of Bruce W. Hodgins' study of *John Sandfield Macdonald* (T., UTP, 1971) deal with the post-Confederation phase of the career of the man who was Ontario's first Premier, but they are sufficient to demonstrate that several enduring themes in Ontario politics date from Confederation. Sandfield's defence of an eastern Ontario point of view emphasizes the regional basis of Ontario politics while Professor Hodgins' discussion of his social and educational policies clearly demonstrates that enlightened programs did not begin with Mowat Liberalism. D. G. Kerr, "The 1867 Elections in Ontario: The Rules of the Game" (*CHR,* 1970) provides a fascinating glimpse of the seamier side of public life, while Margaret Helen Small, "A study of the Dominion and the Provincial Elections of 1867 in Ontario" (M.A. thesis, Queen's University, 1968) is a careful piece of electoral analysis. Richard Splane's 1948 M.A. thesis for the University of Toronto, "The Upper Canada Reform Party 1867-1878," is a thoughtful analysis of political ideas and practices, while the intimacy of the connections between provincial and federal Liberals renders W. R. Graham's "The Alexander Mackenzie Administration, 1873-1878: a study of Liberal tenets and tactics" (M.A. thesis, University of Toronto, 1944) and Dale Thomson, *Alexander Mackenzie, Clear Grit* (T., Mac., 1960) of interest to students of provincial politics.

The most important work on late nineteenth-century political life, "Oliver Mowat and Ontario, 1872-1896: A study in Political Success," a 1967 doctoral dissertation done at the University of Toronto by Margaret Evans, argues that Mowat's role as a defender of provincial rights had little to do with his political success and focuses on Mowat's social and developmental programs, which in her view were usually the most advanced in Canada. Mowat himself appears as a consummate politician, progressive yet conservative, whose brokerage politics set the style followed by almost all his successors. Although Mrs. Evans has made excellent use of government documents and the contemporary press, the absence of any substantial collection of Mowat papers has been severely felt, while her thematic organization seems to lead to a certain aridity which was not lacking in Mowat himself. As well, many of the themes Mrs. Evans' attempts to deal with in terms of Mowat's career resist being extracted from their natural chronological limits. Of the several articles about Mowat published by Mrs. Evans, the most useful is that which appeared in *Profiles of a Province*, briefly summarizing her dissertation. An earlier two-volume biography by C. R. W. Biggar which appeared in 1905 (reprinted, N.Y., AMS, 1971) was written in the old "life and letters" style and, as its author put it, "in a spirit of loyal and affectionate remembrance." Carman Miller's article, "Mowat, Laurier and the Federal Liberal Party, 1887-1897" which appeared in *Oliver Mowat's Ontario*, is an adequate treatment of its subject.

Late nineteenth century religious tensions are examined in their political dimension in: Martin A. Galvin, "The Jubilee Riots in Toronto, 1875" (*Report of the Canadian Catholic Historical Association*, 1959); J. R. Miller, " 'Equal Rights For All'; The E.R.A. and the Ontario Election of 1890" (*OH*, 1973); James T. Watt, "Anti-Catholicism in Ontario Politics: 1894" (*OH* 1967); and Janet B. Kerr, "Sir Oliver Mowat and the Campaign of 1894" (*OH*, 1963). Despite its tendency to read in places like a loosely strung together collection of documents, Franklin A. Walker's *Catholic Education And Politics In Ontario* (T., UTP, 1964) which draws upon a wide variety of Catholic archival material, is by far the most comprehensive study of both the separate schools and French-language education controversies for the years 1867 to the 1930's. The agrarian unrest of the Mowat years is discussed in S. E. D. Shortt's essay "Social Change and Political Crisis in Rural Ontario: The Patrons of Industry, 1889-1896," which appeared in *Oliver Mowat's Ontario*, and in J. D. Smart, "The Patrons of Industry in Ontario in the 1890's" (M.A. thesis, Carleton University, 1970). Douglas O. Baldwin's 1973 York Ph.D. thesis, "Political and Social Behaviour in Ontario, 1879-1891: a quantitative approach" attempts to apply a newer methodology to the study of the Ontario political culture.

PROVINCIAL POLITICS, 1896-1923

Oliver Mowat's leaving the office of Premier in 1896 ended an era, but the new age of Tory progressivism was delayed by the astute political opportunism and brilliant oratory of Sir George Ross. Educator, prohibitionist, businessman, imperialist, Ross played many roles but perhaps was most significant of all as a transitional figure in the province's shift from the agrarian-based, moralistic Liberalism of Mowat to the new style politics of Whitney and Adam Beck. Unfortunately there is no good study of either Ross or his period and the absence of an adequate collection of Ross Papers poses perhaps insuperable difficulties. Two useful M.A. theses are Douglas Dart, "George William Ross, Minister of Education for Ontario, 1883-1899" (University of Guelph, 1971) and David O. Trevor, "Arthur S. Hardy and Ontario Politics, 1896-1899" (University of Guelph,

1973). Some light is thrown on the late 1890s and early 1900s by Charles W. Humphries' well-written Ph.D. thesis, "The Political Career of Sir James P. Whitney" (University of Toronto, 1966) and his interpretation of Tory reformism, which he attributes very largely to pressures from the growing urban middle class reacting against traditional agrarian values, is convincingly summarized in "The Sources of Ontario 'Progressive Conservatism,' 1900-1914" (*CHAR*, 1967). Unfortunately, Professor Humphries' work is overbalanced in the direction of Whitney's opposition years and he pays little attention to a number of important subjects. *Silent Frank Cochrane*, by Scott and Astrid Young (T., Mac., 1973) is a brief portrait of Whitney's powerful Minister of Lands, Forests and Mines. Two essays, "The Gamey Affair" by C. W. Humphries, and "The Cruise of the Minnie M," by B. D. Tennyson, (both in *OH*, 1967) describe the political corruption perpetrated by the dying Ross government.

Newton Wesley Rowell, leader of the opposition between 1911 and 1917, had a career which reflected many of the central currents in Ontario's development. Leading Methodist layman, prohibitionist, social reformer and corporation lawyer, he is the subject of a major biography by Margaret Prang, *N. W. Rowell, Ontario Nationalist* (T., UTP, 1975) and his Ontario role is summarized by her essay in *Profiles of a Province*. Although almost nothing has been written on the major social policies of the Whitney period, the dramatic public power movement has attracted much attention. A. Brady, "The Ontario Hydro-Electric Power Commission" (*CJEPS*, 1936), is a good introduction, while *Adam Beck and the Ontario Hydro*, by W. R. Plewman, (T., Ryerson, 1947) is an informative, pungent and gossipy account by one who knew the incredible Hydro czar well. Although Merrill Denison's *The People's Power, The History of Ontario Hydro*, (T., M&S, 1960) has the faults and many of the virtues of an official history, it does convey some of the excitement of the period and emphasizes the role played in the Hydro movement by small businessmen and municipal reformers. *An Expensive Experiment* (N.Y., 1913), by R. P. Bolton, and *Niagara In Politics* (N.Y., E. P. Dutton & Co., 1925), by James Mavor, are examples of the literature produced by the enemies of Hydro. See too Kenneth C. De-war's 1975 U. of T. Ph.D. thesis, "State Ownership in Canada, The Origins of Ontario Hydro."

The thrust of H. V. Nelles' brilliant study, *The Politics of Development: Forests, Mines and Hydro-electric Power in Ontario, 1849-1941* (T., Mac., 1974), is largely devoted to what might be roughly described as the progressive period in Ontario politics from about the turn of the century to the early 1920's. It provides a fascinating study of the dynamics of the businessman-politician relationship in the exploitation of Ontario's incredibly rich natural resources and attempts to explain the development of indigenous traditions, rooted in Ontario history yet reflecting all the circumstances of the day. The idea of a public interest, prior to and more important than mere private profit, was asserted most successfully in hydro-electric development and with least impact in the more individualistic mining industry. The limitations imposed by the power of private enterprise, the culpability of politicians, the reality of provincial status and the circumstances of an international economy are effectively analyzed, and the consequences of the close relationship between powerful businessmen, often of American origin and with American backing, and provincial politicians, on the province's democratic processes, are assessed. Although some of Professor Nelles' judgments, particularly in his later chapters, are too sweeping and his theory in places crowds unduly upon a reality both more complex and more trite than he would allow, this conceptually powerful volume is the best work on an Ontario subject in many a year and may have salutary effects on the whole field. A different interpretation is argued convincingly in R. Peter Gillis's important article, "The Ottawa lumber barons and the conservation movement, 1880-1914" (*JCS*, 1974). The conservation movement for a later period, from the late 1930s on, is dealt with in Arthur Herbert Richardson's *Conservation by the people: the history of the conservation movement in Ontario to 1970*, ed. by A. S. L. Barnes (T., UTP, 1974), a study which is dry and official in its approach.

There are only fragmentary studies of the impact of World War I on Ontario life. *The Province of Ontario In The War*, by J. Castell Hopkins (T., Warwick Bros. & Rutter Ltd., 1919) provides an introduction in the manner befitting the editor of the *Canadian Annual Review*. T. Gerald Stortz, "Ontario Labour and the First World War" (M.A. thesis, University of Waterloo, 1976) emphasizes the economic dimension of labour discontent and is a useful corrective to earlier accounts of labour's role in this era. B. D. Tennyson's "The Political Career of Sir William H. Hearst" (M.A. thesis, University of Toronto, 1963) and articles by the same author (in *OH*, 1963, 1964, 1965, and 1966) provide an introduction to the issues of the Hearst years. In an article on "The Ontario General Election of 1919: The beginnings of agrarian revolt" (*JCS*, 1969) Professor Tennyson argues that the Hearst administration had governed progressively and that its defeat that year must be attributed to the general spirit of post-war unrest, while Peter Oliver in "Sir William Hearst and the Collapse of the Ontario Conservative Party" (*CHR*, 1972) emphasizes internal decay and political mismanagement. Also concerned with the 1919 election is K. D. Wakefield's (M.A. thesis, Queen's University, 1973) "Measuring one party dominance: a study of Maurice Pinard's theory of third party emergence with reference to the case of the UFO in the Ontario general election of 1919."

Wartime rural unrest is examined in R. W. Trowbridge, "War-Time Discontent and the Rise of the United Farmers of Ontario" (M.A. thesis, University of Waterloo, 1966), and by W. R. Young in "Conscription, Rural Depopulation, and the Farmers of Ontario, 1917-1919" (*CHR*, 1972). The fascinating farmers' movement which took over the government in 1919 has been much studied but the results remain largely in thesis form. The best work is still Jean MacLeod, "The United Farmer Movement In Ontario, 1914-1943" (M.A. thesis, Queen's University, 1958), and her broader "Agriculture and Politics in Ontario Since 1867" (Ph.D. thesis, University of London, 1961). Russell Hann's pamphlet, "Some Historical Perspectives On Canadian Agrarian Political Movements: the Ontario Origins of Agrarian Criticism of Canadian Industrial Society" (T., New Hogtown Press, 1973) is thoughtful and provocative. John David Hoffman, "Farmer-Labor Government In Ontario" (M.A. thesis, University of Toronto, 1959), is an account by a political scientist which emphasizes intra-party relations as does an article by the same author (*CJEPS*, 1961). Martin Robin's volume, *Radical Politics and Canadian Labour 1880-1930* (Kingston, Queen's Univ., 1968), is particularly useful on labour's involvement in the Drury administration and demonstrates how swiftly the spirit of cooperation collapsed. A more general discussion is J. F. Cahan, "A Survey of the Political Activities of the Ontario Labour Movement, 1850-1935" (M.A. thesis, University of Toronto, 1945). Accounts by contemporaries include: L. A. Wood's 1924 volume, *A History of Farmers' Movements in Canada* (T., UTP, 1975); *The Challenge Of Agriculture* (T., Morang, 1921), a study of the UFO by its educational secretary, M. H. Staples; and *Farmer Citizen* (T., Ryerson, 1968), the memoirs of W. C. Good, the UFO's self-styled philosopher. *Farmer Premier, The Memoirs of E. C. Drury* (T., M&S, 1966) is of considerable interest but thoroughly unreliable for the old gentleman was not well served by his editor. W. E. Raney, the Drury administration's Attorney General, is the subject of an article by Peter Oliver entitled "W. E. Raney and the Politics of Uplift" (*JCS*, 1971), which relates the administration's moral reform policies to its rising political unpopularity. The same author's (Ph.D. thesis, University of Toronto, 1969) "The Making of a Provincial Premier, G. Howard Ferguson and Ontario Politics, 1870-1923" has several chapters on the Drury years and examines the circumstances surrounding the Tory return to power in 1923. Oliver has also published a collection of essays, some old and some new, entitled *Public And Private Persons, The Ontario Political Culture 1914-1934* (T., Clarke, Irwin, 1975) in which he seeks to comprehend the relationship between particular figures and the larger political culture.

PROVINCIAL POLITICS, 1923-1973
　　Except for the Hepburn interlude, the Conservative Party has been in office in Ontario since 1923. The political history of that era remains largely unwritten. Richard Alway's, "Mitchell F. Hepburn and the Liberal Party in the Province of Ontario 1927-1943" (M.A. thesis, University of Toronto, 1965), was a sound beginning while Neil F. McKenty's *Mitch Hepburn* (T., M&S, 1967) is a racy account which focuses on key issues such as the liquor question,

separate schools, hydro-electric matters and the Oshawa
General Motors strike, but falls short of being a full biography. McKenty emphasizes the rural outlook which Hepburn
imposed on the Liberal Party but the conclusion both of the
book and of an article, "That Tory Hepburn," in *Profiles of
a Province* that Hepburn was indeed a Tory fails to probe
the full extent of the Premier's demagoguery or to take into
account the contrast in styles between him and such figures
as Howard Ferguson and George Henry. One aspect of the
1937 election is discussed in "A 'Silent' Issue: Mitchell Hepburn, separate-school taxation and the Ontario election of
1937," by Richard Alway, which appeared in M. Cross and
R. Bothwell, eds., *Policy by Other Means* (T., Clarke Irwin,
1972). On the Conservative dynasty which started in 1943,
there is little of interest. The CCF, however, is better
served, particularly by Gerald L. Caplan, who in *The Dilemma of Canadian Socialism, The CCF in Ontario* (T., M&S,
1973), and in two articles (*CHR*, 1963, and *CJEPS*, 1964)
presents a rise and fall theory of the CCF which demonstrates the extent of the party's weaknesses during the depression and attempts an explanation of its striking success
in 1943 and of the disastrous election of 1945. Ian Mac-
Pherson, "The 1945 Collapse of the CCF in Windsor" (*OH*,
1969) throws further light on how internal divisions and
external opposition resulted in the failure of that year. Leo
Zakuta, *A Protest Movement Becalmed* (T., UTP, 1964),
should also be noted.

The essay by John Wilson and David Hoffman, "Ontario, A Three-Party System in Transition," which appeared
in Martin Robin, ed., *Canadian Provincial Politics* (Scarborough, Prentice-Hall, 1972), attempts an interpretation of
the course of Ontario politics since Confederation but
achieves success only for the more recent post-war period in
which techniques of electoral and legislative analysis are
brought to bear on the party structure. "The Liberal Party
in Contemporary Ontario Politics" (*Canadian Journal of
Political Science*, 1970) is a model piece of analysis by the
same authors. Ontario political history remains sadly defi-
cient in work which goes beyond questions of leadership and
results of individual elections, and not until more is done
along the lines attempted by Professors Wilson and Hoff-

man will we begin to have a satisfactory understanding of the province's political structure. In the meantime, Donald C. MacDonald, one of the province's most distinguished politicians, has compiled a collection of essays, *Government and Politics of Ontario* (T., Mac., 1975) and Jonathan Manthorpe has provided a journalistic account, *The Power And The Tories, Ontario Politics—1943 To The Present* (T., Mac., 1974).

FEDERAL-PROVINCIAL RELATIONS

For many years the major and almost the only work in the field was J. C. Morrison's "Oliver Mowat and the Development of Provincial Rights in Ontario: A Study in Dominion-Provincial Relations, 1867-1896." An M.A. thesis done at the University of Toronto under the supervision of D. G. Creighton and published in *Three History Theses* (Ontario Department of Public Records and Archives, 1961), it describes in ample detail if somewhat unsympathetically the classic episodes in Mowat's provincial rights struggle. The brief section on federal-provincial relations in Mrs. Evan's *Mowat* presents a markedly different point of view. Professor Christopher Armstrong, in "The Political Economy of Federalism: Ontario's Relations with the Federal Government, 1897-1941" (Ph.D. thesis, University of Toronto, 1972), takes up the story where Morrison left off chronologically but with a very different approach. The extent of industrialization and urbanization, he suggests, had transformed the nature of the game and ruthless business interests intent on playing one level of government off against the other were now among the principal players. As well, the province had to fight more aggressively than ever for the right to use its natural resources as it saw fit while new social needs in such areas as education and social welfare put enormous strains on provincial finances. In part this is the old story presented so well in the Rowell-Sirois Report but Armstrong succeeds in giving it exciting new dimensions. Another example of the approach is the essay by Professors Armstrong and H. V. Nelles, "Private Property in Peril: Ontario Businessmen and the Federal System, 1898-1911," in Glenn Porter and Robert Cuff, eds., *Enterprise and National Development* (T., Hakkert, 1973). This is not the place to describe the standard accounts of federal-provincial relations written from a national perspective, but two of particular interest to Ontario are Ramsay Cook, *Provincial Autonomy, Minority Rights and the Compact Theory, 1867-1921* (Ottawa, QP, 1969), which demonstrates the major role played by Ontario figures in the early enunciation of provincial rights theory, and Richard Simeon, *Federal-Provincial Diplomacy* (T., UTP, 1972), which uses a case study approach to explore the dynamics of several recent issues. Richard Alway's "Hepburn, King and the Rowell-Sirois Commission" (*CHR*, 1967) and the McKenty biography which deals with the Hepburn-King feud in detail, leave the student puzzled as to whether personal animosities or long-standing provincial interests were more to the fore in provincial policy formation. Finally, the provincial government, believing its cause to be just and not blind to the uses of political propaganda, has always advanced its views in great detail in position papers, budget addresses and elsewhere and these are readily available in most major libraries.

NORTHERN ONTARIO

Separate studies of *Settlement and the Forest Frontier in Eastern Canada*, by A. R. M. Lower, and *Settlement and the Mining Frontier*, by H. A. Innis, are printed together as Vol. IX of the Canadian Frontiers of Settlement series (T., Mac., 1936), and although the bulk of the Innis section is on Northwestern Canada, taken together they provide an invaluable beginning to scholarly analysis of Northern Ontario. Two chapters in Morris Zaslow, *The Opening of the Canadian North 1870-1914* (T., M&S, 1971), are a perceptive and well-balanced general account of settlement, the mining and forestry industries, transportation and the role of government in Northern Ontario and Quebec. Not the least of the merits of Professor Zaslow's work is the useful comparative framework in which it studies the two areas. Nelles' book is a third indispensable source for Northern Ontario. Richard S. Lambert, with Paul Pross, *Renewing Nature's Wealth, A Centennial History of the Public Management of Lands, Forests & Wildlife in Ontario 1763-1967* (Department of Lands and Forests, 1967), is a major effort dealing with much more than Northern Ontario.

The bibliographies in the above works, particularly Zaslow and Lambert, provide full assessments of additional literature which for reasons of space cannot be repeated here. Among the most useful works on mining are *Metals and Men, The Story of Canadian Mining*, (T., M&S, 1957) and *Sudbury Basin*, (T., Ryerson, 1953), both by D. M. Le-Bourdais, and *The Mineral Resources of Canada* (T., Ryerson, 1933) and *The American Impact on Canadian Mining* (T., 1941), both by E. S. Moore. T. W. Gibson, *Mining in Ontario* (Department of Mines, 1937), is a brief factual account by the long-time Deputy Minister of the Department of Mines. O. W. Main, *The Canadian Nickel Industry* (T., UTP, 1955) is a judicious study of an industry of vital importance to the whole province. There are also a number of studies of particular mining camps such as S. A. Pain's study of Kirkland Lake, *Three Miles of Gold* (T., Ryerson, 1960). Settlement studies include G. L. McDermott, "Frontiers of Settlement in the Great Clay Belt of Ontario and Quebec" (*Annals of the Association of American Geographers*, 1961), and Benoit-Beaudry Gourd, "La Colonisation des Clay Belts du Nord-Ouest québecois et du Nord-Est ontarien (*RHAF*, 1973). Although the various works on railways contain sections which describe in passing their impact on Northern Ontario, there is no comprehensive treatment of the Temiskaming and Northern Ontario Railway. O. S. Noct, *Algoma Central Railway* (T., Thomas Nelson, 1975) is a popular study. Northern Ontario has also inspired a number of idiosyncratic yet colourful general accounts by interested parties which interpret development in terms of heroic deeds and individual enterprise. The best of these are O. T. G. Williamson, *The Northland Ontario* (T., Ryerson, 1946), and S. A. Pain, *The Way North* (T., 1964). Denis M. Watson's "Frontier Movement and Economic Development in Northeastern Ontario, 1850-1914" (M.A. thesis, University of British Columbia, 1966) is a first-rate study by a geographer.

THE ECONOMY

Ontario, of course, is part of a larger regional economic system, perhaps best described as Laurentian, which in turn is as closely connected with the Northeastern United States as with the rest of Canada. What has been written to date on the Ontario economy has seldom coincided with the province's political boundaries and the student must turn to national and international studies described elsewhere for an understanding of the province's economic development. Nonetheless, with its own fiscal policies, its energy and industrial strategies and, perhaps most important of all control of its own natural resources, Ontario does constitute an economic region, one which has attracted remarkably little scholarly analysis. This is particularly surprising since the volume and quality of studies devoted to the Quebec economy have revealed how fruitful a provincial approach can be. At present, however, we are restricted to a few books, some published essays and a considerable number of graduate dissertations. As a result we know a good deal about individual railways, about individual entrepreneurs and particular industries but no one as yet has attempted to put it all together in a synthesis which would include as well an assessment of the impact of provincial fiscal and economic policies.

Among the more useful published essays are: W. H. Breithaupt, "The Railways of Ontario" (*O.H.S. Papers and Records*, 1929); W. M. Drummond, "The Impact of the Post-War Industrial Expansion on Ontario's Agriculture" (*CJEPS* 1958); K. A. J. Hay, "Trends in the Location of Industry in Ontario, 1945-1959" (*CJEPS*, 1965); H. A. Innis, "An Introduction to the Economic History of Ontario from Outpost to Empire," in *Profiles of a Province*; J. E. MacNab, "Toronto's Industrial Growth to 1891" (*OH*, 1955); J. T. Saywell, "The Early History of Canadian Oil Companies: A Chapter in Canadian Business History" (*OH*, 1961); A. G. Talbot, "Ontario Origins of the Canadian Explosives Industry" (*OH*, 1964); Margaret Van Avery, "Francis R. Clergue and the Rise of Sault Ste. Marie" (*OH*, 1964); R. G. Hoskins, "Hiram Walker and the Origins and Development of Walkerville, Ontario" (*OH*, 1972); David F. Walker, "Transportation of Coal into Southern Ontario, 1871-1921" (*OH*, 1971); and Walker's "The Energy Sources of Manufacturing in Southern Ontario, 1871-1921" (*Ontario Geography*, 1971). Recent studies of particular railway promotions include R. M. Stamp, "J. D. Edgar and the Pacific Junction Railway" (*OH*, 1963); J. Konarek, "Algoma Central and

Hudson Bay Railway: The Beginnings" (*OH*, 1970); James Eadie, "Edward Wilkes Rathbun and the Napanee Tamworth and Quebec Railway" (*OH*, 1971).

The more important theses are C. A. Hall, "Electric Utilities in Ontario Under Private Ownership, 1890-1914" (Ph.D., University of Toronto, 1968); R. Sauvé, "Economic Growth of Eastern Ontario—Trend and Structural Analysis" (M.A., University of Ottawa, 1971); D. M. Ray, "Settlement and Rural Ontario Migration in Easternmost Ontario 1783-1956" (M.A., University of Ottawa, 1961); I. C. Taylor, "Components of Population Change, Ontario, 1850-1940," (M.A., University of Toronto, 1967); and there are also several studies of economic growth at the county level such as D. J. Hall, "Economic Development in Elgin County 1850-1880" (M.A. thesis, University of Guelph, 1971).

The classic treatise on agriculture is R. L. Jones, *History of Agriculture In Ontario, 1613-1880* (T., UTP, 1946). The more recent *A History of Agriculture in Ontario* by G. Elmore Reaman, (2 vols., T., Saunders, 1970) while bringing the story up to the present is an undistinguished effort. Related studies are: D. A. Lawr, "The Development of Ontario Farming, 1870-1914: Patterns of Growth and Change" (*OH*, 1972); P. M. Ennals, "The Impact of the Penetration of American Agricultural Technology into Southern Ontario During the Nineteenth Century" (Ph.D. thesis, University of Toronto, 1970); and L. Reeds, "The Agricultural Geography of Southern Ontario" (Ph.D. thesis, University of Toronto, 1956).

The pulp and paper industry has long been of pivotal importance to the Ontario economy, and studies of its growth and difficulties include: C. P. Fell, "The Newsprint Industry," in H. A. Innis and A. F. W. Plumptre, eds., *The Canadian Economy and its Problems* (T., 1934); E. A. Forsey, "The Pulp and Paper Industry" (*CJEPS*, 1935); John A. Guthrie, *The Newsprint Paper Industry* (Cambridge, Harvard Univ. Press, 1941); and chapter 7 in V. W. Bladen, *An Introduction to Political Economy* (London, OUP, 1941).

Geographers continue to do much of the research and analysis which will necessarily precede any attempt to formulate a general interpretation, and James Gilmour, *Spatial Evolution of Manufacturing in Southern Ontario, 1851-*

1891 (T., UTP, 1972), is a fine example of such efforts, as are: D. M. Ray, *Market Potential and Economic Shadow. A Quantitative Analysis of Industrial Location in Southern Ontario.* (University of Chicago, Dept. of Geography, Research Papers No. 101, 1965); N. C. Field and D. P. Kerr, *Geographical Aspects of Industrial Growth in the Metropolitan Toronto Region* (Regional Development Branch, Dept. of Treasury and Economics, 1968); and John U. Marshall, *The Location of Service Towns* (T., UTP, 1969). Geographers have also contributed the invaluable *Economic Atlas of Ontario* (T., UTP, 1969), an internationally acclaimed contribution to economic geography. Alan Wilson's *John Northway, a Blue Serge Canadian* (T., Burns & MacEachern, 1965) is a case study in entrepreneurship, and T. W. Acheson's "The Social Origins of Canadian Industrialism: A Study in the Structure of Entrepreneurship 1880-1910" (Ph.D. thesis, University of Toronto, 1971), while national in its scope, casts much light on Ontario traditions of business leadership.

The above items are far from being a comprehensive list, but it is evident that any effort to achieve an ordered regional analysis has been hindered on the one hand by the natural inclination to treat Ontario as part of a larger economic entity and on the other hand by a tendency to write fragmented accounts without any attempt at comprehensiveness or synthesis. As a result, what there is remains scattered and lacking in direction. Until the perspective of the economic historian extends beyond a particular industry and until bolder and more analytic approaches along the lines of Professor Acheson's work or Michael Bliss's "A Living Profit: Studies in the Social History of Canadian Business, 1883-1911" (Ph.D. thesis, University of Toronto, 1972) are attempted on a regional scale, there can be no general economic history of Ontario to compare with that being written for comparable regions elsewhere.

URBAN AND LOCAL STUDIES

It is impossible here to mention, let alone assess, the multitude of studies of cities and towns or even the many county histories which the professional historian tends to underestimate and neglect. While a critical guide to such work is much needed it is a project in itself and the bibliographies noted above must provide guidance. The leading example of the old metropolitan approach to urban history which examined the external relations and internal development of cities as they related to factors of growth is D. C. Masters' solid study, *The Rise of Toronto, 1850-1890* (T., UTP, 1947). Jacob Spelt, *Urban Development In South-Central Ontario* (1955; T., M&S, 1972), has a helpful bibliographical essay by the author. It is a pioneering comparative study of urban growth in the context of general economic development. Donald Kerr and Jacob Spelt, *The Changing Face of Toronto—A Study In Urban Geography* (Ottawa, QP, 1965), uses an historical approach to analyze the growth of a huge metropolitan configuration. More recently, of course, urbanologists have turned from studies of growth to attempts to write the internal history of the city in terms of its social development and the life patterns of its inhabitants. No greater contrast between the old and the new exists than in the extended narrative treatment G. P. de T. Glazebrook gives to *The Story of Toronto* (T., UTP, 1971), and the largely quantitative analysis provided by a geographer, Peter G. Goheen, *Victorian Toronto 1850 to 1900* (University of Chicago, Dept. of Geography, Research Paper No. 127, 1970). While Professor Glazebrook's approach may be deplorably unanalytic and incurably anecdotal, a reviewer suggested that in much of Goheen's book, "the city and its people seem to become incidental to the testing of techniques such as factor analysis, surface trend mapping, and regression analysis." Nonetheless Goheen, who uses a sampling of assessment rolls to develop his conclusion that the largely pre-industrial city of 1870 had little in common with the Toronto of 1899, which by that date had become in many of its patterns more appropriately comparable to the city of recent years, undoubtedly is doing the kind of work which is essential if we ever hope to be able to offer generalizations about the historical experience of Ontario's cities based on valid and sufficient empirical data. Not all good recent work is quantitative, however, as Desmond Morton's biography, *Mayor Howland, The Citizens' Candidate*

(T., Hakkert, 1973), a brief interpretation of urban reform politics in late nineteenth century Toronto, demonstrates. Nor must all quantitative work be as difficult for the layman to comprehend as is Goheen, and the Hamilton project headed by Michael Katz and the Peel County project under David Gagan have successfully used routinely generated records such as census material, birth, death, and marriage certificates, land deeds, wills, assessment rolls and city directories to attempt to reconstruct the life patterns of entire nineteenth-century populations. These are team projects investigating social structure and mobility and attempting to develop new analytic techniques for the social historian. Some of the results of their work is in: M. Katz, "Social Structure in Hamilton, Ontario," which appeared in *Nineteenth Century Cities*, edited by Stephen Sternstorm & Richard Sennett (New Haven, Yale Univ. Press, 1969), and the same author's "The People of a Canadian City" (*CHR*, 1972); H. J. Graff, "Literacy and Social Structure in Elgin County, Canada West, 1861" (*Social History*, 1973); and David Gagan & Herbert Mays, "Historical Demography and Canadian Social History: Families and Land in Peel County, Ontario" (*CHR*, 1973). Such work does not lack for criticism from those who feel that it is done with insufficient regard for traditional local history by people who do not understand the regions they are investigating, and doubts have been raised about the validity of the data base and of the techniques being used to manipulate it. While it is premature to attempt any assessment and while mistakes will undoubtedly be made and results may be less satisfactory than some enthusiasts expect, the above projects are directed by scholars who seem scrupulously cautious about the technical side of their work and careful to present their results in jargon-free prose and with a minimum of obscure graphs and charts. Another important essay is Gilbert A. Stelter, "The Origins of A Company Town: Sudbury in the Nineteenth Century" (*Laurentian University Review*, 1971) while Albert Rose, *Governing Metropolitan Toronto, A Social and Political Analysis, 1953-1971* (Los Angeles, University of California Press, 1973), is a brief but enlightening study of a governmental experiment which has attracted international attention.

SOCIAL HISTORY

In this field one may with some justification be ruth-
lessly selective, partly because so much of the work which
has been done falls short of the standards of contemporary
scholarship. As well, the best writing in areas such as religion and labour history has been within a national and not a
regional framework. Thus there has been a good deal written about the churches and their impact on modern Canada,
and while regional perspectives would undeniably be useful,
the student for the most part must turn to national studies.
One effort which focuses largely on Ontario which might be
singled out for mention is William Magney's sensitive study
of the Methodist Church's response to social change, "The
Methodist Church and the National Gospel, 1884-1914" (*The
Bulletin*, 1968, published for the United Church by Ryerson,
1969). Similarly, in labour history there is little work which
adopts a consistently regional perspective, but Doris French,
Faith, Sweat and Politics, (T., M&S, 1962), a brief biography of D. J. O'Donoghue, a figure of importance in the
labour movement in late nineteenth century Ontario, brings
a sense of personality and excitement to a field in which so
many efforts are pompous and dull. Robert H. Babcock's
Gompers in Canada (T., UTP, 1974) is a work of competent
scholarship, concentrating largely on Ontario, which deals
with the impact of continentalism on the labour movement
prior to the First World War. A good deal of work is underway in the field of working class culture and several of the
better studies focus on Ontario. Gregory S. Kealey and
Peter Warrian, eds., *Essays in Canadian Working Class History* (T., M&S, 1976) includes valuable articles by several
of the provinces abler young historians. *Women at Work,
Ontario 1850-1930* (T., Women's Press, 1974), while flawed
as history, is generally imaginative and useful, while Gregory S. Kealey's pamphlet "Hogtown, Working Class Toronto At the Turn of the Century" (New Hogtown Press,
1974) contains a great deal of information. Again with regard to studies of minority cultures the volume is impressive but the quality is not. No attempt can be made here to
assess the existing work, and for guidance there is the Gregorovich bibliography. One attractive effort dealing with
Toronto which uses photographic evidence is Robert Harney

and Harold Troper, *Immigrants, A Portrait of the Urban Experience, 1890-1930* (T., Van Nostrand, 1975).

The Franco-Ontarians, constituting about ten per cent of the population and occupying a special position as representative of one of the two founding cultures have attracted more attention. The more notable studies include Leopold Lamontagne's essay "Ontario: The two Races," in Mason Wade, ed., *Canadian Dualism* (T., UTP, 1960), and T. H. B. Symons, "Ontario's Quiet Revolution: A Study of Change in the Position of the Franco-Ontarian Community", in Robin Burns, ed., *One country or Two?* (M., McGill-Queen's, 1971), a long essay focussing on educational matters but dealing also with federal-provincial and Ontario-Quebec relations which argues that the changes in Ontario in the 1960s in regard to Francophone citizens were so many and so profound as to constitute a revolution. A large proportion of works dealing with Franco-Ontarians describe their struggle for educational rights and these include: Franklin Walker's *Catholic Education and Politics in Ontario*; C. B. Sissons, *Bi-lingual Schools in Canada* (T., Dent, 1917); Marilyn Barber, "The Ontario Bilingual Schools Issue: Sources of Conflict" (*CHR*, 1966); Margaret Prang, "Clerics, Politicians, and the Bilingual Schools Issue in Ontario, 1910-1917" (*CHR*, 1960); Peter Oliver, "The Resolution of the Ontario Bilingual Schools Crisis, 1919-1929" (*JCS*, 1972); and André Lalonde, *Le réglement XVII et ses répercussions sur le Nouvel-Ontario* (Sudbury, la Société historique du Nouvel-Ontario, 1966). Victor Lapalme, "Les Franco-Ontarians et la politique provinciale" (M.A. thesis, University of Ottawa, 1968), is a political analysis, while M. J. Fitzpatrick, "The Role of Bishop Francis Michael Fallon in the Conflict between the French Catholics and the Irish Catholics in the Ontario Bilingual Schools Question, 1910-1920" (M.A. thesis, University of Western Ontario, 1969), is a revealing and able effort. Robert Choquette, *Language And Religion, A History of English-French Conflict in Ontario* (Ottawa, University of Ottawa Press, 1975) deals primarily with Franco-Ontarian and Irish-Catholic relations between 1900 and 1927. Although it contains much important new material, it retains most of the faults of a hastily published doctoral dissertation.

By far the best study of the development of attitudes and programs in the field of social reform and social welfare is Terrence R. Morrison's brilliant "The Child and Urban Social Reform in Late Nineteenth Century Ontario, 1875-1900" (Ph.D. thesis, University of Toronto, 1970). Emphasizing the secular dimension of the social reform movement and also its elitism, Morrison argues that no significant new social philosophy emerged in the late nineteenth century to grapple with the effects of industrialism and that reform leadership was essentially conservative in its motivation and cautious in its prescriptions. The same author's "Reform As Social Tracking, The Case of Industrial Education in Ontario, 1870-1900" (*Journal of Educational Thought*, 1974) is a good interpretive essay, but his article (*OH*, March, 1976) "'Their Proper Sphere', Feminism, The Family, and Child-Centred Social Reform In Ontario, 1875-1900," falls short of his earlier standards. One indispensable study is Richard B. Splane, *Social Welfare In Ontario* (T., UTP, 1965), which is largely institutional in its approach and explains with considerable clarity the origins and extent of the nineteenth century welfare structure. Margaret K. Strong, *Public Welfare Administration in Canada* (Chicago, 1930), and two books by Harry M. Cassidy, *Unemployment and Relief in Ontario, 1929-1932* (T., Dent, 1932) and *Public Health and Welfare Organization in Canada,* (T., Ryerson, 1945), provide an introduction to the later period. Two important theses are Ian Bain, "The Role of J. J. Kelso in the Launching of the Child Welfare Movement in Ontario" (M.S.W. University of Toronto, 1955) and Dean Ramsey, "Development of Child Welfare Legislation in Ontario" (M.S.W. thesis, University of Toronto, 1949). Stephen A. Speisman's "Munificent Parsons and Municipal Parsimony," (*OH*, 1973) is a study of poor relief in Toronto in the second half of the nineteenth century. Michael Piva's "The Workmen's Compensation Movement in Ontario," (*OH*, 1975) places its subject in a broad perspective.

Prohibition, one of the great social movements of the past century, is examined in political terms in Gerald A. Hallowell, *Prohibition in Ontario 1919-1923* (Ottawa, Ontario Historical Society, 1972) and in a broader social perspective by Graeme Decarie, "Something Old, Something

New. . . . Aspects of Prohibitionism in Ontario in the 1890's," an essay in *Oliver Mowat's Ontario.*

In educational history, the prominence of cultural-religious disputes has ensured that separate schools have been as much studied as French-language matters and among the leading efforts are Walker and C. B. Sissons, *Church and State in Canadian Education* (T., Ryerson, 1959). As for general studies, some of the early attempts to write the province's educational history are valuable for their own sake and as a reflection of contemporary attitudes. These include Walter N. Bell, *The Development of the Ontario High School* (T., UTP, 1918), and John McCutcheon, *John Seath and the School System of Ontario* (T., UTP, 1920). Two general studies of Canadian education which include much Ontario material are C. E. Phillips, *The Development of Education in Canada* (T., Gage, 1957), and J. D. Wilson, R. M. Stamp and L. P. Audet, eds., *Canadian Education: A History* (Scarborough, Prentice-Hall, 1970). While there are several fine essays in the latter effort, the "new education history" seems to have had less impact in Canada than one might have expected. R. M. Stamp, one of the new generation, has published a number of essays: "Educational Leadership in Ontario, 1867-1967," in *Profiles of a Province*; "Urbanization and Education in Ontario and Quebec, 1867-1914" (*McGill Journal of Education*, 1968); "Technical Education, the National Policy, and Federal-Provincial Relations in Canadian Education, 1899-1919" (*CHR* 1971); and "Empire Day in Ontario schools: training young imperialists" (*JCS*, 1973). Robin S. Harris, *Quiet Evolution, A Study of the Educational System of Ontario* (T., UTP, 1967), is a brief introductory survey lacking in analytic rigor. Financial and administrative questions are examined in a political context in an able study by D. M. Cameron, *Schools for Ontario: Policy-making, administration and finance in the 1960's* (T., UTP, 1972). In a category by itself is the eight-volume series by W. G. Fleming, *Ontario's Educative Society* (T., UTP, 1971-72). This enormous chronicle of the education explosion which occurred largely when William Davis was minister is uncritical but indispensable, the obvious starting point for anyone interested in the recent history of education in Ontario. Much of the best work in Ontario educational history is being done by scholars associated with the Ontario Institute for Studies in Education who are studying education as a branch of social history and often call upon quantitative methods to assist them in the task. The fall 1972 edition of the *History of Education Quarterly* was a special issue devoted to "Education and Social Change in English-Speaking Canada," which includes several outstanding examples of this approach. OISE has also published a series of guides to educational records available in the Ontario Archives and elsewhere which are of great assistance to the student of educational history. An example from the series is *Items Relating To Education In Private Papers In The Ontario Archives*, prepared by Roy Reynolds (T., OISE, 1973).

For higher education there exist a substantial number of histories of particular institutions. A few examples are: W. S. Wallace, *A History of the University of Toronto 1827-1927* (T., UTP, 1927); J. J. and R. D. Talman, *"Western"—1878-1953* (London, University of Western Ontario, 1953); and C. B. Sissons, *A History of Victoria University* (T., UTP, 1952). Other colleges and universities have also been studied and there is much on Ontario institutions in the "Studies in the History of Higher Education in Canada" series. Charles M. Johnston's *McMaster University, Volume I, The Toronto Years* (T., UTP, 1976) is a careful and informative account which sets the University's development in its social and political context. *Halfway up Parnassus* (T., UTP, 1974) is a welcome if somewhat anodyne memoir of life at the University of Toronto by that institution's former president, Claude Bissell. E. E. Stewart, "The Role of the Provincial Government in the Development of the Universities of Ontario, 1791-1965" (Ph.D. thesis, University of Toronto, 1970) is an indispensable study particularly valuable for the more recent period. While there is room for much more by way of administrative and institutional studies, what the field needs most at the moment is a social approach which would cut across the story of particular institutions to examine such questions as changing public perceptions of the role of higher education, the expanded func-

tion of the universities in an urban and industrial age and
the impact of the local, national and even international environment on the Ontario University.

CONCLUSION

There has been no effort made in this bibliographic
survey to deal with cultural or intellectual history while a
number of other important themes, including journalism,
sports and recreation and the history of science have also
been ignored. Two important constraints have been lack of
space, and a recognition that to some extent these topics are
treated elsewhere in this volume. More important, however,
is the absence of work on the above subjects which is consciously and explicitly regional. That a book is written in
Ontario by an Ontario author and includes subject matter
which in part at least relates to Ontario must necessarily
give that work a certain regional quality, yet some subjects
cannot and others simply have not been effectively dealt
with in the regional context. To the extent that art, architecture and perhaps even theatre and music have been affected
by the Ontario environment and developed characteristics
which could not have been gained elsewhere, an approach
which seeks to define and explain those characteristics is
not only justified but essential. One stimulating attempt to
deal with the province's intellectual and cultural history is
William Westfall's "The Dominion of the Lord, An Introduction to the Cultural History of Protestant Ontario in the
Victorian Period" (*QQ*, 1976). The many recent excellent
coffee-table books on Ontario furniture, gravestones, art and
architecture, barns, the rural countryside and small towns
will one day be of immeasurable assistance to those attempting a cultural synthesis which will come to terms with the
evolution of the Ontario mind. In a study of attitudes and
ideologies such as Carl Berger's brilliant volume *The Sense
of Power*, which is devoted so largely to figures living in or
nurtured by Ontario, a more explicit analysis of the impact
of that particular environment might or might not have
been helpful. It seems likely, however, that such will be the
direction of future studies in these areas.

This, however, is not necessarily desirable and is far
from inevitable. A major problem for the student of Ontario

history will continue to be that of definition. The sheer bulk of the work cited above should not deceive anyone or lead to the conclusion that the past record in Ontario studies is one of impressive achievement. Too much of the work done remains fragmented, incomplete and even antiquarian; too little attains high standards of scholarship and almost none points in the direction of a convincing regional synthesis. The few exceptions, perhaps most notably the Nelles volume, have been pointed out in the above essay, but the absence of successful overviews and general interpretatons of Ontario society must alert us to the difficulties involved. This goes beyond any mere preoccupation with national history and seems by a curious irony to reflect one of the conundrums faced for so long by national historians. If efforts to achieve a national synthesis have been defeated by Canada's stubbornly intractable regional realities, the very diversity, the size and the lack of definition of Ontario society pose similar problems for provincial historians. Perhaps Arthur Lower was right after all in his puckish assertion that there is no such animal as the "Ontarian." Those who believe, however, that regionalism remains as an important approach to the study of this society must hope that they are not doomed to repeat in their work that search for an elusive provincial identity that proved so frustrating and stultifying when pursued on a national level.

French Canada

Ramsay Cook

Historical writing in French Canada has undergone
significant changes in the past two decades, changes which
in many ways reflect and parallel the altered character of
Quebec society since the 1950s. French-speaking historians
have been asking new questions about their past just as
many Quebeckers have been questioning their present and
speculating about their future. Put rather simply, Quebec in
the years since the Second World War has become an increasingly secular and urban French-speaking North American society. No longer does the Church play a major role in
such social institutions as the educational system, nor does
Roman Catholicism define to any great extent the cultural
values of Quebec. Where once the leading historians in
Quebec were either clerics or trained by clerics, today's historians with very few exceptions are secular in both background and education. Where the role of the Church and
the survival of *la nation canadienne-française* once preoccupied French Canadian historians almost exclusively, the new
historians, while not unconscious of the national question,
are more likely to be engaged in examining economic development, demographic patterns, urban growth, ideological
conflict, and working class organization and life.

To understand this development it is important to say
something about Quebec historical writing in general, and
especially about work on the period before Confederation.
Indeed, it is useful to observe that post-Confederation history in Quebec, while receiving much more attention than at
any time in the past, is still not the main field of interest,
controversy and innovation for French-speaking historians.
It is the period between 1760 and 1850 that has been subject

to the most thorough revision by recent writing and that, in turn, increasingly influences the manner in which the post-Confederation period is approached.

The impact and meaning of the British Conquest has long been the central historical question for Quebeckers. (See my essay entitled "Conquêtisme" in *The Maple Leaf Forever* (T., Mac., 1971).) But until the 1950's, the economic impact of that momentous event had rarely been measured. Since the mid fifties, however, the works of Michel Brunet and Fernand Ouellet have made economics the major concern in discussions of the Conquest.

Out of the controversy over the economic implications of the Conquest came the most important historical work published in Quebec since François-Xavier Garneau launched French Canadians on an unending quest for the true meaning of their past with his *Histoire du Canada* in 1845. Fernand Ouellet's brilliant and provocative *Histoire économique et sociale du Québec, 1760-1850* (M., Fides, 1966), formulated the questions which have since dominated French-Canadian historical writing: the role of French Canadians in the Quebec economy and their attitude to economic matters, sources of capital investment, markets, the viability of the seigneurial system and the adaptation of agricultural techniques, the growth of urban centres and the relationship between economics, politics, religion, and nationalism. Ouellet's work examined in detail, for the first time, the mass of statistical evidence available to the historian with the skill and patience to use it. In a more recent work, *Le Bas Canada 1791-1840. Changements structuraux et crise* (O., Editions de l'université d'Ottawa, 1976, to be translated and published shortly by M&S), Ouellet has added a detailed political and religious dimension to his earlier study, thus providing a fresh understanding of the developments leading up to the Rebellion of 1837 and its aftermath.

Ouellet's interpretation of these tempestuous years has not gone unchallenged. Anyone interested in this fundamental controversy will find the essential issues clearly set out in T. J. A. LeGoff's article "Agricultural Crisis in Lower Canada, 1802-12: A Review of a Controversy" (*CHR*, 1974). Whatever the outcome, the socio-economic approach which Ouellet first developed is now as dominant in the interpretation of Quebec's past as the clerico-nationalist one once was. Such works as Louise Dechêne's *Habitants et Marchands de Montréal aux XVIIe Siècle*, (M., Plon, 1974), at one end of the time scale, and Jacques Rouillard's *Les Travailleurs du Coton au Québec, 1900-15* (M., Les Presses de l'université du Québec, 1974), at the other, both reflect this orientation. Moreover, most Quebec historians have descended from the nationalist pulpits occupied so frequently by their predecessors, leaving nationalist advocacy to such polemicists and simplifiers as Léandre Bérgeron whose popular *Petit Manuel d'histore du Québec* (M., Editions Québécoises, 1969), displayed an almost total innocence of the new trends in French-Canadian historical writing.

HISTORIOGRAPHY, BIBLIOGRAPHY, JOURNALS AND RESEARCH GUIDES

Historiographical essays critically assessing historical writing in Quebec are fairly numerous. The most recent survey is contained in *Recherches Sociographiques*, (1974), an issue entirely devoted to historiographical essays. Of special interest for Post-Confederation historians are Joseph Levitt's careful analysis of Robert Rumilly, the most prolific Quebec historian, and Pierre Savard's judicious "Un quart de siècle d'historiographie québécoise, 1947-1972." Fernand Ouellet's "La Recherche historique au Canada-français," in Louis Baudouin, ed., *La Recherche au Canada Français* (M., Les Presses de l'université de Montréal, 1968) is a clear expression of that seminal historian's viewpoint. My own essays on the subject, "The Historian and Nationalism," in *Canada and the French Canadian Question*, (T., Mac. 1966), and "*La Survivance* French Canadian Style," in *The Maple Leaf Forever* are chiefly concerned with an analysis of nationalism in historical writing. An informed outsider's judgments are found in Robert Mandrou, "L'Historiographie canadienne-française: Bilan et Pérspective" (*CHR*, 1970). Very few of these essays deal exclusively with the post-Confederation period, but all contribute something towards an understanding of the recent evolution of French Canadian attitudes and approaches to the past.

The standard bibliographical aids to the history of French Canada are now slightly outdated. The most useful for history students is René Durocher and Paul-André Linteau, *Histoire du Québec: Bibliographie sélective, 1877-1970* (M., Boréal Express, 1970). *Québec 1940-1969, Bibliographie* (M., Les Presses de l'université de Montréal, 1971), compiled by Robert Boily, is especially rich in social science references. Claude Thibault's *Bibliographia Canadiana* (T., Longmans, 1973), is quite complete but must be used with discrimination and patience. Jacques Cotnam's *Contemporary Quebec: An Analytical Bibliography* (T., M&S, 1973) is useful for what it covers, while the *Guide d'Histoire Du Canada* (Québec, Les Presses de l'Université Laval, 1968), edited by André Beaulieu, Jean Hamelin and Benoît Bernier contains not only a fairly exhaustive list of books and articles, but is introduced by a perceptive survey of Canadian historical writing contributed by Serge Gagnon. *Livres et Auteurs Québécois*, published annually, prints essays and book reviews concerned with history and is indispensible for anyone who wishes to keep abreast of recent writing.

There are several scholarly journals which regularly publish articles, book reviews and bibliographies on French-Canadian topics. The most important of these is *La Revue d'Histoire de l'Amérique française*, founded in 1947 by chanoine Lionel Groulx as an outlet for his clerico-nationalist views. It has developed into a first-class professional journal, published four times a year. Its annual bibliographies are carefully compiled and highly inclusive. *Recherches sociographiques*, published at Laval University, is an interdisciplinary journal providing historians with an opportunity to publish their work alongside that of other social scientists. In Quebec, in contrast to the rest of Canada, sociology and political economy have maintained, to a substantial degree, a firm historical grounding. Consequently the work of sociologists like Fernand Dumont, Jean-Charles Falardeau and Marcel Rioux, economists like Albert Faucher and Gilles Paquet, and political scientists like Léon Dion, André-J. Belanger and Vincent Lemieux, which appears in *Recherches sociographiques* and elsewhere, is of great value to historians. *Histoire Sociale/Social History*, published twice yearly at the University of Ottawa, is perhaps the most interesting historical journal currently published in Canada, though it has not carried much material on post-1967 Quebec. *The Canadian Historical Review*, published quarterly by the University of Toronto Press, is open to historians of both official languages but recently has had very few articles or book reviews in French. The *Annual Report of the Canadian Historical Association*, recently rechristened *Historical Papers*, also contains many important articles on French Canadian history.

There are several valuable publications that research students will find it beneficial to consult. *The Union List of Manuscripts* (Ottawa, QP, 1975), as its title suggests, attempts to include all manuscript collections in public depositories. *L'Etat général des archives publiques et privées du Québec* (Québec, Ministère des affaires culturelles, 1968), should also be consulted. *Répertoire des Publications gouvernementales du Québec, 1867-1964* (Québec, Imprimateur de la Reine, 1968), compiled by André Beaulieu, Jean-Charles Bonenfant, and Jean Hamelin, and the supplements for 1965-68, provide careful guidance to the mass of published government documents. André Beaulieu and Jean Hamelin's *Les Journaux de Québec*, (Québec, Les Presses de l'Université Laval, 1965), is an excellent analytical guide to Quebec newspapers, though it is occasionally incomplete in its details. *Annuaire de Québec/Québec Yearbook*, published regularly since 1914, is a rich store of information about most facets of Quebec life, while the *Canadian Annual Review*, particularly in the years since John T. Saywell revived it in 1961, regularly contains authoritative articles on Quebec politics, economics and constitutional developments.

GENERAL STUDIES

Mason Wade, *The French Canadians* (Revised edition, 2 vols., T., Mac., 1968), remains the only comprehensive study in English despite the fact that over twenty years have passed since the book's first appearance. It is a simple exercise to point out its deficiencies, particularly since many new specialized studies have been published in the intervening years. Nevertheless it remains a useful general account. Wade's study relies heavily on Robert Rumilly's forty-one volume *Histoire de la Province de Québec*, (M., various publishers, 1940-1969). Students of Quebec history will find that the chronologically organized volumes of this work are very useful, especially on political matters. It must be used with some care, however, not merely because of the author's strongly conservative-nationalist bias, but also because the sources of Rumilly's information are frequently not revealed. That reservation is counter-balanced, to some extent, by the recognition that Rumilly has had access to documents which, at least so far, have not been available to other researchers. Rumilly's numerous biographies, notably those of Mgr. Laflèche, Honoré Mercier, Henri Bourassa, and Maurice Duplessis, for the most part simply rework the material contained in the *Histoire* and are subject to the same reservations.

There are several textbooks which contain valuable accounts of French Canadian history. In English, *Canada: Unity in Diversity* (T., Holt, Rinehart and Winston, 1967), by Jean Hamelin, Fernand Ouellet and Paul Cornell, contains several excellent chapters on Quebec. Different in tone and content is Jean-Claude Robert's *Du Canada français au Québec libre: Histoire d'un mouvement indépendentiste* (M., Flammarion, 1975), whose subtitle reveals its central interpretative theme. It places heavy emphasis on recent history. *Histoire des Canadas*, (M., HMH, 1975), by Rosario Bilodeau, Robert Comeau, André Gosselin and Denise Julien organizes the history of Canada within the framework of three colonialisms: French, British and American. For a sound, thoroughly objective general account Jean Hamelin, *et al., Histoire du Québec* (Ste. Hyacinthe, Edisom, 1976) is the best of the textbooks.

CONFEDERATION, THE CONSTITUTION AND MINORITY RIGHTS

Despite the interest of French Canadians in the real and imagined injustices of Confederation, not much has been written on this topic by their historians. Polemic rather than scholarship characterizes much that has been published. That is certainly the case with Lionel Groulx's *La Confédération canadienne* (M., *Le Devoir*, 1918), though that is not surprising since it was written in the midst of the conscription crisis of the First World War. The same author's account of Francophone minority schools, *L'Enseignement française au Canada* (2 vols., M., Granger Frères, 1933), is more dispassionate, though now rather outdated. Jean-Charles Bonenfant's *The French Canadians and the Birth of Confederation*, (Ottawa, Canadian Historical Association Booklet No. 21, 1966) is a balanced summary account, and there is full discussion of Confederation in Andrée Desilets, *Hector Langevin* (Québec, Les Presses de l'Université Laval, 1969). Peter Waite's *The Life and Times of Confederation* (T., UTP, 1962), and W. L. Morton's *The Critical Years* (T. M&S, 1964), include informative chapters. The articles by G. F. G. Stanley and Walter Ullmann, the first on the so-called compact theory of Confederation, and the second on the role of the Quebec bishops in Confederation, found in Ramsay Cook, ed., *Confederation* (T., UTP, 1967), are important.

Père Richard Arès has devoted a great deal of energy to analysing and expounding French Canadian views of Confederation and its development. Two of his books, *Dossier sur le Pacte Fédératif de 1867* (M., Bellarmin, 1967), and *Nos Grandes Options Politique et Constitutionnelles* (M.; Bellarmin, 1972), contain valuable summaries of a very extensive literature. Ramsay Cook's *Provincial Autonomy, Minority Rights and the Compact Theory 1867-1921* (Ottawa, Information Canada, 1969) covers somewhat the same ground, though some of its interpretations stand in need of revision in the light of the still unpublished work of Arthur Silver on Quebec and the Francophone minorities, and by Christopher Armstrong on Ontario's approach to Canadian federalism. The Carleton Library edition of *The Tremblay Report* (T., M&S, 1973), edited by David Kwavnick, is a clear expression of traditional French Canadian nationalism and its constitutional implications. Claude Morin's *Quebec versus Ottawa* (T., UTP, 1976) is a very personal assessment of negotiations between Quebec and Ottawa during the 1960's, while D. V. Smiley's *Canada in Question* (Revised edition, T., McGraw-Hill, 1976) is a thorough account of recent developments in Canadian federalism, including a clear account of Quebec's position.

The history of the rights of the French-speaking minorities outside of Quebec has received a good deal of recent discussion. On the origins of the question in Manitoba, W. L. Morton's *Manitoba: A History* (T., UTP, 1957), and his introduction to *Alexander Begg's Red River Journal* (T.,

Champlain Society, 1956), remain the standard accounts. The documents Morton edited under the title *Manitoba; The Birth of a Province* (Altona, Manitoba, The Manitoba Records Society, 1970) should also be consulted. Arthur Silver's essay, "French Quebec and the Métis Question, 1869-1885," in Carl Berger and Ramsay Cook, eds., *The West and the Nation* (T., M&S, 1976), and the biographies of Louis Riel by G. F. G. Stanley and Hartwell Bowsfield provide important additional material. *The Diaries of Louis Riel*, (Edmonton, Hurtig, 1976), edited by Thomas Flanagan, and the same scholar's edition of *The Prophetic Writings of Louis Riel*, (Ottawa, The National Museum of Man, 1976), are both of great interest.

The conflict over minority school rights is covered in a series of articles in R. C. Brown, ed., *Minority Schools and Politics* (T., UTP, 1969), to which should be added Peter Oliver's excellent "Regulation 17: the Resolution of the Ontario Bilingual Schools Crisis, 1916-1929," in his *Public and Private Persons* (T., Clarke Irwin, 1975). This same controversy is examined in detail in Robert Choquette's *Language and Religion: The History of English-French Conflict in Ontario*, (Ottawa, University of Ottawa, 1975). Paul Crunican's *Priests and Politicians: Manitoba Schools and the Election of 1896* (T., UTP, 1974), M. R. Lupul's *The Roman Catholic Church and the Northwest School Question* (T., UTP, 1974), and George Rawlyk's *Acadian Education in Nova Scotia* (Ottawa, Information Canada, 1970), are all essential to a thorough understanding of the history of minority school problems and the politics of French-English relations. While somewhat dated now, *La Dualité Canadienne/Canadian Duality* (Québec and Toronto, Les Presses de l'Université Laval and UTP, 1960), edited by J. C. Falardeau and Mason Wade, contains several excellent essays on French-English relations in education, politics, economics and constitutional matters. Professor Falardeau's own contribution is especially perceptive.

POLITICS AND INSTITUTIONS

Much work remains to be done in the historical study of Quebec political parties. At present the most satisfactory way to approach the topic is through the biographies of leading political figures. Cartier, Laurier, Bourassa, St. Laurent, Duplessis and Trudeau have all been studied and their biographies are cited in the chapter on National Politics. Similarly the memoirs of Raoul Dandurand, Chubby Power, Georges-Emile Lapalme, Pierre Sevigny and Antonio Barrette are valuable, if read critically. Blair Neatby's *Laurier and the Liberal Party in Quebec: A Study in Political Management* (T., M&S, 1973) is a carefully documented examination of the federal Liberals during a crucial period. Marc LaTerreur's *Les Tribulations des conservateurs au Québec de Bennett à Diefenbaker* (Québec, Les Presses de l'Université Laval, 1973) helps to explain why Quebec has been so strongly Liberal during most of the twentieth century. H. F. Quinn's *The Union Nationale* (T., UTP, 1963), though based only on published sources, and therefore somewhat limited, is the only available published study of the politics of the period between 1935 and 1960, except for Rumilly. Jean-Louis Roy's *La Marche des Québécois* (M., Lémeac, 1976) provides a wealth of economic, social and institutional background to the *Union nationale* period, and argues that the reactionary character of the Duplessis administration has been exaggerated. The most thoroughly studied party in Quebec is the one of perhaps the least significance, Social Credit. That movement has been analysed in two exceptionally able works: Maurice Pinard, *The Rise of a Third Party* (T., Prentice-Hall, 1971), and Michael B. Stein, *The Dynamics of Right Wing Protest: A Political Analysis of Social Credit in Quebec* (T., UTP, 1973). The latter book contains an informative historical section on the origins of *créditisme*. A recent volume of essays entitled *Partis politiques au Québec* (M., HMH, 1976), edited by Réjean Pelletier, presents some new research on Quebec political parties, including an analysis of some aspects of the *Parti Québécois*. For background to that party André D'Allemagne's partisan, but informative, *Le R.I.N. de 1960 à 1963* (M., Editions l'étincelle, 1974) is useful. Vera Murray, *Le Parti Québécois* (M., HMH, 1976), is the first of what will doubtless be a spate of books on the party. Jean Provencher's *René Lévesque: Portrait d'un Québécois* (M., La Presse, 1973) is superior to Peter Desbarats' *René: A Canadian in Search of a Country* (T., M&S, 1976), though both books contribute to an understanding of the *Parti Québécois* leader.

Electoral studies are increasingly numerous but are mainly concerned with recent elections. Two articles provide general surveys: Jean Hamelin, Jacques Letarte and Marcel Hamelin, "Les élections provinciales dans le Québec" (*Cahiers de Géographie de Québec*, 1959-60) and Vincent Lemieux, "Québec: Heaven is Blue and Hell is Red," in Martin Robin, *Canadian Provincial Politics* (Scarborough, Prentice-Hall, 1972). Important electoral studies include Marcel Caya, "Aperçu sur les élections provinciales du Québec 1867 à 1886" (*RHAF*, 1975) and Ronald Rudin, "Regional Complexity and Political Behavior in a Quebec County, 1867-1886" (*Histoire Sociale/Social History*, 1976). More recent elections are examined in Vincent Lemieux, *et al.*, *Quatre Elections Provinciales au Québec, 1956 Duplessis—1960 Lesage—1962 Lesage—1966 Johnson* (Québec, Les Presses de l'Université Laval, 1969). For the very important 1970 election, which saw the collapse of the *Union nationale* and the emergence of the *Parti Québécois*, there is a thorough analysis and interpretation in Vincent Lemieux, Marcel Gilbert and André Blais, *Une Election de réalignement* (M., Editions du Jour, 1970). For details of election returns see Vincent Lemieux, *Le Quotient politique vrai: Le Vote provincial et fédéral au Quebec* (Québec, Les Presses de l'Université Laval, 1969), and for party platforms consult Jean-Louis Roy, *Les programmes électoraux du Québec* (2 vols., M., Lémeac, 1970). André Bernard's collection of essays entitled *Québec: élections 1976* (M., HMH, 1976), is a preliminary contribution to an understanding of the critical election of November 15, 1976.

General studies of Canadian government and federalism are valuable for an understanding of the institutional environment of Quebec public life. For more specific information on Quebec, Louis Sabourin, ed., *Le Système politique de Canada: Institutions fédérales et québécoise* (Ottawa, Editions de l'université d'Ottawa, 1968), contains a wide selection of informative essays. André Bernard's *Réflexions sur la politique au Québec* (M., Editions de Sainte Marie, 1968), and Edmon Orban's *Le Conseil Législatif de Québec, 1867-1967*, (M., Bellarmin, 1967) are informative about special features of Quebec's public institutions. F. W. Gibson, ed., *Cabinet Formation and Bicultural Relations: Seven Case Studies*, (Ottawa, Information Canada, 1970),

R. Desrosier's *Le personnel politique québécois* (M., Boréal Express, 1972) contains two very useful articles, Jean Hamelin and Louis Baudouin, "Les cabinets provinciaux, 1867-1967," and Robert Boily, "Les hommes politiques du Québec." An extremely important work, which attempts to integrate institutions, politics, parties and ideology, is Marcel Hamelin's *Les Premieres Années du Parlementarisme Québécoise, 1867-1878* (Québec, Les Presses de l'Université Laval, 1974). John T. Saywell's *The Office of Lieutenant-Governor* (T., UTP, 1957), contains important material on this office in Quebec. There are several contributions to R. M. Burns, ed., *One Country or Two?*, (M., McGill-Queen's, 1971), that detail the integration of the institutions of Quebec and the rest of Canada, and discuss some of the difficulties that might result from an effort to separate them. Edmond Orban, ed., *La Modernisation Politique du Québec* (M., Boréal Express, 1976) discusses some current institutional problems including an essay by Claude Morin on what he sees as the confining effect that Canadian federalism has had on Quebec's "modernization."

ECONOMICS

Albert Faucher is the father of economic history in Quebec. His studies of the nineteenth century have examined broad questions of technological development, capital investments, the role of the French-Canadian entrepreneur, and the relationship of the Quebec economy to the rest of Canada and to the United States. His two most important books are *Histoire économique et Unité canadienne* (M., Fides, 1970), and *Québec en Amérique au XIXᵉ Siècle* (M., Fides, 1973). Another study of very high quality, a successor to the work of Fernand Ouellet referred to earlier, is Jean Hamelin and Yves Roby, *Histoire économique du Québec, 1851-96* (M., Fides, 1971). W. F. Ryan's *The Clergy and Economic Growth, 1896-1914* (Québec, Les Presses de l'Université Laval, 1966), not only contains some fine economic history but also attempts to come to grips with one of the central controversies of Quebec economic studies: did the church aid or retard industrialization? Ryan's answer, which is not based on an exhaustive study of all parts of Quebec, is affirmative for the areas that interested him,

Three Rivers, and the Chicoutimi-Lac St. Jean region. A solid, if somewhat technical and heavily statistical, account of Quebec economic history is André Raynauld, *et al.*, *Croissance et Structures économiques de la Province de Québec* (Québec, Ministère de l'industrie et commerce, 1961). Maurice Saint-Germain's *Une Economie à libérer—Le Québec analysé dans les structures économique* (M., Boréal Express, 1973) is a provocative socio-economic analysis of Quebec development. Gilles Lebel, *Horizon 1980* (Gouvernement du Québec, Ministère de l'industrie et du commerce, 1970), offers a valuable study of the evolution of the Quebec economy between 1946 and 1968.

There is still much work to be done in writing the history of Quebec's resources and industrial development. John Dales' *Hydroelectricity and Industrial Development: Quebec 1898-1940* (Cambridge, Harvard University Press, 1957) is a first-class account of one major industry. Paul Sauriol, *The Nationalization of Electric Power* (M., Harvest House, 1962), provides much useful information as background to the 1963 decision of the Lesage government to bring the last remaining private power companies under Quebec Hydro. Another important Quebec resource that has been studied in some historical detail is asbestos. Something of its history may be found in Pierre-E. Trudeau, ed., *The Asbestos Strike* (T., Lorimer, 1974). Two older works which may still be read with profit are A. J. de Bray, *L'Essor Industriel et Commercial du Peuple Canadien* (M., Beauchemin, n.d.) and Errol Bouchette, *L'Indépendance Economique du Canada-français* (M., Wilson and Lafleur, 1913). de Bray's book is useful mainly for statistical information, while Bouchette's analyses the reasons for the apparent lack of French-Canadian entrepreneurship in Quebec's industrial development. Some of the essays in Robert Comeau, ed., *Economie Québécoise* (M., Les Presses de l'université de Québec, 1969), deal with this latter topic, though many other subjects are examined, too. All of the essays in René Durocher and Paul André Linteau, *Le "Retard" économique et l'infériorité économique des Canadiens français* (M., Boréal Express, 1971), are devoted to a discussion of the French Canadian's particular economic problems in an industrial economy.

Though the importance of agriculture in the Quebec economy has long been recognized, it has not been studied in detail. The rural economy is considered in a general way by Faucher, and Hamelin and Roby. Useful background may be found in chapter three of R. Cole Harris and John Warkentin, *Canada Before Confederation* (T., OUP, 1974), but for the later period the main source remains Charles Lemelin's unpublished "Agricultural Development and Industrialization in Quebec," (Ph.D. Dissertation, Harvard University, 1951). One section of the thesis is published under the title "The State of Agriculture," in Jean-Charles Falardeau, *Essays on Contemporary Quebec* (Québec, Les Presses de l'Université Laval, 1953). Though by no means an exclusively rural institution, the credit union movement had an impact on both farm and urban life and is discussed with care in Yves Roby, *Alphonse Desjardins et les Caisses populaire, 1854-1920* (M., Fides, 1964). The farmers' own organization, the Union Catholique des Cultivateurs, is outlined in Firmin Létourneau's *l'U.C.C.* (M., l'Action nationale, 1949.)

SOCIETY, RELIGION AND EDUCATION

The social history of modern Quebec, like that of most of Canada, is still in its infancy. Some of the essays in Marcel Rioux and Yves Martin, *French Canadian Society* (T., M&S, 1964), especially those by Jean-Charles Falardeau on the church, Jacques Brazeau on the problems of French Canadians in the public service, Norman Taylor on French-Canadian entrepreneurs, and Hubert Guindon's provocative study of Quebec's social evolution, are useful for historians. There is also some social history in almost every work of political and economic history and the study of labour also entails a look at the larger society. There is much about society in Jean-Louis Roy's book on the Duplessis years, and a collection like Hubert Charbonneau's *La Population du Québec; Etudes retrospectives* (M., Boréal Express, 1973), contains much valuable information about population growth and movement. Though not strictly speaking works of history, and somewhat controversial in their conceptions, two sociological works are very important in understanding Quebec's transformation from a rural to an urban society. These are Horace Miner, *St. Denis: A French Canadian Par-*

ish (Chicago, University of Chicago Press, 1963), and E. C. Hughes, *French Canada in Transition* (Chicago, University of Chicago Press, 1943).

Some Quebec social institutions have been studied. The history of the Roman Catholic Church is briefly surveyed in Nive Voisin, André Beaulieu and Jean Hamelin, *Histoire de l'Eglise Catholique au Canada* (M., Fides, 1971) and more extensively in Herman Plante's *L'Eglise Catholique au Canada* (Trois Rivières, éditions du Bien Publique, 1970), though this book concludes in 1886. Though there are many biographies of bishops and other churchmen most of them are very pious. One of the more interesting biographies is Rolland Litalien's study of Mgr. Moreau of Ste. Hyacinthe, entitled *Le prêtre québécois à la fin du XIXᵉ siècle* (M., Fides, 1970).

There are some special studies of the role of the church in society which are important. William Ryan's study of the church and economic development has already been noted. Jean Hulliger, in *L'Enseignement Social des Evêques Canadiens de 1891 à 1950* (M., Fides 1958), sets out, somewhat uncritically, the Bishops' attempts to apply the teachings of the church to industrial society. Trudeau's *Asbestos Strike*, already mentioned, contains some interesting material on this theme, especially in the contributions of abbé Gérard Dion and Fernand Dumont. P. Hurtubise *et al.* present a series of extremely interesting studies of the role of the layman in the Quebec church in *Le Laïc dans l'Eglise canadienne-française de 1830 à nos Jours* (M., Fides, 1972). The essays by Pierre Savard and René Durocher are particularly rewarding. There is only one published study, based on modern research, of that important topic, the relations of church and state. Antonin Dupont's *Les Relations entre l'Eglise et l'Etat Sous L.-A Taschereau* (M., Guerin, 1973) is strongly critical of Taschereau, and might be read in company with B. L. Vigod, "Qu'on ne craigne pas l'encombrement des compétences: Le gouvernement Taschereau et l'éducation 1920-1929" (*RHAF*, 1974) which is more sympathetic to the Liberal premier. On the place of the church in contemporary Quebec the six volume *Report* of the Commission d'Etude sur les Laïcs et l'Eglise (M., Fides, 1972-74) contains a wealth of material. A thorough survey of recent writing on the history of the church in Quebec is found in Nive Voisine's "La production des vingt dernières années en histoire de l'Eglise du Québec," in *Recherches sociographiques* (1974).

Historically one of the most important responsibilities of the Church lay in the field of education. This subject is surveyed in Louis-Phillippe Audet, *Histoire de l'Enseignement au Québec* (2 vols., M., Holt, Rinehart and Winston, 1971), and in the same author's contributions to J. D. Wilson, R. H. Stamp and L.-P. Audet, *Canadian Education: A History* (Scarborough, Prentice-Hall, 1970). There are some helpful essays in Marcel Lajeunesse, *L'Education au Québec 19ᵉ et 20ᵉ Siècles* (M., Boréal Express, 1971). Contemporary educational problems are best approached through the various volumes of the *Royal Commission on Education*, or Parent Commission, (Québec, Queen's Printer, 1964-66). The establishment of a Ministry of Education was the first result of the Parent Commission, and the controversy surrounding that action is dealt with in Léon Dion, *Le bill 60 et la société québecoise* (M., HMH, 1967).

THE WORKING CLASSES

Labour history is a relatively new field in French Canadian history, and one that is growing in quality and quantity. General histories of Canadian labour, such as those by Logan and Lipton, include some material on the union movement in Quebec. *Le Travailleur québécois et le syndicalisme* (M., Les Presses de l'université de Québec, 1971), by Richard Desrosiers and Denis Héroux, adds much additional detail. Trudeau's *The Asbestos Strike*, and Jean-Paul Lefebvre, ed., *En Grève* (M., Editions de l'Homme, 1963), together cover six major strikes since 1937. Jean Hamelin, ed., *Les Travailleurs Québécois, 1851-1896* (M., Les Presses de l'université du Québec, 1973), contains several excellent essays in labour history, some of which go beyond trade union history to examine the conditions of working class life. Terry Copp's fine study, *The Anatomy of Poverty* (T., M&S, 1974) examines Montreal working-class life and the government policies that were supposed to better that life. His conclusion is that the policies had little effect. Jean de Bonville's *Jean-Baptiste Gagnepetit: Les Travailleurs Montréalais à la fin du*

XIXe Siècle (M., l'Aurore, 1975), though not as thorough as Copp, also merits attention. The essays in Fernand Harvey, ed., *Aspects Historiques du Mouvement ouvrier au Québec* (M., Boréal Express, 1973), are sometimes rather overloaded with sociology but some, notably Harvey's own study of the Knights of Labor in Quebec, are of good quality. L. M. Tremblay's *Le Syndicalisme québécois: Idéologie de la CSN et de la FTQ, 1940-1970* (M., Les Presses de l'université de Montréal, 1972) is useful provided that the reader realizes that there is much more to unions than ideology. Jacques Rouillard's *Les Travailleurs de Coton au Québec, 1900-1915* (M., Les Presses de l'université du Québec, 1974), places the workers' problems firmly in the economic context of the textile industry, giving the work a balance that is sometimes missing in working class history.

One of the main leaders of Quebec trade unionism in this century, Alfred Charpentier, has left a fascinating autobiography, *Cinquante Ans d'Action Ouvrière: Les Mémoires d'Alfred Charpentier* (Québec, Les Presses de l'Université Laval, 1974), though his earlier book, *Ma Conversion au Syndicalisme Catholique* (M., Fides, 1946), remains an extremely revealing document. Finally on workers and politics there is a collection of documents edited by Stanley Ryerson, *et al.*, *L'Action Politique des Ouvrières Québécois (fin de XIXe siècle à 1919)* (M., Les Presses de l'université du Québec, 1976). These documents should be read in conjunction with Jacques Rouillard's "L'action politique ouvrière, 1899-1915," in Fernand Dumont *et al.*, *Idéologies au Canada français* (Québec, Les Presses de l'Université Laval, 1974).

WOMEN

Since Quebec was slower than most parts of Canada to grant women the right to vote and to modify laws which discriminated against women, interest in women's history has only been stirred recently. Catherine Cleverdon's *The Woman Suffrage Movement in Canada*, (T., UTP, 1974), covers the subject adequately in a chapter entitled "The First Shall be Last." Micheline D. Johnson covers the ground again in "History of the Status of Women in the Province of Quebec," in *Studies of the Royal Commission on the Status of Women* (Ottawa, Information Canada, 1971).

A prominent leader of the Quebec feminist movement, Thèrese Casgrain, has told her story with verve in *A Woman in a Man's World*, (T., M&S, 1974). Another autobiography which is essential to an understanding of woman's place in Quebec is Claire Martin's *In An Iron Glove*, (T., Ryerson, 1968). Also of interest is Jennifer Stoddard, "The Woman Suffrage Bill in Quebec," in Marylee Stephenson, ed., *Women in Canada*, (Toronto, 1973).

The traditional view of women in Quebec is analysed by Susan Mann Trofimenkoff, "Henri Bourassa and the Woman Question," (*JCS*, 1975), and in Laure Conan, *Si les Canadiennes le Voulaient* (M., Lémeac, 1974). The views of Mgr. Paquet, Henri Bourassa, Olivar Asselin, Joséphine Dandurand and Marie Gérin-Lajoie are represented in Ramsay Cook and Wendy Mitchison, *The Proper Sphere* (T., OUP, 1976).

The history of women must be seen as part of social history. Some work on Quebec women has begun to move in this direction. D. Suzanne Cross, "The Neglected Majority: The Changing Role of Women in 19th Century Montreal" (*Histoire Sociale/Social History*, 1973), and Marie Lavigne, Yoland Pinard and Jennifer Stoddard, "La Fédération nationale Saint-Jean-Baptiste et les révindications féministe au début du XXe Siècle" (*RHAF*, 1975) are in this category. Somewhat polemical, but still worth reading, is Mona-Josée Gagnon, *Les Femmes vues par Le Québec des Hommes* (M., Editions du Jour, 1974). What is needed most in Quebec social history and women's history is work on the history of the family.

IDEAS AND IDEOLOGY

In recent years historians of modern Quebec have written a great deal about ideas and ideology. Two collections of a rather uneven quality, relying primarily on newspapers and periodicals for ideas about nationalism, religion, politics and society, are Fernand Dumont *et al.*, *Idéologies au Canada français 1850-1900* (Quebec, Les Presses de l' Université Laval, 1971), and Fernand Dumont *et al.*, *Idéologies au Canada français, 1900-1929* (Québec, Les Presses de l'Université Laval, 1974). Two other volumes in the same series cover more specialized but important problems. André-J.

Bélanger's *L'Apolitisme des idéologies québécoise: La grand tournant, 1934-36*, (Québec, Les Presses de l'Université Laval, 1975), is an impressive effort to explain the persistent hostility to politics found in Quebec ideology, especially nationalist ideology. Geneviève Laloux-Jain's *Manuels d'Histoire du Canada au Québec et en Ontario de 1867 à 1914* (Québec, Les Presses de l'Université Laval, 1974), analyses the way in which varying views of nationalism have shaped historical writing. The latter topic, dealing with more recent textbooks, is dealt with in Marcel Trudel and Geneviève Jain, *Canadian History Textbooks: A Comparative Study* (Ottawa, Information Canada, 1969).

The predominant ideology in Quebec has been nationalism. For a selection of nationalist views see Ramsay Cook, ed., *French Canadian Nationalism: An Anthology* (T., Mac., 1970). Pierre-E. Trudeau's opening chapter in *The Asbestos Strike* remains a brilliant, if polemical, essay as does Michel Brunet's, "Les Trois Dominantes dans la Pensée Canadienne-française: l'agriculturisme, l'anti-étatisme et le messianisme," in his *La Présence anglaise et les canadiens* (M., Beauchemin, 1958). Marcel Rioux, "The Development of Ideologies in Quebec," in G. L. Gold and M. A. Tremblay, eds., *Communities and Culture in French Canada* (M., Holt, Rinehart and Winston, 1973), offers an overview from a nationalist viewpoint. A Marxian approach to ideology in Quebec is presented by Gilles Bourque and Nicole Laurin-Frenette, "La Structure nationale québécoise," in *Socialisme québécoise 1971*, and in a rather unsatisfactory abridged version in Gary Teeple, ed., *Capitalism and the National Question in Canada* (T., UTP, 1972).

Any student of modern Quebec nationalism would need to be familiar with the ideas of Henri Bourassa, chanoine Lionel Groulx and André Laurendeau, who spent their lives writing and thinking about the nature of French Canada and its place in North America. While voluminous and sometimes pretentious, Lionel Groulx's *Mes Mémoirs* (4 vols., M., Fides, 1970-74) present a quite extraordinary running commentary on Quebec nationalism and nationalists in this century. An excellent selection of this ideologue's writings has been brought together and translated by Susan Mann Trofimenkoff in *Abbé Groulx: Variations on a Nationalist*

Theme (T., Copp Clark, 1974). The same author's *Action française: French Canadian Nationalism in the Twenties* (T., UTP, 1975) is a thorough study of the organization which was the vehicle for Groulx's views. Some of Bourassa's writings in translation are found in Joseph Levitt, ed., *Henri Bourassa on Imperialism and Biculturalism* (T., Copp Clark, 1970). Supplementary reading should include Levitt's excellent *Henri Bourassa and the Golden Calf* (Ottawa, University of Ottawa Press, 1969), which goes beyond the usual discussions of Bourassa's nationalism and takes stock of his social ideas. There is as yet no full scale study of Laurendeau, the pupil of both Bourassa and Groulx who became editor of *Le Devoir* and Co-Chairman of the Royal Commission on Bilingualism and Biculturalism. There is a short study of his career in Ramsay Cook, *Canada and the French Canadian Question* (T., Mac., 1966), and two very good selections of his writings which complement one another. Phillip Stratford's *André Laurendeau: Witness for Quebec* (T., Mac., 1974), includes the whole of Laurendeau's important *The Conscription Crisis of 1942*, while Ramsay Cook and Michael Behiels, eds., *The Essential Laurendeau* (T., Copp Clark, 1976), provides documents illustrating Laurendeau's intellectual evolution. Finally, attention should be drawn to the nineteenth-century nationalist writer, Jules-Paul Tardivel whose ideas can be studied in his novel translated as *For My Country* (T., UTP, 1975). That edition includes a brilliant introduction by A. I. Silver which is extremely important to an understanding of the dominant clerico-conservative nationalism of the late nineteenth and early twentieth century.

A rather different French-Canadian intellectual tradition, more liberal and less nationalist, can be discovered in Léopold Lamontagne's *Arthur Buies*, (Québec, Les Presses de l'Université Laval, 1957), and Hervé Carrier, *Le Sociologue canadien Léon Gérin* (M., Bellarmin, 1960), which deals with late nineteenth-century figures. Two works which analyse liberal thinkers of this century are Marcel-Aimé Gagnon's *Jean-Charles Harvey: Précurseur de la Révolution Tranquille* (M., Beauchemin, 1970), which sets out the ideas of a non-conformist novelist and newspaperman, and Robert Parisé, *Georges-Henri Lévesque* (M., Alain Stanké, 1976), which expounds the ideas of the founder of the important

School of Social Sciences at Laval University. Finally reference should be made to two collections of short studies of French Canadian thinkers: Laurier Lapierre, ed., *The Four O'Clock Lectures: French Canadian Thinkers of the Nineteenth and Twentieth Centuries* (M., McGill University Press, 1966), and Jean-Charles Falardeau, *"L'Essor des Sciences Sociales au Canada-Français* (Québec, Ministère des affaires culturelles, 1964).

CULTURE

There is no very clear distinction between cultural and intellectual history, and in Quebec nationalism has played as significant a role in cultural as in intellectual life. Three useful studies of Quebec literature examine this aspect of French-Canadian culture. Jean-Charles Falardeau, *Notre Société et son Roman* (M., HMH, 1967), attempts to discover what novels reveal about social evolution. Maurice Lemaire, *Les Grande Thèmes nationalistes du roman historique canadien-français* (Québec, Les Presses de l'Université Laval, 1970), explores the way in which the historical novel in Quebec has been nationalist in content. Jack Warwick's *The Long Journey* (T., UTP, 1968) looks at the fashion in which French Canadian fiction has persistently returned to the theme of the North, in the manner of the *coureur-des-bois*. There are many general surveys of French Canadian literature. The most comprehensive is Pierre de Grandpré, ed., *Histoire de la Littérature française du Québec* (4 vols., M., Beauchemin, 1967-70), while Gérard Tougas, *The History of French Canadian Literature* (T., Ryerson, 1967) is the most useful survey in English.

The history of French-Canadian painting is exceptionally well explained in Jean-René Ostiguy, *Une Siècle de Peinture canadienne 1870-1970*, (Québec, Les Presses de l'Université Laval, 1971). The two most important artists of twentieth-century Quebec are the subjects of studies by Guy Robert. His *Jean-Paul Lemieux* (Québec, Editions Garneau, 1968), is a beautifully illustrated book accompanied by a brief but sound text. His *Borduas* (Québec, Les Presses de l'Université Laval, 1972) is a thorough and engrossing study of the cultural history, and even the intellectual history, of Quebec from the twenties to the fifties. For the popular arts, which have been extremely important in Quebec's culture, there are three especially valuable books: Jean Palardy, *The Early Furniture of French Canada* (T., Mac., 1963), and two volumes by Michel Lessard and Hugette Marquis, *Encyclopédie des Antiquités du Québec* (M., Les Editions de l'Homme, 1971), and *Encyclopédie de la maison Québécoise* (M., les Editions de l'Homme, 1972). Marius Barbeau's *J'ai Vu Québec* (Québec, Editions Garneau, 1957), is still a beautiful reminder of the traditional society that modernization has gradually destroyed.

CONTEMPORARY HISTORY

Books dealing with contemporary Quebec, its socio-economic problems, and the debate over its future relations with the rest of Canada are not, strictly speaking, historical studies. Nevertheless there are many books which those interested in the tumultuous developments in Quebec in the last twenty years will find rewarding. An excellent place to start is with a collection of essays that is now more than twenty years old, *Essays on Contemporary Quebec* (Les Presses de l'Université Laval, 1953), edited by Jean-Charles Falardeau. It includes studies of industrial development, agriculture, religion, politics and ideology which are not only very good in their own right, but which sum up the state of Quebec society on the eve of the Quiet Revolution. It is a book that can be fruitfully compared with a later collection of essays edited by J-L. Migué, *Le Québec Aujourd-hui: Régards Universitaires* (M., HMH, 1971), which covers much the same ground after twenty years of change.

In English the most recent summary and analysis of Quebec developments since 1945 is Dale Postgate and Kenneth McRoberts, *Quebec: Social Change and Political Crisis* (T., M&S, 1976). It is thorough and balanced, and its footnotes provide an up-to-date list of books and articles on a wide variety of current topics in Quebec. A second study which concentrates on these years is Léon Dion's *Nationalismes et Politique au Québec* (M., HMH, 1975), which attempts to distinguish nationalisms according to traditional political categories of conservative, liberal and socialist. Marcel Rioux's, *Quebec in Question* (T., James Lewis and Samuel, 1972), while clearly independentist in outlook, is full of provocative interpretations. *The Decolonization of Quebec* (T., M&S, 1973), by S. H. Milner and Henry Milner, is a Marxian account of recent Quebec history, more sophisticated than Léandre Bergeron's *Petit Manuel d'histoire du Québec* (M., Edition Québécoise, 1969), but nevertheless overly simple in its explanation of complex events.

The interpretation of the past on which the separatist understanding of the present rests is best stated in Maurice Séguin's *L'idée d'indépendance au Québec: Genèse et historique* (M., Boréal Express, 1968). That interpretation is challenged by Fernand Ouellet in "The Historical Background of Separatism in Quebec," in Ramsay Cook, *French Canadian Nationalism: An Anthology* (T., Mac., 1970). Though sometimes ignored, the writings of Pierre Vadeboncoeur, particularly his *La Ligne du Risque* (M., HMH, 1963), and *La Dernière Heure et la Première* (l'Hexagone, 1970) probe deeply into the Quebec psyche and society from a nationalist perspective. Though rather dated now, René Lévesque *et al.*, *Option Quebec* (T., M&S, 1969), is a useful source of *Parti Québécois* ideas. The collection of articles entitled *les québécois* (M., parti pris, 1971), presents the viewpoint of young writers in the sixties whose radicalism derived from Karl Marx, Jean-Paul Sartre, Jacques Berque and Franz Fanon. Malcolm Reid's The *Shouting Sign Painters* (T., M&S, 1972) is an uncritical celebration of that group. Pierre Vallières, *The White Niggers of America* (T., M&S, 1971), is a very personal, radical assessment of Quebec. It is often moving in its autobiographical sections, though its analysis is heavily rhetorical. A very good study of the verbal, and sometimes physical violence, of the left-wing fringe of Quebec nationalism is found in Marc Laurendeau, *Les Québécois Violents* (M., Boréal Express, 1974).

The literature on the FLQ crisis of October 1970 is extensive but far from satisfactory since most of the crucial government documents are still confidential. Gérard Pelletier's *The October Crisis* (T., M&S, 1971), states the federal government's position, while Denis Smith's *Bleeding Hearts ... Bleeding Country* (Edmonton, Hurtig, 1971), critically dissects that position. John T. Saywell's *Québec 70: A Documentary Narrative* (T., UTP, 1971), is an indispensable narrative of the confused events of the autumn of 1970.

Jacques Lacoursière, *Alarme Citoyens* (M., La Presse, 1972), Jean-Claude Trait, *FLQ 70: Offensive D'Automne* (M., Les Editions de l'Homme, 1970), and Gustaf Morf, *Terror in Quebec: Case Studies of the FLQ* (T., Clarke Irwin, 1970) are among the better instant books of the period.

The most effectively argued French-Canadian defence of federalism is Pierre-E. Trudeau, *Federalism and the French Canadians* (T., Mac., 1968), though Gilles Lalande, *Pourquoi le fédéralisme* (M., HMH., 1972), looks at the system in more detail. David Cameron's *Nationalism, Self Determination and the Quebec Question* (T., Mac. 1974), is one of the few books which attempts to set out Canadian controversies over nationalism and federalism in the context of modern European political and social theory. Even if it is somewhat brief in its discussion of Quebec, its early chapters are well-worth serious attention. Léon Dion's *The Unfinished Revolution* (M., McGill-Queen's Press, 1976) is a very thoughtful political scientist's reflections on two decades of rapid change in Quebec. *Le nationalisme québécois à la croisée des chemins* (Québec, Centre québécois de rélations intérnationales, La Collection Choix, 1975) provides a set of widely differing interpretations of the direction of Quebec nationalism. Dale C. Thomson, ed., *Quebec Society and Politics: Views from Inside* (T., M&S, 1973), presents many of the same views, in English. Finally, the volumes of the *Report of the Royal Commission on Bilingualism and Biculturalism*, (5 vols., Ottawa, Queen's Printer, 1965-70), and the many subsidiary studies published by the Commission are all worth consulting though special attention should be paid to volume III which deals with the place of French Canadians in the Canadian social structure.

Few of the books on contemporary events were written by historians. Today the nationalist front lines are more often occupied by sociologists and political scientists than historians, something of a change from the past. Whatever the explanation, it is certainly not that Quebec historians are completely detached from present controversies. Rather it is more likely that, under the influence of new approaches to history, they are simply too excited by the prospect of re-examining their past.

Atlantic Canada

W. B. Hamilton

Anyone interested in the history of the Atlantic Provinces since 1867 soon realizes that the period has received relatively little attention. Preoccupied with what has been aptly described as the "Golden Age" of Maritime historiography, historians have concentrated on the pre-confederation years and the region awaits a latter day John Bartlet Brebner or Daniel Cobb Harvey to unravel its more recent history. While the time span covered by this bibliography has been sadly overlooked, it should not be taken to mean that the student must start from scratch. There are significant books and monographs, key articles tucked away in scholarly journals, valuable material in royal commission reports and informative studies in related fields—most notably political science and historical geography. Hopefully, the entries which follow will point the way to these sources and provide a coherent picture of what is available. In the context of this section of the book the phrase "post-confederation" has deliberately been given a broad interpretation to cover all four provinces since 1867. This approach permits a more balanced view of the subject and aside from simple convenience may help encourage investigation of common themes important in gaining an understanding of the entire region.

BIBLIOGRAPHIC AIDS AND REFERENCE MATERIALS

The student with limited background who approaches a research topic in the history of the Atlantic Provinces may well begin with Douglas Lockhead, ed., *Bibliography of Canadian Bibliographies* (T., UTP, 2nd. ed., 1972). If searching for general leads the index in this volume will

181

bear close study. W. F. E. Morley, *The Atlantic Provinces*
(T., UTP, 1967), another obvious starting point, is an indispensable reference for both general studies and local history to 1950. William B. Hamilton, *Local History in Atlantic
Canada* (T., Mac., 1974), contains a capsule history of the
region along with bibliographical suggestions on a wide
range of topics. The most complete guide is Claude Thibault, *Bibliographia Canadiana* (T., Longman, 1973). Be
forewarned that references to Atlantic Canada are widely
scattered in this massive volume. Use the general index and
do not neglect entries in the Addenda. Norah Story, *The
Oxford Companion to Canadian History and Literature* (T.,
OUP, 1967), provides an annotated bibliography for each
province. See also: Norah Story, *Supplement to the Oxford
Companion To Canadian History* (T., OUP, 1973).

The provincial archives and university libraries of the
region have, from time to time, produced bibliographic
guides. By far the most useful, because of its complete coverage and excellent organization, is Hugh A. Taylor, ed.,
New Brunswick History: A Checklist of Secondary Sources
(Fredericton, Public Archives of New Brunswick, 1971).
Another example, Alice R. Stewart's, *The Atlantic Provinces
of Canada* (Orono, Univ. of Maine, 2nd. ed., 1971), provides
a comprehensive list of major secondary sources. A running
watch should be kept on contemporary research by referring to the Atlantic Provinces section in "Recent Publications Relating to Canada" in the *Canadian Historical Review*. The *New England Quarterly* publishes occasional bibliographies on New England and many of the entries have
significance for Atlantic Canada. Scholarly articles dealing
with the history of the region find their way into a wide
variety of journals. The most important ones directly bear-
ing on the region are: *Acadiensis, Bulletin Société Historique Acadienne, Collections New Brunswick Historical Society, Collections Nova Scotia Historical Society, Dalhousie
Review, New England Quarterly, Newfoundland Quarterly,*
and *Nova Scotia Historical Quarterly*.

Olga Bishop, *Publications of the Governments of Nova
Scotia, Prince Edward Island and New Brunswick*, (Ottawa,
National Library, 1957), is an essential reference for gov-
ernment documents. Unfortunately, there is no comparable

treatment for Newfoundland. John P. Greene, ed., *A Preliminary Inventory* (St. John's, Public Archives of Newfoundland and Labrador, 1970), lists current holdings of that institution.

Throughout this section reference will be made to a number of unpublished theses. Information concerning a number of theses relating to Nova Scotia may be found in Delphin Muise, "Theses on Nova Scotian History" (*Education Office Gazette*, November, 1968). The basic reference for Nova Scotian political figures is C. Bruce Fergusson, *Nova Scotia M.L.A.'s 1758-1958*, (Halifax, Public Archives of Nova Scotia, 1958). None of the other provinces have, as yet, produced like directories. Background on leading Newfoundland politicians may be found in R. Hibbs, ed., *Who's Who In and From Newfoundland* (2nd. ed., St. John's, 1930), and James R. Thomas, ed., *Newfoundland and Labrador Who's Who*, (Centennial Edition, St. John's, E. C. Boone, 1967). A source of contemporary information is *The Atlantic Yearbook*, an annual publication of Unipress, Fredericton, N.B. For the newspapers of New Brunswick consult J. Russell Harper, *Historical Directory of New Brunswick Newspapers and Periodicals* (Fredericton, Univ. of New Brunswick, 1961).

GENERAL STUDIES

In the absence of a comprehensive scholarly history of Atlantic Canada since 1867 one must piece together the history of the region from a variety of sources. Although dated in many respects, Volume XIV of Shortt and Doughty's *Canada and Its Provinces* (Toronto, Glasgow Brook & Co., 1914) presents a useful overview of the three Maritime Provinces down to the early years of the twentieth century. J. R. Smallwood, ed., *The Book of Newfoundland* (St. John's, Newfoundland Book Publishers, I & II, 1937, and III & IV, 1967) provides a *pot-pourri* of Newfoundland history with considerable emphasis on the period since 1867. More interpretative are the articles in R. A. MacKay, ed., *Newfoundland Economic Diplomatic and Strategic Studies* (T., OUP, 1946). St. John Chadwick, *Newfoundland—Island Into Province* (L., Cambridge Univ. Press, 1967), despite a promising title, is only marginally useful for general trends and devel-

opments. Most of the research in Acadian history has concentrated on the Expulsion and the years immediately following that unhappy event; however, Naomi Griffith, *The
Acadians: Creation of A People* (T., McGraw-Hill Ryerson,
1973), devotes some attention to the evolution of a distinct
Acadian nationalism. Much of the history and not a little of
the political rhetoric of Atlantic Canada has concentrated
on questions relating to regional identity and protest. For
contrasting views see George Rawlyk, "Nova Scotia's Regional Protest 1867-1967" (*QQ*, 1968) and C. M. Wallace,
"The Nationalization of the Maritimes" in J. M. Bumsted,
ed., *Documentary Problems in Canadian History* (George-
town, Irwin-Dorsey Ltd., 1969). The overall question of regional identity is surveyed in several essays in Mason Wade,
ed., *Regionalism in the Canadian Community 1867-1967* (T.,
UTP, 1969). An incisive historiographical review is contained in George Rawlyk, "A New Golden Age of Maritime
Historiography" (*QQ*, 1969). Significantly, only two of the
fourteen articles in Rawlyk's *Historical Essays on the Atlantic Provinces* (T., M&S, Carleton Library, 1967) deal
with the post-Confederation period. One of these, A. G. Bailey, "Creative Moments in the Culture of the Maritime
Provinces" (originally published in *Dalhousie Review*,
1949), is a study of the late nineteenth century milieu which
produced the Fredericton school of poets. General historiographical information is in Carl Klinck, *Literary History of
Canada* (T., UTP, 1965). For some Newfoundland "chinks
in Klinck" see: G. M. Story, "The St. John's Balladeers"
(*The English Quarterly*, 1971).

POLITICAL HISTORY

Nova Scotia

The classic work on Nova Scotian politics is Murray
Beck, *The Government of Nova Scotia* (T., UTP, 1957).
Three theses which survey political trends in nineteenth
century Nova Scotia are K. G. Pryke, "Nova Scotia and
Confederation 1864-70" (Ph.D., Duke University, 1962), Del-
phin Muise, "Elections and Party Development: Federal
Politics in Nova Scotia 1867-87" (Ph. D., University of
Western Ontario, 1971), and Phyllis Blakeley, "Party Gov-
ernment in Nova Scotia 1878-97" (M.A., Dalhousie Univer-

sity, 1945). In the same context K. G. Pryke, "The Making of a Province: Nova Scotia and Confederation" (*CHAR*, 1968), may be cited. The immediate post-Confederation repeal movement is covered in R. H. Campbell, "The Repeal Agitation in Nova Scotia 1867-69 (*Collections Nova Scotia Historical Society*, 1942), and Donald Warner, "The Post Confederation Annexation Movement in Nova Scotia" (*CHR*, 1947). Phyllis Blakeley, "The Repeal Election of 1886" (*Collections Nova Scotia Historical Society*, 1945), carries the question down to 1890 when it temporarily faded from the scene. A systematic analysis of nineteenth century federal elections in Nova Scotia may be found in Delphin A. Muise, "Parties and Constituencies: Federal Elections in Nova Scotia 1867-1896" (*CHAR*, 1971). In this important article Muise puts forward the thesis that Nova Scotia was "not a smouldering hot bed of anti-confederation sentiment." That "great fever in the lower provinces—the fisheries", as John A. Macdonald put it, is discussed in R. S. Longley, "The Fisheries in Nova Scotian Politics 1865-71" (*Collections Nova Scotia Historical Society*, 1942). Additional information is provided in Ronald Tallman, "Peter Mitchell and the Genesis of a National Fisheries Policy" (*Acadiensis*, 1975). For the pivotal federal election of 1896 see Kenneth McLaughlin, "The Canadian General Election of 1896 in Nova Scotia" (M.A., Dalhousie University, 1967). More readily available is K. M. McLaughlin, "W. S. Fielding and the Liberal Party in Nova Scotia 1891-96" (*Acadiensis*, 1974). E. R. Forbes, "The Rise and Fall of the Conservative Party in the Provincial Politics of Nova Scotia 1922-23" (M.A., Dalhousie University, 1968), takes a look at one of the rare periods of Conservative rule in that province—the Rhodes-Harrington government of 1925-33. Other than the entries listed below under the headings "Biographical Studies" and "Economic History" there has been little serious research in twentieth century Nova Scotian politics. Unfortunately a similar gap exists in the political history of New Brunswick and Prince Edward Island.

New Brunswick

The standard treatment of political development in New Brunswick is Hugh G. Thorburn, *Politics in New Brunswick* (T., UTP, 1961). The manoeuvring which surrounded the Smith-Wilmot government formed to oppose the inclusion of New Brunswick in Confederation and the anti-Confederation movement through to 1882 is treated in Carl Wallace, "Albert Smith—Confederation and Reaction in New Brunswick" (*CHR*, 1963). For the role of Arthur Hamilton Gordon (lieutenant-governor, 1861-66) in the Confederation dilemma see J. K. Chapman "Arthur Gordon and Confederation" (*CHR*, 1956). Two articles by A. G. Bailey throw additional light on the Confederation question in the province: "Railways and the Confederation Issue in New Brunswick" (*CHR*, 1940), and "The Basis and Persistence of Opposition to Confederation in New Brunswick" (*CHR*, 1942). Further discussion of late nineteenth century New Brunswick politics will be found in four theses: Esther Greaves, "Peter Mitchell, A Father of Confederation" (M.A., University of New Brunswick, 1958), D. L. Poynter, "The Economics and Politics of New Brunswick 1878-83" (M.A., University of New Brunswick, 1961), M. Gordon, "The Andrew G. Blair Administration and the Abolition of the Legislative Council of New Brunswick, 1882-92" (M.A., University of New Brunswick, 1964) and J. I. Little, "The Federal Election of 1896 in New Brunswick" (M.A., University of New Brunswick, 1964).

Prince Edward Island

The centenary of Prince Edward Island's entry into confederation inspired considerable research in political history; however, Frank MacKinnon, *The Government of Prince Edward Island* (T., UTP, 1951), remains the best account of Island politics. A full and extremely informative study, Francis W. P. Bolger, *Prince Edward Island and Confederation* (Charlottetown, St. Dunstan's Univ. Press, 1964), surveys the crucial decade prior to 1873. For initial reading there is D. C. Harvey, "Confederation in Prince Edward Island" (*CHR*, 1933). A fascinating account of an American mission to "talk fish and trade" is unfolded in Ronald D. Tallman, "Annexation in the Maritimes—The Butler Mission to Charlottetown" (*Dalhousie Review*, 1973). Lorne C. Callbeck, *The Cradle of Confederation* (Fredericton, Brunswick Press, 1964) treats the full sweep of Island history. Three books inspired by the 1973 centennial are Francis W.

P. Bolger, ed., *Canada's Smallest Province*, and David Weale and Harry Baglole, *The Island and Confederation: The End of an Era* (Summerside, Williams & Crue, 1973). For a satirical look at the 1973 Centennial along with a host of related topics see: Harry Baglole and David Weale, *Cornelius Howatt: Superstar!* (Summerside, 1974).

Newfoundland

References to late nineteenth century Newfoundland politics are scattered; however, Frederic F. Thompson, *The French Shore Problem in Newfoundland* (T., UTP, 1961), covering one of the most vexing diplomatic and political issues, touches on broader matters. The following articles provide wide-ranging analyses of some of the major events: Fred J. Newhook, "Newfoundland's First Rejection of Confederation: The Election of 1869" (*(Newfoundland Quarterly*, 1961); G. F. G. Stanley, "Further Documents Relating to the Union of Newfoundland and Canada" (*CHR*, 1948); Harvey Mitchell, "Canada's Negotiations with Newfoundland 1887-95" (*CHR*, 1959); and Harvey Mitchell, "Constitutional Crisis of 1889 in Newfoundland" (*CJEPS*, 1958). There are three M.A. theses at Memorial University which help in unravelling the intricacies of post-1867 Newfoundland politics: E. C. Moulton, "The Political History of Newfoundland 1865-74" (1963); and Kenneth J. Kerr, "A Social Analysis of the Members of the Newfoundland House of Assembly, Executive Council and Legislative Council for the period 1855-1914" (1973). In addition, J. K. Hiller, "A History of Newfoundland 1874-1901" (PhD. Thesis, Cambridge University, 1971), places the last quarter of the century in perspective. The twentieth century is well served by two important books. S. J. R. Noel, *Politics in Newfoundland* (T., UTP, 1971) is an informative study characterized by completeness and good style. Peter Neary, *The Political Economy of Newfoundland* (T., Copp Clark, 1973), authoritatively documents the period 1929-72. Insight into particular issues is provided by: G. O. Rothney, "The Denominational Basis of Representation in the Newfoundland Assembly 1919-62" (*CJEPS*, 1962), G. E. Panting, "The Fishermen's Protective Union of Newfoundland and the Farmers Organizations in Western Canada" (*CHAR*, 1963), Ian Mc-

Donald, "W. F. Coaker and the Fishermen's Protective Union in Newfoundland Politics" (Ph.D. thesis, University of London, 1971), Henry B. Mayo, "Newfoundland's Entry Into Confederation" (*CJEPS*, 1949), and Parzival Copes, "The Fishermen's Vote in Newfoundland" (*Canadian Journal of Political Science*, 1970). Not surprisingly, much emphasis has been placed on the fall of responsible government and the role of the Commission of Government. A concise introduction to the topic is G. E. Panting, "Newfoundland's Loss of Responsible Government," in J. M. Bumsted, ed., *Documentary Problems in Canadian History.* More detailed information is contained in two theses, H. A. Cuff, "The Commission of Government in Newfoundland: A Preliminary Survey" (M.A., Acadia University, 1959), and R. A. Clarke, "Newfoundland 1934-1949 – A study of the Commission of Government" (Ph.D., University of California (Los Angeles), 1951). Volume III of J. R. Smallwood, ed., *The Book of Newfoundland,* outlines the events which culminated in Confederation in 1949 (See also references to Smallwood in "Biographical Studies" below). A provocative treatment of post-1949 Newfoundland politics is presented in three articles by Peter Neary, "Democracy in Newfoundland: A Comment" (*JCS*, 1969), "Party Politics in Newfoundland 1949-71: A Survey and Analysis" (*JCS*, 1971), and "Party Politics in Newfoundland: The End of the Smallwood Era" (*JCS*, 1972).

Local Government and Maritime Union

The peculiarities of local government in the Atlantic Provinces are discussed in C. Bruce Fergusson, *Local Government in Nova Scotia* (Halifax, Public Archives of Nova Scotia, 1961), H. J. Whalen, *The Development of Local Government in New Brunswick* (Fredericton, QP, 1963), J. C. Crosbie, "Local Government in Newfoundland" (*CJEPS*, 1956), and H. J. Finnis, *Local Government In the Changing Economy of Cape Breton* (Antigonish, St. Francis Xavier Univ., 1968). Recent administrative changes in New Brunswick are examined in an excellent study by Ralph R. Krueger, "The Provincial-Municipal Revolution in New Brunswick" (*Canadian Public Administration*, 1970). In 1864 the concept of Maritime Union lay behind the Charlottetown

Conference; since that time it has periodically surfaced as a panacea for the political and economic ills of the area. For the historical background see J. M. Beck, *History of Maritime Union: A Study of Frustrations* (Fredericton, 1969), and C. Bruce Fergusson, "Maritime Union" (*QQ*, 1970). For the most recent scheme advocating Maritime Union see *Maritime Union Study* (Fredericton, QP, 1970).

BIOGRAPHICAL STUDIES

Despite an impressive roll call of prominent personalities, including four of Canada's fifteen prime ministers (Thompson, Tupper, Borden and Bennett) scholarly biographical studies are conspicuous by their absence. A few of the early figures are covered in Volume X of the *Dictionary of Canadian Biography* and subsequent volumes of this series will be awaited with interest. Joseph Howe belongs, in part, to the "Golden Age"; however, for his participation in the Confederation debate see J. M. Beck, "Joseph Howe and Confederation: Myth and Fact" (*TRSC*, 1964). Balanced general accounts by the same author appear in *Our Living Tradition*, (fourth series, T., UTP, 1962), and "Joseph Howe Anti-Confederate" (Ottawa, Canadian Historical Association, 1965). Some of the conflicting views concerning Howe are surveyed in George Rawlyk, ed., *Joseph Howe Opportunist? Man of Vision? Frustrated Politician?* (T., Copp Clark, 1967). Other leading personalities in the Confederation debate in Nova Scotia are analyzed in Volume XXXVI of the *Collections Nova Scotia Historical Society* (A. G. Archibald, R. B. Dickey, P. S. Hamilton, W. A. Henry, Jonathan McCully, J. W. Ritchie, Charles Tupper and M. I. Wilkins). Arthur Hamilton Gordon is the subject of a complete biography, J. K. Chapman's *The Career of Arthur Hamilton Gordon* (T., UTP, 1964). James Hannay's *Sir Leonard Tilley* (T., Morang & Co., 1911) is worth consulting; however, a more objective treatment will be found in a thesis by Carl Wallace, "The Career of Sir Samuel Leonard Tilley" (Ph.D., University of Alberta, 1972). For references to Peter Mitchell see "Political History" above. The best treatment of both Tupper and Thompson is found in theses: A. W. MacIntosh, "The Career of Sir Charles Tupper in Canada 1864-1900" (Ph.D., University of Toronto, 1960), and J. D. Heisler, "Sir

John S. D. Thompson 1844-94" (Ph.D. University of Toronto, 1955). An earlier biography of Thompson, J. Castell
Hopkins, *Life and Work of Rt. Hon. Sir John Thompson*
(Brantford, 1895), is unsatisfactory from the viewpoint of
modern scholarship. Be particularly wary of Sir Charles
Tupper's carefully "laundered" *Recollections of Sixty Years
in Canada* (T., Cassell & Co., 1914). W. S. Fielding, a lead-
ing political figure of the period has attracted attention in
C. Bruce Fergusson, *The Mantle of Howe* (Windsor, Lance-
lot Press, 1970), and *Mr. Minister of Finance* (Windsor,
Lancelot Press, 1971). The life and times of Sir Robert Bor-
den may be traced in his own *Memoirs*, published posthumously in 1938 and now available in a second edition in the
Carleton Library Series, 1969. A short essay by James A.
Gibson in *Our Living Tradition* (Second and Third Series)
(T., UTP, 1959) serves as a general commentary. R. Craig
Brown's biography *Robert Laird Borden* (T., Mac., 1975),
although short on his early life is the definitive study of the
career of Canada's eighth prime minister. Sir Frederick
Borden, Sir Robert Borden's contemporary and relative, is
examined in Carmen Miller, "The Public Life of Sir Freder-
ick Borden" (M.A. thesis, Dalhousie University, 1964). W.
Stewart Wallace, *The Memoirs of Rt. Hon. Sir George Foster*
(T., Mac., 1933), provides some insight into a career which
spanned the years from 1882 to the 1920s. E. M. Macdonald,
Recollections Political and Personal (T., Ryerson, 1935), is
a gossipy though informed view of the politics of the 1920s
and 30s. Ernest Watkins, *R. B. Bennett* (L., Secker & War-
burg, 1963), surveys the life of Canada's eleventh Prime
Minister. It should be used in conjunction with J. R. H.
Wilbur, ed., *The Bennett New Deal: Fraud or Portent?* (T.,
Copp Clark, 1968), which critically analyzes Bennett's han-
dling of the Depression.

Two books useful in charting the career of Angus L.
Macdonald are *Speeches of Angus L. Macdonald* (T., Longmans Green, 1960), and John Hawkins, *The Life and Times
of Angus L.* (Windsor, Lancelot, 1969). Macdonald, once
described as a "poet in politics" is, perhaps, his own best
interpreter. Hawkins' biography suffers because it verges
on hagiography; nevertheless, it has some merit because of
considerable research among Macdonald's close associates.

The Nova Scotian trait of "following the leader" is examined in Fulton Logan, "Personality as an issue in Nova Scotian Politics" (M.A. thesis, Dalhousie University, 1972), which analyzes this phenomenon through the careers of Fielding, Murray, Macdonald and Stanfield. For Stanfield's provincial career see Peter Aucoin, "The Stanfield Era: A Political Analysis" *(Dalhousie Review*, 1967), and E. D. Haliburton, *My Years With Stanfield* (Windsor, Lancelot, 1972). A recent biography—pro Stanfield and generally quite fair—is Geoffrey Stevens, *Stanfield* (T., M&S, 1973). The politician in Atlantic Canada whose career looms largest in recent history is J. R. Smallwood. We are too close in time to have an objective portrait of his remarkable life; however, the student is directed to Richard Gwyn, *Smallwood: The Unlikely Revolutionary* (T., M&S, 1968), and the subject's own *I Chose Canada* (T., Mac., 1973). See also Peter Neary, "Joey Smallwood: He's One of We" (*Canadian Forum*, 1973).

ECONOMIC HISTORY

T. N. Brewis, *Regional Economic Policies in Canada* (T., Mac., 1969), is an important starting point for research in the recent economic history of the region. Appropriate chapters in general texts such as W. T. Easterbrook and H. G. J. Aitken, *Canadian Economic History*, (T., Mac., 1961), or A. W. Currie, *Canadian Economic Development* (T., Thomas Nelson, 1960), will help set the stage. Peter Neary, *The Political Economy of Newfoundland*, is an essential reference for economic matters in Newfoundland from the Depression years to the present. More specialized studies will be found in Stanley A. Saunders, *The Economic History of the Maritime Provinces* (Ottawa, 1939 [Issued as a study for the Royal Commission on Dominion Provincial Relations]), Stanley A. Saunders, *Studies in the Economy of the Maritime Provinces* (T., Mac., 1939), B. S. Keirstead, *Economic Effects of the War on the Maritime Provinces* (Halifax, Dalhousie University, 1944), Alexander K. Cairncross, *Economic Development and the Atlantic Provinces* (Fredericton, Atlantic Provinces Research Board, 1961). and J. F. Graham, *Fiscal Adjustment and Economic Development: A Case Study of Nova Scotia* (T., UTP, 1963). An important commentary and critique of recent developments in New Brunswick is contained in Thomas J. Plunkett, "The Report of the Royal Commission on Finance and Municipal Taxation in New Brunswick" (*Canadian Public Administration*, 1965). A reprint of the same article appears in D. C. Rowat, ed., *The Canadian Municipal System* (T., M&S, 1969). Economic development in the Atlantic region has been greatly influenced by federal policies—perhaps to a greater extent than in other parts of the country. For a discussion of the impact of the "National Policy" see Stanley A. Saunders, "The Maritime Provinces and the National Policy: Comments Upon Economic Regionalism in Canada" (*Dalhousie Review*, 1937), and T. W. Acheson, "The National Policy and the Industrialization of the Maritimes 1880-1910" (*Acadiensis*, 1972). Additional insight may be obtained from K. G. Pryke, "Labour and Politics: Nova Scotia at Confederation" (*Social History*, 1970), and Brian D. Tennyson, "Economic Nationalism and Confederation: A Case Study in Cape Breton" (*Acadiensis*, 1972). David G. Alexander, "A New Newfoundland: The Traditional Economy and Development to 1934" (Paper presented to the Canadian Historical Association, Kingston, 1973), offers a fresh interpretation of the economic history of Newfoundland and is illustrative of the impressive research now being undertaken by the Maritime History Group at Memorial University. An important study of shipping, shipbuilding and Maritime industrial history generally is to be found in Basic Greenhill and Ann Giffard, *Westcountrymen in Prince Edward's Isle* (T., UTP, 1967). Useful and current information may be obtained from *The Atlantic Economy: Annual Review* (Halifax, Atlantic Provinces Economic Council, 1967 onward). There are also a number of specialized studies touching on economic matters published by the Queen's Printer, Fredericton, for the Maritime Union Study of 1970. Publications of the Institute of Social and Economic Research at Memorial University have significance for any enquiry into the socio-economic history of the region. Some representative titles are: Tom Philbrook, *Fisherman, Logger, Merchant, Miner: Social Change and Industrialism in Three Newfoundland Communities*, Shmuel Ben-Dor *Makkovik: Eskimos and Settlers in a Labrador Community. A Contrastive Study in Adaption*, Noel Iverson and

D. Ralph Matthews, *Communities in Decline: An Examination of Household Resettlement in Newfoundland*, Cato Wadel, *Marginal Adaptions and Modernization in Newfoundland: A Study of Strategies and Implications of Resettlement and Redevelopment of Outport Fishing Communities*, Cato Wadel, *Now Whose Fault Is That? The Struggle For Self Esteem in The Face of Chronic Unemployment*, and Ottar Brox, *Maintenance of Economic Dualism in Newfoundland.*

Royal Commission Reports

One of the most ready sources for the economic history of the region is royal commission reports, as witnessed by the fact that since 1867 Atlantic Canada has been subjected to over one hundred federal investigations alone. (See return tabled in the House of Commons, March 12, 1969). Some of the most important are Industrial Unrest of Steelworkers at Sydney (Ottawa, 1924), Fisheries of the Atlantic Provinces (Ottawa, 1925), Maritime Claims (Duncan Report) (Ottawa, 1926), Newfoundland Royal Commission (Amulree Report) (1933), Dominion-Provincial Relations (Rowell-Sirois Report) (Ottawa, 1939), Canada's Economic Prospects (Gordon Report) (Ottawa, 1957), Report of the Royal Commission for the Preparation of the Case of the Government of Newfoundland for the Revision of the Financial Terms of Union (St. John's, 1957), Report of the Royal Commission on Newfoundland Finances (Ottawa, 1958), Coal Industry (Donald Report) (Ottawa, 1960), and Report of the New Brunswick Royal Commission on Finance and Municipal Taxation (Byrne Report) (Fredericton, 1963).

Industrial Studies

Over the years the fishing industry has attracted the attention of both historians and economists. H. A. Innis' monumental *The Cod Fisheries: The History of An International Economy* (T., UTP, 1954), especially chapters 11-14, is invaluable. The early international entanglements surrounding the industry are surveyed in Charles S. Campbell, "American Tariff Interests and the Northeastern Fisheries" (*CHR*, 1964). Of particular concern to Newfoundland is Shannon Ryan, "The Newfoundland Cod Fishery in the

Nineteenth Century" (M.A. thesis, Memorial University, 1971). An abridged version of the thesis was presented to the Canadian Historical Association June, 1973. Two articles by Parzival Copes, containing much useful material, are "Community Resettlement and Rationalization of the Fishing Industry in Newfoundland" (Paper presented to the Canadian Economics Association, June, 1971), and *The Resettlement of Fishing Communities in Newfoundland* (Ottawa, Canadian Council on Rural Development, 1972). For the ups and downs of the coal industry see: Eugene Forsey, "Economic and Social Aspects of the Nova Scotia Coal Industry" (T., 1926), F. W. Gray, "Fifty Years of the Dominion Coal Company" (*Dalhousie Review*, 1942-43), and the Donald Royal Commission Report cited above. The most scholarly work concerning the strife between management and labour in Cape Breton is Donald W. McGillivrary, "Industrial Unrest in Cape Breton 1920-25" (M.A. thesis, University of New Brunswick, 1970). Although verging on the melodramatic, *The Peoples History of Cape Breton* (privately published, Halifax, 1971), is useful. The result of an OFY grant funded by the federal government, *The Peoples History* leans heavily upon a series of articles on "labour and politics in Cape Breton" by Paul MacEwan, originally published in the *Cape Breton Highlander* (1966-68). More comprehensive is Paul MacEwan's *Miners and Steelworkers: Labour In Cape Breton* (T., Hakkert, 1976); however, the latter chapters dealing with contemporary politics are less than objective. A good understanding of the impact of the cooperative movement may be obtained from *The Social Significance of the Cooperative Movement* (Extension Department, St. Francis Xavier University, Antigonish, 1960), and Alexander Laidlaw, ed., *The Man From Margaree: Writings and Speeches of M. M. Coady* (T., M&S, 1971). The Maritime cooperative movement in its national context is surveyed in Ian MacPherson, "The Origins of The Canadian Cooperative Movement 1900-1914" (*CHAR*, 1972). Three books which take a critical look at recent trends in the economy of Nova Scotia are: Roy E. George, *A Leader and a Laggard: Manufacturing Industry in Nova Scotia, Quebec and Ontario* (T., UTP, 1970); John T. Sears, *Institutional Financing of Small Business in Nova Scotia* (T., UTP, 1972), and Roy E.

George, *The Life and Times of Industrial Estates Limited*, (Halifax, Dalhousie Institute of Public Affairs, 1974).

Urban Studies

Serious research in urban history is still in its infancy in the Atlantic Provinces. An important introductory study of Saint John, Halifax and St. John's is J. M. S. Careless, "Aspects of Metropolitanism in Atlantic Canada," in *Regionalism in the Canadian Community* (T., UTP, 1969). Halifax, the largest city in the region, has not been given the attention which its long and colorful history warrants. Thomas Raddall's oft quoted *Halifax Warden of the North* (T., M&S, 1965) suffers by comparison with his other works. Phyllis Blakeley, *Glimpses of Halifax* (Belleville, Mika Publishing Co., 1973), covers the years 1867-1900, while Michael J. Bird, *The Town That Died* (T., Ryerson, 1962), gives a popular treatment of the explosion of 1917. Worth consulting are Parzival Copes, *St. John's and Newfoundland: An Economic Survey* (St. John's, St. John's Board of Trade, 1961), and E. Roy Harvey, *Sydney: An Urban Study* (T., Clarke Irwin, 1971).

RELIGIOUS HISTORY

Most of the denominational histories concentrate upon the nineteenth century; however, relevant portions of Philip Carrington, *The Anglican Church in Canada* (T., Collins, 1963), and A. A. Johnston, *A History of the Catholic Church in Eastern Nova Scotia* (Antigonish, St. Francis Xavier Univ. Press, 1971), summarize some of the more recent highlights. George E. Levy, *The Baptists of the Maritime Provinces* (Saint John, 1946), takes that denomination through to the twentieth century. The earlier D. W. Johnson, *History of Methodism in Eastern British America* (Sackville, Tribune Publishers, n.d.), is of value for the pre-1925 years. A more recent survey of the Presbyterian Church may be found in: Archibald D. MacKinnon, *History of the Presbyterian Church in Cape Breton* (Antigonish, Formac, 1975). The influence of deep-rooted religious trends, particularly as they touch on educational matters, may be traced in chapters dealing with the Atlantic Provinces in C. B. Sissons, *Church and State in Canadian Education* (T., Ryerson, 1959). There are also a number of informative local church histories, e.g., R. V. Harris *The Church of St. Paul*, [Halifax] (T., Ryerson, 1949), or G. M. Story, *George Street United Church: One Hundred Years of Service* (St. John's, 1973). Because religious and educational questions are so completely entwined, note the entries which follow under educational history. A significant article which covers a wide range of twentieth century social and religious history is: E. R. Forbes, "Prohibition and the Social Gospel in Nova Scotia" (*Acadiensis*, 1971).

EDUCATIONAL HISTORY

G. A. Frecker, *Education in The Atlantic Provinces* (T., Gage, 1956), provides a summary of general information. More helpful are two provincial studies, K. F. C. Mac-Naughton, *The Development of the Theory and Practise of Education in New Brunswick* (Frederiction, University of New Brunswick, 1947), and F. W. Rowe, *The History of Education in Newfoundland* (T., Ryerson, 1952). Excellent coverage of mid-nineteenth century developments in Prince Edward Island will be found in Sister Mary Olga McKenna, "The Impact of Religion and Politics in the Structure of Education in Prince Edward Island" (*Canadian Association Foundations of Education Annual Report*, 1967), and Ian Robertson, "Education, Politics and Religion in Prince Edward Island" (M.A. thesis, McGill University, 1968). General trends in the educational history of all four Atlantic Provinces may be traced in chapters 5, 6 and 7 by William B. Hamilton in *Canadian Education: A History* (Scarborough, Prentice-Hall, 1970). George Rawlyk and Ruth Hafter, *Acadian Education in Nova Scotia* (Ottawa, Information Canada, 1970), a study prepared for the Royal Commission on Bilingualism and Biculturalism, is a comprehensive survey of Acadian education down to 1965.

HISTORICAL GEOGRAPHY – DEMOGRAPHIC STUDIES

An excellent overview of the historical geography of the region is contained in Alan Macpherson, ed., *The Atlantic Provinces* (T., UTP, 1972). A full and extremely informative analysis of the geography and agricultural history of Prince Edward Island is contained in Andrew Hill Clark,

Three Centuries and the Island (T., UTP, 1959). One ethnic minority which has received considerable scholarly attention is the Black population of the region. Much of Robin W. Winks' *The Blacks in Canada: A History* (New Haven, Yale University Press, 1971) deals with Atlantic Canada. Other sources of information are Robin W. Winks, "Negroes in the Maritimes: An Introductory Survey" (*Dalhousie Review*, 1968-69), and "Negro School Segregation in Ontario and Nova Scotia" (*CHR*, 1969), by the same author. See also George Rawlyk, "The Guysboro Negroes: A Study in Isolation" (*Dalhousie Review*, 1968), and D. H. Hill, *Negro Settlement in Canada* (a report presented to the Royal Commission on Bilingualism and Biculturalism, 1966), and *The Black Man in Canada* (Teach-in Report, St. Francis Xavier University, 1969). W. A. Spray, *The Blacks in New Brunswick* (Fredericton, Brunswick Press, 1972), is a well-researched history of black settlement in that province. Frances Henry's ethnographic analysis *The Blacks of Nova Scotia* (T., Longmans, 1973) suffers by comparison with Professor Spray's book. Charles W. Dunn, *Highland Settler: A Portrait of the Scottish Gael in Nova Scotia* (T., UTP, 1953), is a penetrating study of the impact of emigration on a folk culture. Raymond MacLean, *Beyond the Atlantic Roar* (T., M&S, 1974), takes a cross disciplinary approach in tracing the evolution of Scottish settlement in Nova Scotia. John J. Mannion, *Irish Settlement in Eastern Canada* (T., UTP, 1974), examines Irish settlement patterns in the Avalon Peninsula (Newfoundland), Miramichi Valley (New Brunswick) and Peterborough (Ontario) areas. It is a classic study of cultural transfer and may well serve as a model for further research in Atlantic Canada.

The North: A Brief Note

J. L. Granatstein

There are three basic studies on the Canadian North.
Morris Zaslow's *The Opening of the Canadian North 1870-1914* (T., M&S, 1971) is an absolutely first class book by one
of Canada's most underrated historians. Rich in documentation, well-written, well-argued, this book sets out in full detail the ways in which Canada took possession of the great
lands to the west and north. A second volume, carrying the
story up toward the present, is in preparation. Of similar
value is R. St. J. Macdonald's edited collection, *The Arctic
Frontier* (T., UTP, 1966). Included in this book are several
fine essays, including an exhaustive analysis of Canadian
sovereignty in the Arctic by Gordon Smith and a fine, stimulating piece on the strategic significance of the North by
the late R. J. Sutherland. The third basic book is K. J. Rea,
The Political Economy of the Canadian North (T., UTP,
1968) an examination of development through to the 1960s.
Any student culling the footnotes in these books will find
virtually everything of value about Canada's arctic domain.

Primary sources that are readily available include material in the *Documents on Canadian External Relations*
series, published (in eight volumes to date) by the Department of External Affairs. The House of Commons *Debates*
are available in every good library and debates on departmental estimates provide a wealth of information about Canadian disinterest. Reports of the various departments are
usually published annually; geological surveys appeared
regularly.

Among scholarly articles on the north are the following: R. J. Diubaldo, "Wrangling over Wrangel Island"
(*CHR*, 1967); D. H. Dinwoodie, "Arctic Controversy: the

1925 Byrd-MacMillan Expedition Example" (*CHR*, 1972); V. K. Johnston, "Canada's Title to the Arctic Islands" (*CHR*, 1933); J. E. G. de Domenico, "The Strategic Importance of Canada's North" (*Canadian Army Journal*, 1960); John Gellner, "Problems of Canadian Defence" (*Behind the Headlines*, 1958); Ivan Head, "Canadian Claims to Territorial Sovereignty in the Arctic Regions" (*McGill Law School Journal*, 1962-63); and A. D. Pharand, "Innocent Passage in the Arctic" (*Canadian Yearbook of International Law*, 1968).

As can be gathered from those titles, much of the writing about the North has been concerned with establishing and protecting sovereignty, both through legal means and through military measures. This theme is also developed in the essays in E. J. Dosman, ed., *The Arctic in Question* (T., OUP, 1976), a good collection that gathers together some of the best scholars in the field. Particularly interesting are Dosman's own contributions, most notably his informed study of the crisis of 1968-70 between Canada and the United States over northern sovereignty. In Dosman's view, the elephant and the mouse were eyeball to eyeball and the mouse blinked—and panicked. Dosman has developed this theme in far more detail in his book *The National Interest: The Politics of Northern Development 1968-75* (T., M&S, 1975), the best and most detailed examination of the way Canada has lost control of its frontier.

This theme is the subject of a number of other works. Richard Rohmer, prolific novelist, publicist and political wheeler-dealer, has written *The Green North* (T., Maclean-Hunter, 1970), and *The Arctic Imperative* (T., M&S, 1973). Robert Davis and Mark Zannis are the authors of *The Genocide Machine in Canada* (M. Black Rose, 1973), a book advancing the thesis that Canada's north is part and parcel of the American war machine. Very valuable is Jim Lotz, *Northern Realities* (T., New Press, 1970), a good overview of problems and possibilities.

Among more technical studies the publications of the Arctic Institute of North America must be cited. The Institute's studies cover the flora and fauna, as well as administration and geology. According to critics, the Institute's work is also funded by American military sources. Also useful is K. J. Rea, *The Political Economy of Northern Development* (Science Council of Canada Background Study No. 36, 1976), a work that updates Rea's standard study.

Other volumes, voluminous in number, deal with the development of oil exploration in the north, pipelines, and native peoples. These cannot be cited here.

Index